India Assam

Physical and political geography of the province of Assam

India Assam

Physical and political geography of the province of Assam

ISBN/EAN: 9783337134600

Printed in Europe, USA, Canada, Australia, Japan

Cover: Foto ©Suzi / pixelio.de

More available books at **www.hansebooks.com**

PHYSICAL AND POLITICAL GEOGRAPHY

OF THE

PROVINCE OF ASSAM.

(Reprinted from the Report on the Administration of the Province of Assam for the year 1892-93, and published by authority.)

SHILLONG :

PRINTED AT THE ASSAM SECRETARIAT PRINTING OFFICE.

1896.

Price—One Rupee.

CONTENTS.

CHAPTER I.

PHYSICAL FEATURES OF THE COUNTRY, AREA, CLIMATE, AND CHIEF STAPLES.

Page

Section 1. Area and Boundaries, and Physical Features ... 1
,, 2. Geological Features ... 10
,, 3. Climate ... 18
,, 4. Chief Staples ... 25
,, 5. Commercial Staples ... 31
,, 6. Manufactures ... 44
,, 7. Trade and Commerce ... 47
,, 8. Mines and Minerals ... 53

CHAPTER II.

HISTORICAL SUMMARY.

Section 1. Assam Proper ... 62
,, 2. Goálpára ... 75
,, 3. Cachar ... 77
,, 4. Sylhet and Jaintia ... 80
,, 5. The Hill Districts ... 82
,, 6. Formation of the Chief Commissionership ... 97

CHAPTER III.

FORM OF ADMINISTRATION.

Section 1. General Administrative System and Staff ... 99
,, 2. Legislative Authority ... 110
,, 3. Education ... 112
,, 4. Immigration and Labour Inspection 120

Section 5. Public Works ... 133
,, 6. Local Self-Government.. 138
,, 7. Finance ... 144

CHAPTER IV.

CHARACTER OF LAND TENURES AND SYSTEM OF SETTLEMENT AND SURVEY.

Section 1. Land Tenures ... 154
,, 2. Waste Land Tenures ... 167
,, 3. System of Survey and Settlement ... 172

CHAPTER V.

CIVIL DIVISIONS OF BRITISH TERRITORY.

Civil Divisions of British Territory 181

CHAPTER VI.

DETAILS OF THE LAST CENSUS.

Details of the Last Census ... 186

CHAPTER VII.

FRONTIER RELATIONS AND FEUDATORY STATES.

Frontier Relations and Feudatory States 207

Physical and Political Geography.

CHAPTER I.

Physical Features of the Country, Area, Climate, and Chief Staples.

SECTION 1.—AREA AND BOUNDARIES AND PHYSICAL FEATURES.

1. The Province of Assam lies on the north-east border of
Bengal, on the extreme frontier of the Indian

Area and boundaries.

Empire, with Bhutan and Thibet beyond it
on the north, and Burma and Manipur on the east. It comprises
the whole of the valley of the Brahmaputra down to the point
where that river, emerging on the Bengal delta, takes a sudden
southward curve, and the greater portion of the valley of the
Surma, nearly to the junction of that stream with the great estuary
of the Megna, together with the intervening range of hills which
forms the watershed between them. It lies between latitude 28° 18′
and 23° 15′ North, and longitude 89° 46′ and 97° 4′ East, and contains
an area of 49,004 square miles, of which 28,755 square miles are
plain and 20,249 square miles are hilly country.* The immediate
boundaries of the province are, on the north Independent Bhutan,
a tract inhabited by Bhutias under the direct Government of Lhassa,

Section 1.

Area and Boundaries and Physical Features.

* These figures represent the area of the plains and hill districts, respectively, the
North Cachar subdivision being treated for this purpose as a hill district. The real
plains area is somewhat greater, as a portion of the Gáro Hills district (473 square miles)
is plain and so also a small part of the Nága and the Khási and Jaintia Hills districts.
On the other hand, it must be remembered that the area classed above as plain includes
the Mikir Hills in Nowgong, and also some low ranges of hills in the south of the Cachar
and Sylhet districts.

The North Lushai Hills are not included in these figures, as, although that tract of
country is now practically part of Assam, it has not yet been actually formed into a district
and incorporated in the ordinary administration of the province. An account of this
tract and of its occupation will be found in Chapter VII.

B

SECTION I.
*Area and
Boundaries
and
Physical
Features.*
known as Towang, and a range of sub-Himalayan hills, inhabited, first by two small races of Bhutia origin, who are believed to be independent, and further eastwards by the savage tribes of Akas, Dallas, Miris, Abors, and Mishmis; on the north-east the Mishmi Hills, which sweep round the head of the Brahmaputra Valley; on the east the Pátkoi range, the intervening ranges, inhabited chiefly by various tribes of Nágas, and the Native State of Manipur; on the south the Lushai Hills, Hill Tippera, and the Bengal district of Tippera; on the west the Bengal districts of Mymensingh and Rangpur, and the Native State of Kuch Bihar.

2. Assam Proper, or the valley of the Brahmaputra, is an alluvial plain, about 450 miles in length, with

Brahmaputra Valley.

an average breadth of about 50 miles, lying almost east and west in its lower portion, but in its upper half trending somewhat to the north-east. To the north is the main chain of the Himalayas, the lower ranges of which rise abruptly from the plain; to the south is the great elevated plateau, or succession of plateaux, known as the Assam Range, much broken at its eastern and western extremities and along its northern face, but in its central portion, from the eastern border of the Gáro Hills to the watershed of the Dhansiri, a region of table land and rolling uplands. The various portions of this range are called by the names of the tribes who inhabit them,—the Gáro, the Khási, the Jaintia, the North Cachar, and the Nága Hills. At several points on the southern side of the valley the hills of the Assam Range abut on the river, and at Goálpára, Gauháti, and Tezpur it has spurs belonging to this group on the north, as well as on the south bank. The broadest part of the valley is where the river divides the districts of Sibságar and Lakhimpur, below which the isolated block of the Mikir Hills to the south (a mass of mountains cut off from the main Assam Range by the valleys of the Dhansiri, Lángpher, and Jamuna rivers), and the projecting group of the Dalla Hills to the north suddenly contract it. Forty miles lower down it widens out, but at the lower end of the Nowgong district it is again encroached upon by the Khási Hills, among the spurs of which the river makes its way in front of the station of Gauháti, and it is almost completely shut in just to the west of that town, below the temple-crowned hill of Niláchal or Kámákhyá, where the stream is not 1,000 yards broad. Beyond this point the hills recede again, and the mountains do not approach the Brahmaputra until the station of Goálpára, situated on a spur of the Gáro Hills, is reached. Here, at the confluence of the Manás and between the rocks of Jogighopa and Pagla Tek, is the "Gate of Assam," to the east of which Assamese is spoken, and to the west of it Bengali. Beyond this point the valley again widens, and at Dhubri opens out into the great delta of Bengal.

3. Throughout its course the Brahmaputra receives a vast number of affluents, great and small, from

The Brahmaputra and its affluents.

the hills to the north and south. The greater of the northern streams are snow-fed, while those from the south (except the Dihing) depend upon the annual rains for their volume, and shrink to small dimensions in the dry season. On the north the chief tributaries of the Brahmaputra are the Dibong, Dihong, Subansiri, Bhoroli, Bornadi, and Manás; on the south the greater affluents are the new and old Dihings, the Disang, the Disoi, and the Dhansiri. A short distance below the junction of the last named a considerable body of water separates itself from the Brahmaputra, and, under the name of the Kallang, goes on a tortuous course through the Nowgong district, rejoining the main stream about 10 miles above Gauháti. The Kallang receives, in the Kopili, the whole drainage of the North Cachar and the Jaintia Hills, besides several minor streams from the Khási Hills. Below Gauháti, the Kulsi and the Jinjiram are the chief southern affluents of the Brahmaputra.

The Dihong, which emerges from the Himalayas through the hills inhabited by the Abors, has been proved by Mr. Needham to be the same stream as the Sanpo, the eastward course of which, along the north of the great Himalayan barrier, has been traced by explorers to a point where it turns southwards into the range. The Brahmaputra itself, so far as is known, has but a short course beyond the limits of British territory, and above Sadiya is far inferior in volume to the Dihong.

Except at the points already mentioned, where hills impinge upon the Brahmaputra, the river flows between sandy banks, which are subject to constant changes for a breadth of about 6 miles on either side of the stream. Within this belt there is no permanent cultivation, nor any habitation but temporary huts erected by people who grow mustard on the *chur* lands during the cold weather. Beyond, the level of the alluvium rises, and tillage and population take the place of sandy flats covered with long grass. Little of this is seen from the river, and the traveller up the Brahmaputra receives the impression that the country is a wilderness untenanted by man, except at the few points where, rock giving permanency to the channel, towns and villages have been established along the stream. These points are Dhubri, the capital of the Goálpára district, Goálpára, Gauháti, the capital of Kámrúp, Tezpur, the capital of Darrang, Koliabar, the port for Nowgong, from which it is distant 32 miles, and Biswanath, in the Darrang district. Between the last named place and Sadiya, close to the point where the river emerges from the hills, a distance of about 200 miles, there is no town or large village on the banks, Golághát being 20 miles, Jorhát 10, Sibságar 8, and Dibrugarh 5, away from the cold-weather channel. Proceeding inland from the belt just described, through which the river flows, one finds a country consisting mainly of alluvial flats, much of which is untilled and covered with long grass, and in the eastern portion of the valley with forest, but much also is under cultivation. The most thickly populated part of the valley is North Kámrúp ; the most thinly, Darrang, west of Tezpur, Lakhimpur, north of the Brahmaputra, and the forests in the extreme east and south of the latter district. To the peopled belt on either side of the valley succeeds another where population again falls off, and extensive forests and grass savannahs reach to the foot of the hills on the north and south. The Brahmaputra is navigable by large steamers as far as Dibrugarh throughout the year, and by smaller vessels as far as Sadiya. Many of its affluents are also navigable in the rains by steamers, and at all seasons by boats of small burthen.

4. The southern, or Surma, valley, which constitutes the second

main division of the province, and comprises the two districts

The Surma Valley.   of Cachar and Sylhet, presents many points
of contrast with that of the Brahmaputra.

It is much smaller in extent, covering only 7,886 square miles,
against 20,869 in the latter. This, however, excludes a portion
of it which lies south of the Gáro Hills and east of the old Brahmaputra, and which, though geographically a part of the Surma
Valley, is not included in the Province of Assam, but forms part
of the Bengal district of Mymensingh. Its mean elevation above
sea level is much lower, the cold-weather zero of the Surma at
Sylhet being only 22·7 feet above the sea, while that of the
Brahmaputra at Gauháti is 148·36 feet. The course of the numerous rivers which traverse it is thus exceedingly sluggish, while
the stream of the Brahmaputra is swift. While the latter river
hurries rapidly along, through a waste of sandy *churs*, making and
unmaking its banks year by year, the rivers of the Surma Valley
find their way to the great estuary of the Megna by extremely
tortuous channels, the banks of which, reinforced by the annual
deposition of silt, are the highest ground in the alluvial area,
and as such are the most populous and best cultivated portions.
To the north of the valley stands the steep face of the Khási and
Jaintia Hills, the plateau of which rises very abruptly from the
plain to a height of 4,000 feet, the table land presenting, when
seen from Sylhet, an almost level line. Near the eastern boundary
of Sylhet, the plateau recedes into the interior of the hills, and
a new barrier, the angular and serrated range of the Baráil,
or "Great Dyke," takes its place as the northern boundary of
the valley. This range gradually increases in height and precipitous character as one proceeds eastwards, and at the eastern
extremity of Cachar takes a curve to the north-east, thereafter
forming the main axis of the Nága Hills, and eventually merging
in the Pátkoi. To the east the valley is shut in by the mountains
of Manipur, a continuation of the succession of parallel ridges, lying
north and south, into which the Arrakan Yoma range divides
as it approaches the Himalayas. On the south also these parallel
ridges extend for some distance into the alluvial plain, gradually

Section 1.

Area and
Boundaries
and
Physical
Features.

retreating as the river emerges from Cachar into Sylhet, but still preserving their uniform meridional direction, until the Bengal district of Tippera is reached.

Throughout this great alluvial plain, except in the western portion adjoining Mymensingh, the surface is broken by frequent groups of isolated hills of small height, called *tilas*. These may be regarded as continuations below the alluvium of the southern ranges of Tippera and the Lushai Hills. The most notable are the groups about Chhátak and north of Sylhet, and the Chiknagul hills in Jaintia. In Cachar, the ridges from the south touch the Surma, or Barák, at Badarpur and at the northern end of the Tilain range, and many isolated hills rise throughout that district, chiefly to the south of the river. Except where the *tilas* and the southern ranges project, the whole valley is a vast deltaic expanse, covered with a perplexing network of sluggish streams, and liable to deep flooding in the rains. The highest ground is on the river banks, from which the surface slopes backward into great hollows, called *haurs*, all of which are lakes, some of great extent, in the rains, and in the greater of which water lies in some part throughout the cold season. In the deeply-flooded but populous country to the west, the villages are built on artificially-raised sites along the river margins, and the ground which is thus obtained is so precious that the houses are crowded together in a manner very unlike the straggling aspect of a village in Assam.

5. The Surma, or Barák, river rises in the Baráil range to the north of Manipur. Its sources are among the

The Surma river.

southern spurs of the great mountain mass called Jápvo, on the northern slopes of which are situated the most powerful villages of the Angámi Nágas. Thence its course is south, with a slight westerly bearing, among the Manipur hills, where it receives numerous tributaries before entering British territory. At Tipaimukh, the trijunction point of Manipur, Cachar, and the Lushai Hills, it turns sharply to the north, and, after, emerging from the Bhuban range near Lakhipur, takes a very tortuous course, with a generally westward direction, through the district. A short distance below Badarpur, on the western

boundary of Cachar, it divides into two branches, the northern of
which is known as the Surma, and flows westwards, more or less,
closely under the Khási Hills, having on its banks the important
centres of Sylhet and Chhátak, till it turns southwards at Sunámganj; the southern, called at first the Kusiára, has a south-westerly
direction, and near the confluence of the Manu river from the
south again divides into two branches, the southern of which
reassumes the original name of the whole river, Barák, and,
passing by the towns of Nabiganj and Habiganj, rejoins the Surma
a short distance to the west of the latter place. The other arm,
called first the Bibiána and afterwards the Kalni, also rejoins the
Surma, north of the confluence of the Barák, at Abidabad.

The chief affluents of the Surma on the north, after it enters
British territory, are the Jiri and Jatinga from the North Cachar
Hills, the Luba, Hari, Piyáin, Bogapáni, and Jadakáta, from the
Jaintia and Khási Hills, and the Maheshkáli from the Gáro Hills.
On the south it receives the Sonai, Dhaleswari, and Kátákhál from
the Lushai Hills, and (in its southern branch, the Kusiára-Barák)
the Langai, Juri, Manu, and Khwáhi from the Tippera Hills. At
Bhairab Bázár, in Mymensingh, 20 miles below the Sylhet
frontier at Lakhai, it unites with the old Brahmaputra, and
becomes known thenceforward as the Megna. The Surma is
navigable by steamers as far as Silchar in the rains; in the cold
weather, however, these vessels do not ascend above Chhátak
on the northern and Fenchuganj on the southern branch. Boats
of considerable burthen traverse the whole river system as far
as Banskandi, east of Silchar, throughout the year, and in the
rains are the most usual vehicle of traffic.

6. The hilly tracts included in the Province of Assam consist
of the Assam Range, which is interposed
between the Brahmaputra and Surma Valleys,
the North Lushai Hills, and the ridges, generally of low elevation, which run northward from Hill Tippera
and the Lushai Hills into the Surma Valley. No part of the
Himalayas fall within British territory. These hilly tracts have
already been summarily described. The remarkable plateau of

The Hill tracts.

The Assam Range.

SECTION 1.

Area and Boundaries and Physical Features.

the Gáro-Khási-North-Cachar Hills, which, with the sharply-serrated range of the Baráil and its spurs, constitutes the Assam Range, is joined at its eastern extremity by the Pátkoi to the Himalayan system, and by the mountains of Manipur to the Arrakan Yoma. At its western end, in the Gáro Hills, it attains an elevation of more than 4,600 feet in the peak of Nokrek, above Tura, but falls again before the Khási boundary is reached. The highest points of the Khási-Jaintia table land are the Shillong Peak, 6,450 feet, the Dingyei, 6,077, Rábleng, 6,283, and Suér, 6,390 ; but these are only the most elevated portions of a plateau, hardly any portion of which falls below 6,000 feet, and which is all inhabited and cultivated. To the east the level again falls, the highest summits not much exceeding 5,000 feet in the Jaintia Hills, and considerably less in the Cachar Hills north of the Baráil. The latter range, commencing on the south-east margin of the Khási-Jaintia plateau, where the Hári river issues from the hills, rises by sudden leaps to a considerable height, and among the hills bordering the Jatinga Valley summits of from 5,000 to 6,000 feet are found. The range then curves north-eastwards, and attains a still greater height, where it forms the boundary between the Nága Hills district and the State of Manipur. Here the greatest elevation (in British territory) is reached by the peak of Jápvo, which is a little less than 10,000 feet above the sea. To the north-east of this point the mountain system of the Baráil is broken up, by the influence of the meridional axis of elevation prolonged from the Arrakan Yoma, into a mass of ranges having a general north-east and south-west direction until the Pátkoi is reached. The highest points in this portion are from 8,000 to 9,000 feet. Snow is frequent on Jápvo and in its neighbourhood, but is not known further west. It is also seen to cover the hills lying about the upper course of the Dihing as far as the Pátkoi, a country as yet insufficiently explored.

Between the main axis of the Assam Range and the valley of the Brahmaputra the average height of the hills varies considerably. The country is deeply cut into by river channels, and is covered with dense forest. The isolated block of hills already referred

Section i.

Area and
Boundaries
and
Physical
Features.

to, lying to the east of Nowgong, called the Mikir-Rengma Hills, is cut off from the main range by low-lying valleys, and has within it summits attaining a height of 4,000 feet. Its interior is little known, the population is very sparse, and the country is densely wooded. The hills lying south of Sibságar and Lakhimpur, and peopled for the most part by the tribes of Nágas which have not yet been brought under British administration, consist of small broken ranges, running generally north-east and south-west, or having irregular spurs leading down into the plains, usually steep on the northern side, with a more gradual slope on the south. The greater part of this tract (in which very extensive and valuable seams of coal exist) is uncultivated and forest-clad, the outer ranges being chiefly uninhabited.

On the southern face the Gáro and Khási Hills rise very abruptly from the plains, and present a succession of precipitous faces, into which the rivers, fed by the enormous rainfall of this region, have cut deep gorges as they issue upon the swamps of North Sylhet. The level line forming the horizon of the plateau is not broken until the Baráil is reached, where the contour becomes rugged and irregular, though the sides are still precipitous. In the Gáro Hills, the lower portions of the Khási and Jaintia Hills and the Baráil range, the slopes are forest-clad. In the upper and central plateau of the Khási Hills, and the greater portion of North Cachar, the landscape is one of undulating grassy hills, with occasional groves of pine and oak. It is believed that the forests here have been destroyed or kept down by the custom of annually burning, either for pasture or for cultivation, the long grass with which the surface is covered. Where fires are excluded, thick forests of young pine and mixed leafy trees spring up.

7. The Lushai Hills, which divide Assam from Burma, consist

The southern hills.

of sandstones and shales of tertiary age thrown into long folds, the axes of which run a nearly north and south direction. From the general character of the deposits, it seems probable that they were laid down in the delta and estuary of an immense river issuing from the Himalayas, to the north-east of Assam during tertiary times, and flowing due south through the country now occupied by the Nága and the Lushai Hills. The hills are for the most part covered with dense bamboo jungle and rank undergrowth, but in the eastern portion, owing probably to a smaller rainfall, open grass-covered slopes are found, with groves of oak and pine interspersed with rhododendrons. These hills are inhabited by the Lushais and cognate tribes, but the population is extremely scanty. The outlying slopes in the Cachar district constitute a great forest reserve; in Sylhet they are now being largely opened out for the growth of tea. Till lately, however, they have been left to be roamed over by Tipperas and Kukis, whose annual *jhúms* were the only cultivation which they supported.

SECTION 2.—GEOLOGICAL FEATURES.

8. The Province of Assam contains within its boundaries, as

Division of the subject.

already mentioned, two great alluvial plains, separated by a central mass of mountains called the Assam Range, and further defined,—the Brahmaputra Valley by the Himalayas on the north, and the Surma Valley by the meridional ranges, the prolongation of the Arrakan hill system, on the south. To the east of both valleys is the great extension of the mountain system of Northern Burma, which eventually unites with the Himalayas in the Pátkoi. The geology of this region, therefore, falls apart into that of the hill tracts, which are being denuded, and of the alluvial plains, which are being formed by the same process.

9. Of the Himalayan system which lies to the north of the

The Himalayas.

Brahmaputra Valley we know very little. Such observers as have explored it have been unable to penetrate further than the exterior zone. In this, however, are found the same characteristic formations as distinguish the sub-Himalayan rocks throughout their whole length from the Indus to the eastern limit of observation. These rocks consist of great thicknesses of soft massive sandstones, of tertiary age and fresh-water origin, the dip of which is towards the interior zone of metamorphic rocks. In the western portion of the range, among the Bhutan hills, it is believed that a gap exists in these sub-Himalayan sandstones, or, at any rate, that the outer zone of rocks found elsewhere along the chain, and known as the Siwáliks, is wanting; but further east, in the Dafla hills, and in the Abor mountains north of Dibrugarh, there are the usual two well-marked ranges of sub-Himalayan hills, with an intervening Dún. As in the Siwáliks, nests and strings of lignite are frequently found in these rocks, and have given rise to expectations, proved on enquiry to be baseless, that useful coal might be discovered in them.

10. Of the rocks which close in the valley on the east nothing

The eastern range.

is known, except that limestone is found among them. This occurs in the shape of boulders and pebbles in the river-beds east of Sadiya, whence it is conveyed by boat down the Brahmaputra, and forms almost the sole lime-supply of Upper Assam.*

11. The Assam Range, which divides the Brahmaputra and

The Assam Range.

Surma Valleys, is separated by well-marked physical and geological features into two great regions, the boundary between which follows the line of the Dhansiri Valley and the Barái range to the point where the latter commences at the south-eastern corner of the Jaintia Hills. The mountains to the west of this boundary, which include the Gáro, the Khási, the Jaintia, and the Mikir Hills, with so much of North Cachar as lies north and west of the Barái, have been described by geologists under the name of the Shillong plateau. The area to the east of this boundary, including the Barái, the ranges of Manipur, and the Nága Hills, is orographically a part of the Burmese mountain system, and of a widely different geological character.

12. The Shillong plateau consists of a great mass of gneiss,

I. The Shillong plateau.

bare on the northern border, where it is broken into hills, for the most part low and

* It is, however, not obtainable in large quantities at remunerative rates, and the demand of the Assam-Bengal Railway, now under construction, for limestone in the Nowgong and Kámrúp districts are being met from the quarries on the southern face of the Khási Hills, from which the stone is brought by river, via Chhátak and Narainganj, to Gauháti.

very irregular in outline, with numerous outliers in the Lower Assam Valley, even close up to the Himalayas. In the central region the gneiss is covered by transition or sub-metamorphic rocks, consisting of a strong band of quartzites overlaying a mass of earthy schists. In the very centre of the range, where the table land attains its highest elevation, great masses of intrusive diorite and granite occur; and the latter is found, in dykes piercing the gneiss and sub-metamorphic series, throughout the southern half to the boundary of the plains. To the south, in contact with the gneiss and sub-metamorphics, is a great volcanic outburst of trap, which is stratified, and is brought to the surface with the general rise of elevation along the face of the hills between Shella and Thariaghat south of Cherrapunji: this has been described as the "Sylhet trap." South of the main axis of this metamorphic and volcanic mass, and almost at the edge of the central intrusive dykes of granite and diorite, fossiliferous strata commence belonging to two well-defined series; (1) the cretaceous, and (2) the nummulitic. On their northern margin both rest conformably on the metamorphics, and rapidly increase in thickness as one proceeds southwards. On the south the whole series bends downwards in a monoclinal flexure, and south of Cherrapunji disappears below the alluvium of the Surma Valley.

The cretaceous series, where last seen, occupies about 1,500 feet between the Sylhet trap and the nummulitic limestone; it varies much in the character of the deposits, consisting chiefly of sandstones, locally massive, coarse, earthy, or ochreous, with intervening dark and pale shales and some layers of flaky, earthy limestone. The series includes several beds of coal, of which the best known are the Maobehlarkar * coal, a few miles south of Mauphlang, whence the station of Shillong is supplied, the extensive and valuable coal-field of Darrangiri, on the Someswari river in the Gáro Hills, and some coal close to the level of the plain at the *débouchure* of the Jádukáta river near Laur in Sylhet; another outcrop to the west of the last-mentioned, on the Maheshkháli river in the Gáro Hills, is very possibly continuous with the latter,

* Described in "Records of the Geological Survey of India," Volume VIII, page 86.

and, if so, promises to be of great value. An isolated specimen of the same series is found on the Námbar stream, on the extreme eastern margin of the Shillong plateau, in the Mikir Hills, a few miles east of Borpathár. This cretaceous coal is brown in colour, compact, splintery, with a conchoidal fracture, and contains numerous specks and small nests of fossil resin.

The nummulitic series, which overlies the cretaceous, varies greatly in thickness in different parts of the range. In the Gáro Hills west of the Someswari it is insignificant; in the Khási Hills it is much more massive. Below Cherrapunji it has a thickness of 900 feet in the Tharia river, consisting of alternating strata of compact limestones and sandstones. It is at the exposure of these rocks on their downward dip from the edge of the plateau that are situated the extensive limestone quarries of the Khási Hills, whence Eastern Bengal is supplied with lime of the best quality. On the level of the plateau above the same strata are found, but have undergone extensive denudation owing to the solubility of the limestone rock in water and the enormous rainfall of that region. In the whole of the southern face of these hills are found numerous caves and underground watercourses due to this cause; and on the plateau of Cherrapunji, while the nummulitic series survives in the rocks on which the Khási village is built, and in the ridge to the west of the old station, the site of the station itself has been swept perfectly clear of it, with the exception of a few rounded hills composed of tumbled fragments of the Larder sandstones which alternated with the calcareous beds.

Before the upthrust of the Barail range the nummulitic beds, like the other members of the series, retire in a north-easterly direction, and their eastern limit has not been traced satisfactorily.

This series also includes coal-beds, several of which have been worked. The best known are the Cherra mines, in a seam situated in the nummulitic mass to the west of the station, and the Lakadong mines in the Jaintia Hills. The nummulitic coal is black, bright, with a cuboidal fracture, and very bituminous.

11. Barail range.

13. There is evidence that, as the nummulitic series overlies the cretaceous, the former was in its turn overlain (perhaps only on its outer margin) by a third, or upper tertiary, series. These rocks have been traced from the western margin of the Gáro Hills, along their southern face (where, south of the Someswari, the tertiary zone is 14 miles wide), and beneath the scarp of the Khási Hills, where they have been almost entirely removed from the plateau by denudation. East of Jaintiapur the soft massive greenish sandstones of this formation appear again in force, and they rise rapidly from this point into the Baráil range. To this series, apparently, belong also the *tilas* of the Sylhet and Cachar plain, and the low meridional ranges of the Tippera and the Lushai Hills, which run up into it on the south; and the valley of Cachar seems to be excavated out of the broken ground where these two conflicting strikes, the west-east of the Baráil, and the south-north of the southern ridges, meet. West of Cachar, the Baráil curves north-eastwards, and the southern ranges take the same direction, till eventually the two lines are found in confluence.

Of this second great division of the Assam Range we know something of the north-western face, looking down upon the Sibságar and Dibrugarh plains, but of the interior very little. A reconnoissance was made in the cold weather of 1881-82 through the eastern and northern portions of Manipur and the district of the Nága Hills, which gave some information regarding the rocks of these regions.

The whole of the western portion of this division of the Assam Range, from the rise of the Baráil in south-eastern Jáintia to the peak of Jápvo in the neighbourhood of Kohima, would appear to be composed of the same tertiary sandstones as have already been mentioned; and the same rocks seem to be continued along the south-eastern margin of the Brahmaputra Valley in Sibságar and Lakhimpur. To these succeed a series of hard sandstones, slates, and shales, with quartzose beds, supposed to be identical with the "axials" of the Northern Arrakan group. Still further east is a considerable trappian intrusion, consisting of serpentine dykes running north and south, identical in composition with those of Burma. Of the Pátkoi itself, and of the junction between it and the Himalayas in the Mishmi Hills, we have at present no information.

14. The north-western face of this region, lying along the Dibrugarh and Sibságar districts, contains several very important coal-fields, which constitute the chief mineral resource of the province. The rocks in which the coal measures occur are, with one exception, situated to the south-west of a great fault, in some places a short distance within the hills, and in others constituting their escarpment towards the plains, which is conjectured to have a throw of from 10,000 to 15,000 feet. They consist of an enormous thickness of sandstones, the upper series of which are topped by conglomerates and clays containing fossil wood ; the coal measures have a thickness of some 2,000 feet, and are succeeded by fine hard sandstones overlying splintery gray shales, several thousand feet thick. The exception is the Jaipur field, in the Tipam hills in the southern corner of the Dibrugarh district, which is north of the fault. Along the Buri Dihing, and near the exit from the hills of the Dikhu, Safrai, Jhanzi, and Disoi rivers, the coal measures are exposed. The greatest of the fields is that of Makum, on the Dihing ; here there is a seam 100 feet thick, containing at least 75 feet of solid coal, and some very large seams have been traced for more than a mile without diminution.

Coal fields of Upper Assam.

The age of these important and extensive coal measures is still uncertain. The coal is of superior quality, and not unlike the nummulitic coal of the Khási Hills, though quite different from the cretaceous coal of the same region ; but the place of the coal in the series where it occurs in Upper Assam renders it extremely difficult to correlate it with the nummulitic coal of Cherra and Lakadong. It is possible that it belongs to the third series, already noticed, along the southern face of the Shillong plateau ; but the associated rocks have not as yet yielded any fossils by which their relations can be studied.*

* "Records of the Geological Survey of India," Volume XV, page 58.

15 Turning now to the alluvium, the marked difference in the physical geography of the Brahmaputra and Surma Valleys, both of which belong to the great Indo-Gangetic plain, has already been noticed. The former is at a considerably higher elevation above sea level than the latter, and the fall is consequently greater. The following are the heights above mean sea level of the chief points (at the surface of the alluvium) in the Brahmaputra Valley.

	Feet.		Feet.
Sadiya	440	Buramukh, near Tezpur	256
Dibrugarh ...	348	Gauháti ...	163
Sibságar ...	319	Goálpára ...	150
Dhubri ...		... 118 feet.	

The valley has thus, in a distance of about 450 miles, a fall exceeding 300 feet. In the Surma Valley, on the other hand, the following are the heights :

Silchar	... 87 feet	Sylhet	... 48 feet.
Chhátak ...		... 41 feet.	

In consequence of this greater fall, the rivers in the Brahmaputra Valley tend to cut away their banks, while those in the Surma Valley tend to raise them. The former is, indeed, most correctly described as in great part a gigantic *khádar*, or strath, within which the river oscillates to and fro, while the latter is a delta in the process of formation. Nearly the whole of the central portion of the Brahmaputra Valley consists of fine greyish-white sand, lightly covered by a layer of clay ; this is diversified near the rocks which occasionally impinge upon the river by beds of strong sandy clay, derived from their detritus. Away from the river the alluvium is more consolidated, and clay, due to the decomposition of the sand, predominates. Throughout this surface there are found here and there (as in the southern portions of the Sibságar district, in the plain of Biswanath, and in the ridge of Tezpur) more elevated tracts, which seem to represent a more ancient *bhángar*, or older alluvium, the greater part of which has disappeared. Such places, where they have been laid bare by the river, are easily distinguishable, by their closer and heavier texture and by their higher colour, from the shifting grey sands of which the rest of the trough is composed, and are often indicated by a name chosen for their peculiar features (*Ranga-mati*, " coloured earth," *Ranga-gora*, " coloured bank ").

In the Surma Valley the process of deltaic formation (whether because depression of the surface has proceeded *pari passu* with alluvial accretion, or because the deposition of silt is slower and less copious than in the central portion of the Gangetic delta) is less advanced than anywhere else in the great alluvial plain. As already explained, the river banks are almost the only high land (always, of course, excepting the *tilas* and hill ranges) in the valley, and behind them lie great basins, or *háurs*, which are deeply covered with water half the year. In the flood season the rivers drain into these *háurs*, and there deposit their silt, the water emerging when the river falls perfectly clear. This process results in a very noticeable raising of the level of these basins ; the Chátla *háur*, a great depression in South Cachar, which receives the floods of the Barák, is said to have risen 18 inches in the ten years ending 1882-83, and almost another foot during the last decade ; the extensive Hakaluki *háur* in South Sylhet, which receives the Langai, is likewise steadily diminishing in depth. One remarkable event in the history of Western Sylhet was the diversion of the Brahmaputra, which, till the commencement of the present century, flowed east of Mymensingh, and of the great tract of old raised alluvium called the Madhupur Jungle, into a new course far to the west. Previously to this diversion, which has now brought the Brahmaputra, as a delta-forming agency, into direct competition with the Ganges, the former river threw the greater portion of its lighter silt into the *bils* of West Sylhet, and thus co-operated in raising that region. Now the Surma Valley depends for its accretions on the purely rain-fed floods of the minor rivers which traverse it, and which are, of course, far inferior as silt-bearers to the great glacier-fed streams that drain the mighty chain of the Himalayas.

SECTION 3.—CLIMATE.

16. The climate of the Assam Province, both in the Brahmaputra and Surma Valleys, is marked by extreme

General remarks.

humidity, the natural result of the great water surface and extensive forests over which evaporation and condensation go on and the close proximity of the hill ranges which bound the alluvial tracts, and on and near to which an excessive precipitation takes place. The cloud proportion throughout the year, even in those months which in the rest of India are generally clear, is very large, dense fogs being characteristic of the cold weather both north and south of the Assam range. It is frequently asserted that the monsoon may be said to begin in Assam two months before its commencement in the rest of India. This, however, is probably a mistake, the exceptionally heavy rainfall of April and May, which is characteristic of the province, and which, aided in the Brahmaputra Valley by the melting of the Himalayan snows, causes a sudden rise of the rivers in those months, being due to local causes, to storms and local evaporation. The spring rains are commonly succeeded by a break, more or less prolonged, of dry weather with westerly winds, before the true monsoon is ushered in, as in most other parts of India, about the beginning of June.

17. Systematic observations have unfortunately been regularly

Observing stations.

taken at only a few points in the province, and the record of its meteorology leaves much to be desired. The places where meteorological observatories have been long established are Sibságar and Silchar; that at Goálpára was closed at the beginning of 1881, and Dhubri was chosen in its stead. At other stations, only the rainfall has hitherto been registered.

18. The mean temperature of the plains portion of the province

Temperature.

is, for a sub-tropical country, generally low. The following are the latest figures for

Sibságar and Dhubri in the Brahmaputra, and Silchar in the
Surma, Valley :

Average monthly mean temperature.

—	January.	February.	March.	April.	May.	June.	July.	August.	September.	October.	November.	December.	Whole year.
Sibságar ..	57·8	61·1	67·6	72·1	77·3	81·5	83·2	82·5	80·8	76·2	67·6	78·7	72·3
Dhubri ..	62·2	61·5	71·6	75·2	77·6	79·3	81·6	80·6	79·1	75·9	70·1	61·5	71·2
Silchar ..	63·3	66·5	73·1	77·7	79·5	81·6	82·2	82·4	81·15	79·1	72·6	65·7	75·5

It will be seen that Sibságar, in the upper half of the Assam Valley, has a lower cold-weather, and higher rainy-season, temperature than Dhubri in the lower half ; and that there is a general coincidence throughout the year between the monthly means for the latter station and Silchar. These points may probably be taken as typical of the greater portion of the plains of Assam.

19. The wind circulation differs considerably in the two valleys. In the Surma Valley, the general
Winds. direction is the same as that in the Gangetic delta, south-west, changing to east towards the head of the valley, for the greater part of the year, with a north-north-east direction during the months of April and May. Over the western portion of the Assam Range the south-west wind from the Bay of Bengal sweeps with considerable force throughout the spring months, preserving a remarkable uniformity of direction. During the rains the direction changes somewhat towards south and south-east, with an occasional northing. In the Brahmaputra Valley, on the other hand, north-east winds are prevalent during the cold-weather and spring months in the upper portion, south-west winds taking their place during July and August. At Goálpára, in the lower half of the valley, the north-east wind also prevails during the greater part of the cold weather ; but for the rest of the year south-east winds are the general feature. Thus, the monsoon winds of the Assam Valley are a back-current of the south-west monsoon, which undoubtedly blows across the hill range to the south. Both in the cold weather

and rains calms are frequent in both valleys, though seldom of long continuance.

Storms often occur in the spring months, generally accompanied by high winds and heavy local rainfall. The valleys and hills of the Shillong plateau assist in the formation, and determine the direction, of these disturbances, which are most common in the lower portion of the Assam Valley. Cyclones from the Bay of Bengal frequently visit and give heavy rainfall to the western portion of the range and the plains at its foot ; they most often occur at the close of the rainy season.

20. The average monthly mean relative humidity of the three observing stations in the two valleys is shown below :

Humidity.

—	January.	February.	March.	April.	May.	June.	July.	August.	September.	October.	November.	December.	Whole year.
Sibsagar	86	81	79	87	82	81	84	84	86	85	81	85	84
Dhubri	76	64	61	68	80	88	86	87	83	80	77	76	78
Silchar	74	70	72	76	80	82	85	85	84	80	77	75	79

This distribution of humidity resembles that of the Bengal delta, and differs greatly (except, of course, in the rainy season) from the data afforded by stations whose relative place in the Ganges Valley resembles those of the three stations selected in Assam. Taking the year as a whole, the humidity of the climate of Sibsagar is exceeded by that of no other meteorological station in India,* and is equalled only by Darjeeling.

21. The following figures show the recorded averages of cloud proportion (complete overclouding being represented by 10) at each of the three observing stations month by month :

Cloud proportion.

—	January.	February.	March.	April.	May.	June.	July.	August.	September.	October.	November.	December.	Whole year.
Sibsagar	5·4	5·5	6·1	6·9	7·8	8·4	8·5	8·5	8·	6·5	4·5	4·4	6·7
Dhubri	1·9	1·6	2·4	3·3	4·6	7·3	6·9	7·4	6·5	2·7	1·4	1·2	3·9
Silchar	3·2	3·1	4·4	5·3	6·2	7·4	7·9	7·9	7·1	4·8	3·4	2·9	5·3

* Excluding Ceylon. The humidity of Galle and Newera Eliya in that island is slightly greater than that of Sibsagar, and that of two other stations is exactly equal to it.

Out of 81 stations at which cloud observations have been taken in India, Sibságar stands at the head of the list,[*] being approached only by Darjeeling. This peculiarity is probably due to the regular prevalence of dense fogs (which are counted as cloud in the table) during the cold weather in the Assam Valley, and to the copious spring rainfall. In the Surma Valley, fogs are decidedly less prevalent, and less dense when they occur, than in that of the Brahmaputra, and are also less common in the upper part of the valley, where Silchar is situated, than in the western half.

22. The distribution of rainfall in Assam is that portion of the meteorology of the province which is best known, and also that in which it differs most remarkably from other parts of India. Besides the observations taken at district and subdivisional headquarters, a rain-gauge is, as a rule, kept, and the rainfall is recorded at every tea garden. There are thus abundant materials for the study of the subject. The table below has been constructed to show separately the rainfall of the three seasons into which the year falls apart, in the Brahmaputra and Surma Valleys and the intervening hill region, respectively. The stations chosen are those at which observations have been recorded for the longest time :

Rainfall.

		Cold-weather rainfall.				Spring rainfall.			Monsoon rainfall.					
—		November.	December.	January.	February.	March.	April.	May.	June.	July.	August.	September.	October.	Whole year.
BRAHMAPUTRA VALLEY.														
Dhubri	..	0·12	0·16	0·42	0·52	1·02	5·14	14·67	25·57	14·63	12·37	12·68	4·23	90·95
Goálpára	..	0·20	0·27	0·52	0·54	2·24	6·46	13·01	24·65	17·76	12·13	11·43	4·18	94·02
Cauhátí	..	0·60	0·27	0·64	0·90	2·42	6·05	9·53	12·91	12·54	10·80	8·00	2·07	65·00
Tezpur	..	0·80	0·39	0·65	0·84	2·3	6·05	9·45	13·56	15·01	12·45	9·31	3·07	74·23
Nowgong	..	0·50	0·26	0·57	1·03	2·44	5·52	8·34	13·16	16·08	14·9	11·21	3·94	79·83
Sibságar	..	1·21	0·60	1·22	2·15	4·54	9·23	11·24	14·04	15·13	15·01	11·73	5·11	90·15
Dibrugarh	..	1·27	0·94	1·47	2·29	5·54	9·74	13·53	18·86	19·52	18·11	13·93	5·90	111·72

* The cloud proportion at Batticaloa in Ceylon is exactly equal to that at Sibságar.

SECTION 3.

Climate.

			Cold weather rainfall.				Spring rainfall.				Monsoon rainfall.			
		November.	December.	January.	February.	March.	April.	May.	June.	July.	August.	September.	October.	Whole year.
HILL DISTRICTS.														
(Assam Range.)														
Tura	..	..	0·45	0·12	0·68	0·71	1·80	6·10	15·92	26·46	23·31	20·8	10·75	7·05	105·23
Shillong	..	..	1·05	0·50	0·50	0·74	1·70	3·75	10·54	18·55	13·55	13·5	10·11	6·11	84·76
Cherra Punji	..	..	1·55	0·25	0·5	2·32	9·65	29·50	51·57	114·55	115·55	86·0	51·56	12·45	475·61
Kohima	..	..	1·25	0·47	0·71	1·10	2·42	4·51	7·31	14·4	15·67	14·2	10·15	3·17	77·03
SURMA VALLEY.														
Sylhet	..	..	1·06	0·27	0·37	1·45	6·32	11·75	21·51	32·55	25·33	20·15	20·75	7·56	158·13
Silchar	..	..	1·11	0·61	0·67	2·3.	8·25	13·25	15·91	19·51	25·5	18·2.	13·87	5·54	150·55

This table exhibits, in a very conspicuous manner, the chief feature of the Assam climate, both in the Brahmaputra and Surma Valleys, *viz.*, its copious rainfall between March and May, at a season when throughout Northern India generally precipitation is at its minimum. It also indicates the existence, in the Brahmaputra Valley, of a middle region (Gauhâti, Tezpur, Nowgong), where the spring and monsoon falls are less than at either extremity of the valley. This may possibly be due to the fact that south of this portion lies the most lofty part of the Shillong plateau, on the southern face of which (at Cherra Punji) and over the central table land the monsoon currents are drained of their humidity. To the west of this central plateau the valley is open to the winds of the Bengal delta ; and to the east the average height of the range falls greatly, admitting the south-west monsoon, by the gorge of the Jatinga Valley, over the low uplands of North Cachar and down the long valley of the Dhansiri, into the great plain of Sibsâgar and Lakhimpur.

In the Surma Valley, the copiousness of the spring rainfall is even more conspicuous than in Assam Proper. The recording stations here are, unfortunately, rather close to the southern face of the Assam range, so that they do not very accurately represent the mean rainfall of this region.

The few stations for which observations have been recorded in the hill region have the character of their rainfall determined very largely by local conditions. Tura, the chief town of the Garo Hills, is situated (at an elevation of only 1,323 feet above the sea) on the northern skirts of the range which forms the main axis of the hills, and rises south of the station to a height of 4,652 feet in the peak of Nokrek. It is thus greatly sheltered from the monsoon currents, which expend their moisture upon the ridge at its back. Similarly, Shillong, though only 30 miles distant from Cherra, where the greatest recorded rainfall in Asia is found, has the clouds drained of their humidity long before they reach it by the immense precipitation along the southern edge of the plateau and in the central table land, which lies some 1,500 feet above the site of the station. Cherra Punji, on the other hand, is so placed as to exemplify all the conditions needed for a great rainfall. It stands, immediately overlooking the plains at a height of 4,455 feet, on a small plateau of thick-bedded sandstones, bounded on two sides by 2,000 feet of sheer descent, which close in gorges debouching southwards on Sylhet, which is practically at sea-level. The south-west wind, sweeping over the inundated alluvial tract, blows up these gorges, as well as on the southern face of the general scarp, and, having reached the heads of the gorges, ascends vertically. The plateau is thus during the summer months surrounded, or nearly so, by vertically-ascending currents of saturated air, the dynamic cooling of which is the cause of the enormous precipitation. It lies, moreover, at the elevation of 4,000 feet, which is found in the Himalayas to be that of maximum precipitation. The annual average varies greatly in different parts of the station, although the whole extent of the plateau is not much more than a couple of square miles. Some of the earlier registers, which were those of rain-gauges near the edges of the plateau, show a higher precipitation than those kept in recent years nearer its centre. The fall has varied greatly from year to year: 805 inches were recorded in 1861, and in the month of July of that year 366 inches fell. In 1884 the total fall was only 276 inches.

Kohima is situated on a ridge north of the great mountain

mass of Jápvo (9.890 feet high), and is thus, like Tura and Shillong,
protected from the full force of the monsoon currents.

23. These being the general characteristics of the climate of
Assam, it will readily be understood that in
its effects upon human health and economic

Effect of climate on
health.

conditions, it presents the usual features of
a cool, equable, humid, sub-tropical region. *Kála-azár*, malarial
diseases, and cholera are the most prevalent forms of sickness.
Kála-azár was once thought to be due to the effects of malaria,
but recent enquiries have shown that it is caused by the attacks
of a parasite (*Dochmius duodenalis*), to the development of which
the humidity of the atmosphere is peculiarly favourable.* The
heavy mortality from this cause was first noticed in 1882 in certain
villages along the northern terai of the Gáro Hills, and in 1884
the number of deaths became so great that a special relief work
was organised. Since that date the disease has spread gradually
through the Goálpára subdivision, and throughout that portion of
the Kámrúp district which lies on the south bank of the Brahmaputra. It has now reached the Nowgong district, and for several
years past a number of deaths in North Kámrúp and Mangaldai
have also been reported to be due to this disease. The mortality
attending its progress has been terrible, and tracts, which before
its advent were covered with thickly-peopled and prosperous
villages, have been left by it deserted and uncultivated. Whole
villages have thus disappeared, and large areas of land have been
thrown out of cultivation. Malaria lurks chiefly in the broken
country forming the skirt of the Assam Range, where the long low
valleys are seldom stirred by the strong winds which blow on the
southern face. In the open country away from the hills it is
seldom severe; and the plains of Sibságar and Dibrugarh, with the
southern portion of Sylhet, are probably throughout the whole of
India, outside of the hills, the tracts which are most suited for
habitation by Europeans, who generally enjoy excellent health.
Notwithstanding the great water surface of Sylhet, and the deep

* Further enquiries have, however, thrown doubt on the correctness of this view. See
Assam Sanitary Reports for 1893 and 1894 and Chief Commissioner's Resolutions thereon.

flooding which it undergoes in the rains, it is, on the whole, a very healthy district. Cachar, which is more confined by hills, is less so. The climate of the hills is healthy or the reverse according to their elevation. The whole of the central plateau of the Shillong range is very salubrious, and the same is the case with the Nága Hills. The Gáro and North Cachar Hills, on the other hand, are low and feverish.

The copiousness of the spring rains, and the steady prevalence of moisture throughout the year, are *and on crops.* extremely favourable to the two great crops of the province : rice and tea. The cultivation of the former resembles in its main features that of the same staple throughout Bengal. But in Assam and Sylhet, tea yields more largely, and can be plucked and manufactured more continuously, than in any other part of India.

Famine, or even scarcity, due to drought, is unknown in the province ; losses from inundation occasionally happen.* But excessive floods are seldom of long duration, and the submerged lands can usually be re-sown ; in any case, a bumper crop the next season invariably follows upon the destruction of one harvest by flooding.

24. Under this section may be mentioned the earthquakes to *Earthquakes.* which the province, or at least the eastern half of it, is subject. Several severe shocks have been recorded, but none such have occurred during the last decade. A full account of the Cachar earthquake of the 10th January 1869 has been published in the "Memoirs of the Geological Survey," Volume XIX. Another severe shock occurred in September 1875, which did some damage to houses in Shillong and Gauháti ; and Silchar was again visited by an earthquake in October 1882.

SECTION 4.—CHIEF STAPLES.

25. The principal and almost the only food-grain of the plains *Food-grains.* portion of the province is rice. The production of this staple is carried on generally under the same conditions as in Bengal ; but the times of sowing

---

* In the Lushai Hills great scarcity has occasionally been caused by the ravages of rats.

and reaping, and the names given to the several crops, vary much in different parts of the province.

One exception to this barbarous system of agriculture is found among the Angámi Nágas. The powerful villages of this people, which lie about the skirts of the central mass of Japvo, are surrounded by admirably-constructed terraced rice-fields, not, as in the Khási Hills, cut in the gentle slope of the valleys and embanked with earthen dykes, but built up with stone retaining-walls at different levels, and irrigated by means of skil-fully-engineered channels, which distribute the water over each step in the series. These remarkable works appear to be peculiar to the group of villages mentioned, their neighbours following the ordinary system of cultivation by *jhúm*. They have doubtless been produced by the necessity of their position. Living in con-stant warfare with one another and with their neighbours, and maintaining their supremacy by military force, these ruling villages were formerly compelled to keep their food-supply in the immediate vicinity of their habitations, and thus to make the utmost of the productive powers of the valley bottoms, instead of carrying their tillage over the wide hill-sides in a rotation of many years, as is done by hillmen elsewhere. Another reason for their resort to irrigation appears to be that their hills are too densely peopled to admit of *jhúm* cultivation, as, although the latter seems to yield a larger outturn for the years during which the cultiva-tion is carried on, the land rapidly becomes exhausted, and, after two or three years' cultivation, requires a long rest before it recovers its fertility; a tribe cultivating on the *jhúm* system thus requires a much greater area of land for its support than one resorting to irrigation.

26. In the Brahmaputra Valley generally there are only two great rice crops,—the *áhu*, (*ásu*, *áus*) and the *sáli* (*háli*). The *áhu*, or early rice, is generally sown broadcast (though it is sometimes transplanted) upon higher lands in February and March, and is reaped soon after the setting in of the rains, from June to August. The *sáli*, on the contrary, is sown first in nurseries in June, and is trans-

Brahmaputra Valley.

planted in July and August into fields which can be flooded in the rains ; it is reaped in December and January.*

The following table will serve to show comparatively the area under these two descriptions of rice and that under other crops in the districts of the Brahmaputra Valley. It represents only lands amalgamated with the mauza, that is, in charge of the local fiscal officers, and does not include in Goálpára the permanently-settled portion of the district, or, in the other districts, the estates of revenue-free holders, grantees of waste lands devoted to tea cultivation, or large privileged holders who pay only half the ordinary rates of revenue, but, though for these reasons not exhaustive, it sufficiently indicates the relative proportions of rice and other cultivation in the districts of the valley :

District.	Early rice.	Late rice.	Mustard.	Cane.	Pulse.	Other crops.	Basti.	Fallow.	Total.	Deduct twice cropped.	Total cultivated area.
	1	2	3	4	5	6	7	8	9	10	11
	Acres.	Acres.	Acres.	Acres.	Acres.	Acres.	Acres.	Acres.	Acres.	Acres.	Acres.
Goálpára ..	17,689	40,896	8,192	49	656	1,057	5,193	611	74,343	8,149	66,194
Kámrúp ..	201,327	357,179	87,240	4,110	28,361	37,284	55,591	86,487	840,581	121,684	719,197
Darrang ..	40,159	146,315	11,576	2,123	12,563	10,618	23,287	39,131	286,172	10,127	276,045
Nowgong ..	44,894	158,490	61,781	2,315	19,911	4,656	26,028	11,440	326,555	42,101	284,454
Sibságar ..	10,585	230,949	12,552	7,661	9,003	28,373	50,619	58,081	429,125	9,936	418,191
Lakhimpur ..	11,611	84,160	3,957	3,468	1,840	4,581	10,614	7,316	126,447	1,915	124,532
Total ..	329,569	1,018,089	154,608	19,716	72,134	86,549	171,734	203,066	2,682,825	193,912	1,858,613

* The names in this paragraph designate harvests rather than kinds of crop. In Kámrúp, for instance, the *áhu* includes (1) the *dhulia áhu*, sown early in dry pulverised fields, which gives the best outturn ; (2) *ásrá*, sown broadcast in fields reduced to a puddle by the early rains ; and (3) *kharma* (called *pharma* in Upper Assam), which is transplanted. The last two are less productive than the first. Under *sáli* is included *báo*, a kind of rice sown early in the season in hollows which fill too deeply with water for *áhu* or ordinary *sáli* ; it is reaped about a month before the latter, and yields a very heavy outturn. *Báo* is sometimes sown broadcast and is sometimes transplanted ; in some districts the area under this crop is considerable. It is sometimes sown together with *áhu*, and if the inundation drowns the latter, the cultivator at least gets his crop of *báo* ; if the rains are moderate, both crops may be reaped, the *áhu* first, the *báo* springing up after the other has been taken away ; lastly, if the rains are scanty, the *báo* hollows give an excellent crop of *sáli* rice. *Sáli*, properly so called, is again divided into " *láhi* " and " *bor* " *dhán* : the former includes the finer varieties, which are grown on comparatively high land where the supply of water is somewhat scanty ; the latter is planted on land which is liable to be more heavily flooded.

Thus, out of the total cultivation, 53·7 per cent. is late rice, or *sáli*, and 17·4 per cent. early rice or *áhu*, the two together making up 71·1 per cent. of the whole of the cultivation in the valley. The remainder is distributed between mustard 9·7 per cent., pulse 3·8 per cent., sugarcane 1·04 per cent., the balance consisting of other crops, such as *til* or sesamum, several varieties of pulse or *dál*, Indian-corn, tobacco, betel, plantations of *sum*-trees (*machilus odoratissima*) for rearing silk, vegetables for household use, &c.

Of the land shown as cropped twice in the year, no portion is included in that occupied by *sáli* rice or sugarcane. *Áhu* rice, mustard, and *mátikalai* (*phaseolus radiatus*), the most common variety of *dál* or pulse grown in Assam) to some extent occupy the same land, that cultivated in the spring with the first-named yielding a winter crop of either of the two latter. But mustard is chiefly grown in the low inundated country of Nowgong, Kámrúp, and Darrang, known as the *chápuri maháls*, on the light soil left after the inundation has subsided. The grass is pressed down and left to wither, after which it is burnt, the soil lightly stirred, and the seed put in. The crop is reaped about February.

27. For the Surma Valley, owing to the fact that the greater part of Sylhet is permanently settled, and that Cachar is settled for a term, while in neither district do *mufassal* establishments corresponding to the *patwaris* of Upper India or the *mandals* of the Brahmaputra Valley exist, we have no accurate statistics of the relative area under different kinds of crop. But here also rice is so much the most important staple that it is unnecessary to notice any other. There is proportionately much less mustard grown in this valley than in Assam Proper, and there is but little export of it to Bengal. Besides mustard, a variety of radish, or *muli*, with a white flower, is cultivated as an oil seed in Sylhet. The various kinds of pulse are also insignificant in area. Sugar is produced in some quantity in the south-west corner of the district, and has a local reputation.

The great crop of rice in Sylhet is the late rice, *áman* and *sail*: the first of these two names is applied chiefly to rice sown broadcast, while the latter (which corresponds in name and character

to the *sáli* of Assam) is transplanted. This crop is reaped from
the middle of November to the end of January. The *áus* (*ásu* or
áhu of Assam) is a comparatively small crop; it is harvested
between the 1st June and the middle of September. In the
western and central parts of the district, which are subject to deep
flooding, a cold-weather rice, called *sáil bura*, is grown in marshy
land, and reaped in April and May. This variety is only locally
of importance.

In Cachar, the rice crops resemble those of Sylhet, consisting of the early and late *áus* (both minor crops), harvested between
June and September, and the *sáil* and *ásrá* (the latter answering
to the *áman* of Sylhet), reaped in November and December.

28. In the hill districts, rice holds a less exclusive place
among the crops cultivated. There are great
differences in different parts of the province
in the crops grown and the system of cultivation adopted; these
differences are determined partly by the character of the country
and partly by the degree of civilisation possessed by the tribe.
Among the Khásis the system of agriculture is comparatively
elaborate, and carefully adjusted to the productive powers of the
soil. In the flattish valleys, with which the central plateau
abounds, rice is grown in terraced and well irrigated fields, and
such fields are found also on the northern margin of the district
wherever the conformation of the surface admits of them. With
this exception, however, the rest of their crops are grown on hill
sides, the turf and scrub upon which are burnt after being previously arranged in beds, and the seed sown in the ashes, which
serve as manure. In this way are raised unirrigated rice, potatoes,
various kinds of millet [the three principal being *soh-riu* or Job's-
tears (*Coix lacrima*), *rai-tru* (*Eleusine coracana*), *rai-sháng* (*Digi-
taria sp.?*)], and a crop called *sohphláng* (*Flemingia vestita*), a
leguminous plant with a red flower, which produces large numbers
of tubers about the size of a pigeon's egg among its roots: these
are eaten raw by the Khásis.

The crops just described are those of the central plateau;
besides these, chiefly on the northern slopes of the hills towards

Hill districts.

Kámrúp and Nowgong, cotton is grown in forest clearings, or *jhúms*, where the soil is enriched by burning the felled trees and scrub. On the southern face of the hills, and on the slopes stretching into Sylhet, are produced the crops to which the wealth of the Khásis is so largely due,—oranges, betel-nuts, and pine-apples. The orange and betel-nut trees grow together, in care-fully kept and regularly renewed groves, and bear in immense profusion. The pine-apple grows like a weed in this region, and is extraordinarily cheap and abundant. Besides these field crops, every Khási village on the plateau has its carefully hedged home-stead lands, in which fine crops of potatoes, Indian-corn, vege-tables, and pulses are raised, with occasional plots of sugarcane.

No others among the hill races can compete with the Khásis in the value of their staples, or the enlightened character of their agriculture. The Gáros to the west, and the Mikirs, Kacharis, and Kukis to the east, cultivate entirely by *jhúming*, clearing the forest with axe and fire, and growing in the space thus secured, among the ashes of the trees and undergrowth, mixed crops of long-stemmed rice, chillies, cotton, millets, and gourds. Some of these tribes are less untidy than others in their mode of tillage, and devote a *jhúm* to a single crop, as rice, cotton, or millet: others mix their crops, which come to maturity at different times during the year. But such a *jhúm* at best is a repulsive sight with its rotting or half-burnt trunks of trees lying as they were felled, and the crop struggling with the weeds of the jungle. Land thus *jhúmed* is nowhere occupied longer than three years, and often less, after which it requires from ten to twenty years to recover its fertility and to become reclothed with forest. All the cotton grown in the province is raised by the hill tribes in this manner, and is remarkable for its short staple and harsh woolly fibre; indeed, it so much resembles wool that it has found a demand in Europe for mixing with wool for the manufacture of carpets.

29. For a series of years, numerous experiments were made annually with a view to ascertaining the average outturn of the different crops grown in Assam. The result of experiments continued over eight years

Average outturn of crops.

seems to be that *sáli* on the average yields a crop of about 20 maunds per acre, *áhu* 17 maunds, and *bao* 16 maunds.* In Sylhet, the outturn of *áman* is nearly 19 maunds and that of *áus* 14 maunds per acre. The yield of *áus* (*dumai* and *murali*) in Cachar is 15 maunds per acre ; the experiments in other varieties of rice in that district have not been sufficiently numerous to furnish a reliable average.

For mustard, the same series of experiments shows an average outturn of 6½ maunds per acre. A particularly interesting feature of the experiments in the outturn of this crop is the proof afforded by them that the yield on land cultivated for the first year is greater than that for the second year, and that in subsequent years the annual outturn falls rapidly. The figures for five years' experiments on lands cultivated for the first, second, and third years are 574 pounds, 501 pounds, and 378 pounds, respectively.

The average yield per acre of other crops is—sugarcane 1,515 pounds, *mátikalai* 401 pounds, linseed 433 pounds, rapeseed 328 pounds, uncleaned cotton 283 pounds, *til* 274 pounds, jute 1,045 pounds, and onions 1,625 pounds.

SECTION 5.—COMMERCIAL STAPLES.

30. The most important commercial staple of Assam is tea.

Tea.

The plant is indigenous to the province, being found wild in the forests south of the Dihing, in the Nága Hills to the south of Sibságar, and in Manipur, North Cachar, and the Lushai Hills. The following paragraphs, extracted from a memorandum written by Mr. (now Sir John) Edgar in 1873, give in a brief and convenient form a sketch of the growth and progress of the tea industry in this province from its commencement down to that year :

There have been lively disputes as to the first discoverer of tea in Assam, and the date of its discovery. It is probable that a Mr. C. A. Bruce, who

---

* Unfortunately, the experiments of earlier years failed to distinguish between the different varieties of *sáli* and *áhu*. But from the figures for 1888-89 it appears that while the *bor dhán* variety of *sáli* yielded 1,821 pounds per acre, *láhi* yielded only 1,159 pounds. Similarly, transplanted *áhu* or *kharma dhán* gave an average outturn of 1,380 pounds, against 1,300 pounds for *áhu* sown broadcast.

SECTION 5.
Commercial Staples.

commanded a division of gunboats in Upper Assam during the first Burmese war, brought down from Upper Assam some plants and seed of the indige* nous plant in 1826, and he actually received a medal from the English Society of Arts. But his claim to have been the first discoverer of tea was disputed by a Captain Charlton, who asserted that the existence of tea in Assam had been first established by himself in 1832. In 1834, a committee was appointed to enquire into, and report on the possibility of introducing the cultivation of tea into India. In 1835 the first attempt was made by Government to establish an experimental plantation in Lakhimpur, but it failed, and the plants were afterwards removed to Jaipur, in the Sibságar district, and a garden established, which was sold to the Assam Company in 1840. This Company, which was formed about 1839, was the first, and is still very much the greatest, concern for the cultivation of tea in Bengal. It was not, however, very prosperous during its early years, and in 1846-47 its shares are said to have been almost unsaleable. Its prospects began to improve about 1852, and in 1859 it was reported officially to have a cultiva-ted area of about 3,967 acres, with an estimated outturn of over 760,000 pounds of tea. Meantime, tea cultivation had been commenced in many other districts. In 1850 a garden was started by Colonel Hannay near Dibrugarh, and in 1853, when Mr. Mills of the Sudder Court visited Assam, he found three private gardens in Sibságar and six in Lakhimpur. In 1851, the first gardens were started in Darrang and Kámrúp. In 1855 indigenous tea was found in Cachar, and the first garden in the district was commenced in the cold season of that year. In the following year (1856) tea was discovered in Sylhet, but no attempt at cultivating it was made for some time after.

It may be said generally that the foundations of the present tea indus-try were laid between 1856 and 1859. In the latter year the labour difficulty began to be seriously felt in Assam and Cachar; but, although Colonel Jenkins, Commissioner of Assam, recorded a serious warning, no one else seemed able to foresee the formidable dangers into which the too rapid progress of the industry would bring it. Later still, in 1862-63, officials as well as planters seem to have indulged in visions of fabulous prosperity, which only deepened the gloom of the miserable time that was so soon to come on them. The Land Revenue Administration Report for that year contains extracts from reports from Assam, Cachar, Sylhet, and Darjeeling, written in the most hopeful spirit; indeed, the two former are written in an exalted tone that contrasts curiously with the usual sobriety of official reports. But even at the time of publication of these reports suspicions had begun to arise about the soundness of this condition of affairs, which was apparently so brilliant. An Act for the regulation of the transport of native labourers emigrating to Assam and Cachar, passed in 1863, was expected to remedy many hideous evils which were discovered to exist in the importation of labourers required to supplement the scanty local supply. But it soon came to light that the condition of these labourers on many gardens in both districts was most deplorable, while the mortality among them was appalling. The evil first fruits of the reckless way in which waste lands had been dealt with, in the belief that Government was fostering tea cultivation thereby, were being gathered in the shape of increasing hostility to Government and its officials, caused by difficulties about surveys, boundaries, title-deeds, and the like, which all had arisen out of the mistaken policy of giving vast tracts of land to anyone choosing to ask for them, without enquiry and without precaution of any kind.

In 1865, an Act was passed for the regulation of the relations of employers and imported labourers after the arrival of the latter in the districts of Assam, Sylhet, and Cachar. Here I shall only say that, though at first at least it did little to improve the condition of the labourers, I am convinced that it had not the slightest connection with the temporary collapse of the tea industry which took place in the following year. The cause of the crash of 1866 was the utterly unsound foundation on which the fabric of the tea industry had been based, and not directly the action of Government, as at the time it was the fashion of even usually well-informed persons to assert. At the same time, we should never lose sight of the fact that the industry might never have got into the ruinous state of inflation that it was in previous to 1866, had it not been for the unwise attempts of Government to foster it at the outset by sacrificing the most necessary safeguards in dealing with land. The depression of the industry consequent on the collapse of so many concerns in 1866 was, of course, intensified by the ignorance of the general body of proprietors of tea shares, who, as was remarked by me in a paper written in 1867, showed as much folly in their hurry to get out of tea as they had a few years before in their eagerness to undertake the speculation.

This depreciation of tea property continued during the years 1866, 1867, and 1868; but about 1869 things began to look brighter. It was seen that people who had worked steadily for years with a view to make gardens that would yield a profit had been rewarded, while much of the property of the collapsed companies had turned out well under careful management. In fact, it was again found out that tea would pay, and ever since it has been steadily progressing in popular estimation, and, as a general rule, in profit to those engaged in it.

F

SECTION 5.

Commercial
Staples. There cannot be the slightest doubt that the industry is in an infinitely better and safer position now than it was ten years ago. The existing gardens are, as a general rule, well filled with plants, highly cultivated, and carefully managed. The amount of tea produced per acre, although falling far short of the sanguine expectation of the first days of tea-planting, is satisfactory in all the more important districts, while the prices obtained this season show that the average quality must be very good. There is every reason to hope that the labour difficulty is disappearing in Cachar, and, in spite of the complaints from Assam, there are evident signs of improvement in that province.

Tea is now cultivated in all the plains districts of the province, and there is one garden in the Khási Hills. The following figures give the total area under tea in each district, and the estimated outturn in pounds, according to the last returns, those of 1892:

		Area in acres.			Approximate outturn in pounds.
		Mature plants.	Immature plants.	Total.	
Brahmaputra Valley.					
Goálpára	...	380	36	416	144,825
Kámrúp	...	4,604	218	4,822	769,384
Darrang	...	20,885	3,745	24,630	11,275,835
Nowgong	...	10,856	1,146	12,002	3,209,496
Sibságar	...	50,503	7,441	57,994	18,094,557
Lakhimpur	...	32,793	7,391	40,184	15,567,207
Total	...	120,021	19,997	139,998	49,061,304
Surma Valley.					
Sylhet	...	40,300	7,574	47,874	18,649,385
Cachar	...	53,184	6,106	59,290	16,506,444
Khási Hills	...	20	10	30	4,000
Total	...	93,504	13,690	107,194	35,159,829
Grand total	...	213,525	33,667	247,192	84,221,133

When the industry was first undertaken, the land which was supposed to be best suited for the plant was hill or undulating ground, such as the spurs of the Khási Hills, in South Kámrúp, and the *tilas* of Sylhet and Cachar. Now, however, it has been found in the Surma Valley that, with good drainage, the heaviest crops of tea can be raised from low-lying land, even such as formerly supported rice cultivation. In the Assam Valley, the most suitable soil is considered to be the old alluvium, or *bhángar*, such as is found in the south of Sibságar district and in the north of Darrang. This is a rich loam, capable, by reason of its undulating surface, of excellent drainage, and very heavy crops are obtained from such gardens. The average outturn per acre was in 1892 returned as 376 pounds for Sylhet and Cachar, and 409 pounds for the Assam Valley.

31. There is ample space still available for the extension of the tea industry. Besides the 247,192 acres shown in the above statement as already occupied with tea, some 797,792 acres have been taken up for plantation purposes, much of which will, no doubt, in due time, be planted, though a good deal may be unsuitable for tea. Prices have fallen considerably during the last decade, but the introduction of labour-saving machinery and of improved methods of cultivation, together with careful attention to economic working, have combined to reduce the cost of production to such an extent that the profits from the better class of gardens are considerably larger, and the position of the industry generally is now much more assured and satisfactory than it was ten years ago.

Prospects of the tea industry.

32. There are four varieties of domesticated silkworms in Assam. The smaller or multivoltine *pát* worm (*bombyx cræsi*), and the larger or univoltine worm of the same name (*bombyx textor*), both feed on the mulberry, and produce a white silk, which was in considerable demand in the days of the Ahom kings. The cultivation of these silkworms is, however, decreasing, and there is little prospect of its revival. The *muga* worm (*antherœa Assama*) feeds on the *súm* tree (*machilus odoratissima*), and on the *sualu* (*tetranthera monopetala*), as also on a variety of other trees, but the silk yield-

Silk.

F 2

ed by the *súm*-fed worm is the best. The worm is a multivoltine, yielding as many as five broods in the year, but usually only three of these are used for the manufacture of silk ; and in Upper Assam breeding is discontinued during the rainy season, and is resumed on the approach of the cold weather with cocoons imported from Kámrúp and Nowgong. In Upper Assam, the worms are frequently fed on patches of natural forest, but in the western districts land is planted out with *súm* trees for this purpose. The worms are placed on the trees as soon as they are hatched, and are watched night and day during the whole period of their life in the open air. When ready to spin their cocoons, they descend the tree, and are removed by the cultivator. The cocoon is about $1\frac{1}{2}$ inch long by $\frac{3}{4}$ths of an inch in diameter, and yields a soft silk of a bright yellow colour, with a beautiful gloss. The silk is wound off the cocoon by an extremely primitive process of reeling. In 1837, Mr. Hugon calculated that an acre of trees would support worms yielding 50,000 cocoons, capable of being reeled into 12 seers of silk ; but a careful estimate prepared by the Deputy Commissioner of Sibságar in 1882 places the outturn per acre at only a quarter of this quantity,—a difference which may partly be explained by supposing that Mr. Hugon was speaking of plantations, while the Sibságar estimate relates to natural *súm* forest, where the trees grow much more sparsely. The area of such forests in the Assam Valley (where alone the *muga* is produced) is believed to be about 300 square miles ; but this great area is used for breeding silkworms only as the alluvial lands of the Brahmaputra are used for growing mustard, that is to say, parties of men make clearance of the undergrowth in patches, and cultivate silkworms for a year or two, after which they move to another spot. The fourth kind of silkworm reared in Assam is that called *eri*, from its feeding on the *eri* (*endi*) or castor-oil plant. This is bred chiefly by Kacharis, Mikirs, Gáros, and Kukis, both in the Assam Valley and on the northern and southern skirts of the central range of Assam, as also in the low hills to the south of Sylhet and Cachar. It is a multivoltine worm, reared entirely indoors, and yielding five broods in the year. The cocoon is smaller than that of the *muga*, and its colour is either white or a deep brick-red, both red and white cocoons being produced indifferently by worms of the same brood. The silk is never reeled, but is spun off by hand.

The demand for *eri* silk is rapidly increasing, but all attempts at producing it on a commercial scale have hitherto failed, the main reason being that the castor-oil plants, on which the worm feeds, are peculiarly liable to destruction by caterpillars when grown in large quantities. As regards the *muga* cocoon, no method of reeling it has yet been introduced which will enable it to be sold at remunerative prices, and its chief sale continues, as heretofore, to be for the purpose of embroidering the hand-made muslins manufactured at Dacca.

33. Cotton is grown in large quantities along the slopes of the

Cotton.

Assam range, especially in the Gáro and Mikir Hills; it is also grown in the hilly country in South Cachar and Sylhet. It forms, except in the Khási Hills, almost the only produce which the hillman has to barter for the necessaries which he buys at the submontane markets, where a large business in it is done. The staple is, as already mentioned, short and harsh, and the main demand for the hill cotton comes from within the province. (A certain quantity, however, is exported, and 68,435 maunds were exported during 1892-93, against only 14,199 maunds during the corresponding year of the last decade. The demand outside the province seems, therefore, to be increasing.)

34. One of the most valuable products of Assam is India-

Rubber.

rubber, which is obtained almost exclusively from *Ficus elastica*, the outturn from other local species being inappreciable.

The rubber tree, which formerly was found in greater or less abundance in many parts of the province, is now restricted to the most inaccessible forests of the Lakhimpur, Darrang, and Khási Hills districts, and in the last of these this tree is now fast disappearing, owing to the wasteful and destructive methods employed by the tappers for obtaining the rubber. There is also good reason

SECTION 5.
Commercial
Staples.
for supposing that the rubber forests situated in territory beyond the Assam frontier, and from which the larger portion of the total outturn is obtained, are gradually becoming less productive than formerly, and that the more accessible of these forests have been completely worked out. When the last decennial report was compiled in 1882-83, the outturn of rubber was returned as 10,000 maunds per annum. But since then there has been a large falling off, the average output during the past ten years having only slightly exceeded 5,000 maunds, and even this comparatively low average has not been attained during recent years, as will be seen from the following figures :

					Maunds.
Outturn in 1889-90	...	...	...	3,419
,, 1890-91	...	...	...	3,076
,, 1891-92	...	...	...	4,227
,, 1892-93	...	...	...	3,250

Within the last year, the old system of leasing out the product over certain areas, known as *maháls*, was abolished, and replaced by a duty of Rs. 12 per maund, which is imposed on all rubber brought from beyond the frontier, or collected in the Government forests. This change of system, however, did not come into force until November 1892, which accounts for the sudden falling off exhibited in the figures of 1892-93, which must, therefore, be considered as abnormally low. The receipts from rubber during the past ten years have averaged Rs. 33,079 a year, but a considerable increase on this sum may be expected to result in future years from the collection of the abovementioned duty.

The amount of rubber exported from Assam during the past three years has been 4,844 maunds in 1890-91, 5,903 maunds in 1891-92, and 4,006 maunds in 1892-93. Its selling price in the Assam markets is from Rs. 50 to Rs. 60 a maund ; in Calcutta it fetches as much as Rs. 100.

35. Indigenous lac is found in the Assam forests, but the staple is also largely cultivated by artificial propagation. The lac insect is chiefly reared on two kinds of fig (*Ficus cordifolia* and *Ficus laccifera*), which are planted on a large scale near villages in the Kámrúp and Darrang

districts. The form in which the great bulk of the lac is exported
is stick lac, the crude product, consisting of small twigs surrounded
by cylinders of translucent orange yellow gum, in which the insects
which deposited it are embedded. A small export exists of shell
and button lac, and of lac-dye, the result of a process of purifica-
tion applied to the stick-lac. The twigs are first separated, and
the gummy envelope is then scraped and rubbed by hand under
a stream of water till the colouring matter has been thoroughly
extracted; this consists of the dead bodies of the insects buried in
the gum, and gradually precipitates itself to the bottom of the
water when left to settle. The water is then drained off, and the
sediment, after being strained, pressed, and dried, becomes lac-dye,
ready for the market. The gummy exudation is meanwhile dried
in the sun, and then melted, in bags of cotton cloth, over a charcoal fire. It is then squeezed out, either in thin sheets upon an
earthen cylinder, when it becomes *shell-lac*, or in dabs upon a
plantain stalk, when it is called *button-lac*. The exports of lac
and lac-dye during the last three years have been as follows: in
1890-91, 9,337 maunds; in 1891-92, 14,753 maunds; and in 1892-
93, 15,376 maunds.

36. Mustard forms a very important commercial staple in the
Assam Valley, where, as shown in the
preceding section, it is largely grown in the
inundated country of Kámrúp and Nowgong. It is manufactured
to a small extent into oil within the province; but this product is
consumed almost exclusively by the immigrant population. The
following are the exports of mustard-seed during the past three
years from the Assam Valley: •

Mustard.

					Maunds.
1890-91	...	...	...	...	8,69,571
1891-92	...	...	...	...	12,77,217
1892-93	...	...	...	...	11,28,996

But little mustard is exported from Sylhet and Cachar. The
figures are—

					Maunds.
1890-91	...	...	...	...	25,974
1891-92	...	...	...	...	24,958
1892-93	...	...	...	...	18,759

37. Jute is grown for export in Goálpára and Kámrúp, but hardly at all in other districts of the Assam Valley. There is also a little jute in South Sylhet. The following are the figures showing the export of this staple for the past three years:

					Maunds.
1890-91	...	...	...	...	3,10,678
1891-92	...	...	...	...	2,24,595
1892-93	...	...	...	...	2,16,479

Nearly the whole of the above came from the Assam Valley.

38. Potatoes are very largely grown in the Khási Hills, but in no other part of the province, as a commercial staple. They were introduced into this district by Mr. David Scott, Governor General's Agent, in 1830, and are now cultivated throughout the upper plateaux of the Khási Hills Proper, though not in the Jaintia country. Two crops are produced yearly, the first being sown in February and March and reaped in July, and the second put down in August and taken up in November and December. The latter crop is chiefly used for seed, and the export is wholly derived from the former. Large quantities are carried down by cart to Gauháti for the supply of the Assam Valley. But the main channel of export to Bengal is *riâ* Cherra Punji and Sylhet, whence the potatoes are conveyed by boat. The exports reached the highest point known in 1881-82, when they amounted to 1,26,981 maunds. In 1886-87, they were returned at 1,04,910 maunds, but in that year the tubers were attacked for the first time by a disease due to the presence of a fungus (*Phytophthora infestans*), and in the following year the crop was reported to have rotted in the ground. Owing to this disease, the exports continued to fall from 41,548 maunds in 1887-88, and 24,386 maunds in 1889-90 to 12,016 maunds in 1890-91. The disease is now reported to have disappeared to a large extent and the exports have increased in consequence. In 1891-92 they were returned at 29,321 maunds. In the following year (1892-93), however, the exports fell again to 10,776 maunds in consequence of diminished cultivation and increased local consumption.

39. Another article of considerable traffic 'which is exported
from the Khási Hills consists of oranges.
Oranges.
These are produced in great abundance, and
of excellent quality, on the slopes of the hills bordering on Sylhet,
where there is a continuous fringe of orange-groves belonging to
the Khási proprietors from the Bogapani river to the exit of the
Piyá in at Dauki Bázár. The higher plateaux produce lemons of
the best quality in profusion, but these are not largely exported.
The exports of oranges from Sylhet during the last three years
are shown below :

					Maunds.
1890-91	...	...	...	...	1,06,854
1891-92	...	...	...	...	1,13,694
1892-93	...	...	...	...	25,259

40. As might be expected from the character of its surface
and climate, the area of forest in Assam is
Forests.
very extensive, and it is the home of many
extremely valuable timber trees. The head of the Assam Valley.
including the Lakhimpur district and part of the Sibságar and
Darrang districts, is a forest country, the greater portion of the
land not under cultivation being stocked with dense and chiefly
evergreen forest. The middle and lower portion of the valley,
on the other hand, is a comparatively open tract with vast expanses
of grass savannah, and forest only in the vicinity of the hills,
on the extensive tracts of high land and on the isolated hills which
are found in this part of the valley. In the Surma Valley there
is little forest in Sylhet, except on the southern hills stretching
up from Tippera, and in the great valley of the Langai and Singla
rivers, in the south-eastern corner, where there is a forest tract
of 170 square miles. In Cachar the whole of the south of the
district bordering on the Lushai Hills, measuring more than 700
square miles, is a forest reserve, whence the populous district of
Sylhet draws its timber supply ; there are also 38 square miles of
reserve in the north of this district. In the hill districts there is
less good forest than might be expected, though there is no lack
of wooded country ; the habits of the hill races do not permit

G

except in isolated spots to which their *jhúms* have not extended, of the growth of valuable timber. Forest fires and *jhúming* have denuded the interior of the hills, where the people chiefly live, of most of its forests ; but along the northern and southern skirts there are large areas of natural forest still untouched. The following is a statement of the forest area as it stood in each district on the 31st March 1893, classed either as (1) reserved or (2) unclassed forests in which no special measures of protection are in force, but Government asserts its right to the trees, and does not allow them to be felled without payment :

	Forest reserves.	Unclassed State forests.
	Sq. miles.	Sq. miles.
Cachar	752	719
Sylhet	170	241
Goálpára	673	17
Kámrúp	128	468
Darrang	298	191
Nowgong	143	213
Sibságar	848	603
Lakhimpur	429	3,529
Gáro Hills	133	217
Khási and Jaintia Hills	52	100
Nága Hills	......	

The most valuable trees in the forests of Assam are *ajhar* (*lagerstræmia regina*) and *sam* (*artocarpus chaplasha*), which are found throughout the Assam Valley, *nahor* (*mesua ferrea*), which does not grow in the plains of the Brahmaputra Valley west of the Mikir Hills, though common in the evergreen forests of the Gáro and Khási Hills, *sal* (*shorea robusta*), which is found only in the lower part of the valley, in Goálpára, Kámrúp, Darrang, and Nowgong, and the Gáro and Khási Hills, *sissu* (*dalbergia sissoo*) which is not found east of the Manas river, and *khair* (*acacia catechu*), which extends eastwards to Charduar in Darrang. In the Surma Valley, *nahor* (there called *nagesar*), *ajhar* (there called *jarul*), and *cham* (the *sam* of Assam) are the most important trees.

The only trees which are important articles of export are *sal*, *sam*, and *ajhar*, which are largely floated down the Brahmaputra into Bengal, and from Cachar into Sylhet, chiefly for boat building. The exploitation of the Cachar forests for the service of Sylhet has always been active and is extending, while that of the Brahmaputra forests in Goálpára and Kámrúp has lately appeared to be stationary. The upper part of the Assam Valley is too remote from a market for its timber resources to be yet regularly exploited ; the only use made of the forests is to yield posts and beams for house building, trees for *dugouts* (the only kind of boat made in the Brahmaputra Valley), charcoal, chiefly for tea manufacture, and soft woods for tea boxes. The time, however, will doubtless come when, with the improvement of communications and the spread of population, these valuable forests will play their part in the development of the province.

The timber exported from Assam in 1892-93 was valued at Rs. 11,76,234.

41. Among the "commercial staples" of Assam, elephants should also be mentioned. These valuable animals abound in the forests of the Assam Valley, on the lower slopes of the Assam Range, and in South Cachar and South-Eastern Sylhet. The Government khedda establishment from Dacca have annually hunted the Gáro Hills forests for several years past, and large numbers of animals have been captured by this agency. When not required for the purposes of the Government khedda, the elephant *maháls* (or right of hunting within certain defined tracts) are leased by auction sale to the highest bidder. Besides the price of the *mahál*, the lessee has to pay a royalty of Rs. 100 on each animal captured. In 1890-91 259 elephants were caught by lessees, in 1891-92, 66, and in 1892-93, 103. The number of elephants caught by lessees has been falling off of late years, owing to the large captures effected by the Government khedda establishment, which have resulted in a considerable decline in the market value of elephants.

Elephants.

SECTION 6.—MANUFACTURES.

42. Tea is the only important article of manufacture in Assam.

Tea.

The total quantity of tea produced in 1892 is returned as 84,221,133 pounds, of which 35,159,829 pounds were manufactured in the Surma Valley and 49,061,304 pounds in the Assam Valley. A sketch of the tea industry has been given in the preceding section.

43. In proceeding to consider the native manufactures of Assam, it is necessary to remember that the

Native manufactures generally.

province possesses no large cities where artisans can find scope for employment, and that the common industrial classes of other parts of India, such as carpenters, blacksmiths, wheelwrights, or masons, are represented in Assam by workers imported from Bengal, and paid at extremely high rates. The list of indigenous Assamese manufactures comprises only silk, thread, and fabrics, coarse cotton fabrics woven mostly from imported thread, brass utensils, oil expressed from the seeds of mustard and *til*, coarse sugar, a few kinds of jewellery, some ornamental articles in ivory, and common domestic pottery and agricultural implements. The Assamese, in fact, are singularly wanting in mechanical genius, and, although the occupation of an artisan is one of the most remunerative in the province, the industrial school established at Jorhát has always suffered from a lack of appreciation by the people whom it was intended to benefit.

44. The silk fabrics are the produce chiefly of the Assam

Silk.

Valley. The various kinds of silk have been described in the preceding section. It is difficult to say whether their production, on the whole, is increasing or decreasing. The common opinion is that it is largely on the decline, and this is probably true of the silk yielded by the *pat* or mulberry silkworms, which was more largely in vogue under the native Government of the Assam Valley than it is in the present day, when it is being supplanted by the cheaper *tussar* of Bengal. The price of the *mugá* and *eri* silks has also risen fourfold within the last fifty years ; but this circumstance is probably due in part to the influx of money into the province, while it is by no means certain that these silks were at any time more easily procurable than they are now. The earliest mention of them is to be found in Muhammad Kasim's chronicle of Mir Jumla's invasion of Assam in 1662, and it was then observed that the silks, though good, were produced in quantities sufficient only for domestic consumption. This is exactly the case at the present time, and as the population of the Assam Valley is certainly greater now than it was in 1662, it would seem to follow that the production of silk is not less than it was in the most flourishing days of the Ahom kingdom. The *muga* silk is used as an article of dress by the wealthier classes in the Assam Valley, and is largely exported to the southern hills, where it is much sought after by the Gáros, Khásis, and other hill tribes. *Muga* thread is also exported to Bengal. *Eri* silk is, perhaps, even more extensively manufactured than *muga*. Unlike the latter, it is not exported in the form of thread, but considerable quantities of the cloth are purchased by the Bhutia traders, who descend into the northern part of the Goálpára, Kámrúp, and Darrang districts every winter. *Eri* cloth is now largely made up into coats, &c., for summer wear by Europeans, and the demand for it on this account is increasing every year. It is generally worn in the cold months by the peasantry of the Assam Valley. The thread is produced also by Kakis and Mikirs in the lower parts of the central range of Assam, and is woven into the striped cloths which form the ordinary dress of all the tribes inhabiting those highlands. It is impossible to give even an approximate estimate of the quantity of *muga* or *eri* produced annually in any part of the province. The value of *eri* thread is Rs. 5 to Rs. 7 per seer; of *muga* thread, Rs. 8 to Rs. 12; while good *eri* cloth sells at Re. 1-8, and good *muga* at Rs. 2-4 per square yard. The manufacture of both kinds of silk is purely domestic. There are no large filatures, nor is there any system of breeding the worms on an extensive scale. The raiyat breeds silkworms enough to yield him a few chhataks of thread, which he either weaves himself, or disposes of at the village fair. There is no regular trade in silk yarns or fabrics, nor any stated market where they can be bought in large quantities.

45. The cotton fabrics of Assam deserve no particular mention.

Cotton.

By the hill tribes and by the Miris in the plains, they are woven from cotton locally grown, and gaily coloured with native dyes. Elsewhere English thread is generally used. A kind of rug or blanket is made by the Kukis and Miris, with cotton ticking on a backing of coarse cloth. The cotton cloths of the Nágas are very substantial and tastefully coloured.

46. Brass utensils are made by the Morias, a low Muhammadan

Brass.

caste found chiefly in the districts of Sibságar and Nowgong. These are of the rudest kind, without any attempt at finish or ornamentation. A style of vessels somewhat superior to these is made at Gauháti and at Sárthibári in Kámrúp.

47. The manufacture of mustard oil is of recent introduction.

Oil and sugar.

The mill used is the ordinary bullock-mill of Upper India, and is gradually supplanting the domestic oil-press, which consists simply of a short beam loaded with a heavy stone. *Gur*, or coarse sugar, is entirely an article of domestic manufacture. It is made by the rudest method, is never exported, and its consumption within the province is but small.

48. The common jewellery of Assam is clumsy and ungraceful,

Jewellery.

consisting chiefly of pieces of coloured glass roughly set in gold or silver. Some beautiful gold filigree-work is, however, made in Barpeta, and the art of enamelling is still preserved in Jorhát. The Khási bracelets, necklets, and earrings in gold and silver are handsome ornaments, though somewhat heavy in design ; and the Manipuri jewellery, or similar patterns, is imitated in Sylhet.

49. The district of Sylhet is noted for its ivory, mats, and fans,

Sylhet manufactures.

and the manufacture of shell-bracelets gives employment to a large number of artificers in the town of Sylhet. These bracelets are cut out as solid rings from large white conch-shells obtained from many places on the sea coast in and near India. They are of graceful appearance, and command a ready sale. In pargana Patharia, in this district, there is a considerable manufacture of *agar attar*, a perfume distilled from the resinous sap of the agar tree (*aquilaria agallocha*). This perfume is much esteemed by Oriental nations, and is exported, *viâ* Calcutta, to Turkey and Arabia. Iron work inlaid with brass, *talwars* and *dāos*, and such like articles, are manufactured in Rajnagar and Lashkarpur in Sylhet. Boat building is also carried on to a considerable extent in that district.

Jorhát, in the Sibságar district, still enjoys some local reputation for its ornamental carved work in ivory. This town is also the only place in Assam where ornamental pottery is made.

50. The boat-making of Barpeta ought, perhaps, to be mentioned in a catalogue of provincial industries.

Boats.

The roughly-hollowed logs are floated across from the Gáro Hills, and, after being further excavated till the thickness of the outer skin is reduced to about an inch and a quarter, they are subjected to a steaming process in the boat-builder's hands, being smeared with liquid mud and inverted over a line of burning embers. While thus softened, the future boat is widened by the insertion of thwarts. If, as usually happens, it splits in the process, the rent is patched with a piece of wood fastened in by clamps holding its bevelled edges to those of the aperture. In this way boats sixty feet long by six or seven feet in breadth are constructed, capable of lasting, if the wood be good forest timber, for ten years or even longer. The same process is followed elsewhere in the valley where boats are made. No such thing as a built boat has probably ever been attempted in the Brahmaputra Valley.

SECTION 7.—TRADE AND COMMERCE.

51. In the preceding sections an account has been given of the most important commercial staples which are produced in the province. It remains to describe the general course of provincial trade, the classes by whom it is conducted, the routes which it follows, and the markets where transactions are concluded.

Introductory.

52. The trade of Assam is carried on in two different directions: first, and chiefly, with the neighbouring province of Bengal; and, secondly, with the foreign States and tribes which surround

Nature of trade in Assam.
Trade routes.

British territory on three sides. Both descriptions of trade are
registered, the first at the stations of Dhubri on the Brahmaputra
and Bhairab Bázár on the Surma, by which channels nearly all
the merchandise from or for Bengal enters or quits the province :
and the second, either by special agency on the channels of
communication, or by the collection of statistics at the various
fairs or marts in the frontier districts to which the neighbouring
tribesmen resort.

The traffic conveyed by the boats and steamers that ply on the
Brahmaputra and Surma represents by far the most important
part of the trade between Bengal and Assam, in which as yet
railways have no share. A certain amount of road traffic also
takes place, but this is not large enough to justify the retention
of a special establishment for the purpose of registering it.
Figures are, however, collected by the police at Sidli and Baida,
but, as they receive no special pay for this work, the figures
supplied are not very reliable. The river traffic is carried on
both by boat and by steamer. Mail steamers run daily on the
Brahmaputra river, between Dibrugarh and Goalundo, and on the
Surma between Goalundo and Silchar during the rainy season
and between Goalundo and Fenchuganj in the cold weather. A
considerable amount of cargo is carried in these steamers, but
special cargo steamers with large flats also run, and carry goods
whose bulk renders them unsuitable for carriage by the smaller
and more speedy mail steamers. Statistics of the goods carried
by these vessels are transmitted by the companies to which they
belong, through the Government of Bengal.

The boat traffic is registered by special establishments, which
were located in 1879 at the two points already mentioned. The
quantity of the goods carried is all (except in a few instances)
that these establishments record ; values are applied to these
quantities in the offices of the Deputy Commissioners of Dhubri
and Sylhet, according to the prices ruling for the articles at those
stations. The figures furnished by the steamer companies are
treated in the same way.

Boats monopolise the greater part of the trade between Assam
and Bengal in lime, rice, gram, kerosine and other oils, salt, sugar,

tobacco, oranges, and potatoes, but the more expensive articles of merchandise, such as tea, piece-goods, liquors, and metals, and also coal and mustard, are for the most part carried by steamer. A curious feature in the returns is that whereas in the Brahmaputra Valley in 1882-83 steamers carried 85 per cent. of the total value of the inter-provincial trade, in 1892-93 they carried only 82·63 per cent., while in the Surma Valley the value of goods carried by steamer has increased from 45 per cent., at the commencement of the decade to 61·89 per cent. at its close. In the case of the latter valley, however, the increase in the proportional values of articles carried by steamer is more than accounted for by the traffic in a single article, tea. Not only is none of that article now carried by boat, but the total value of the tea exported has increased by more than the absolute increase in the value of goods carried by steamer.

Taking the province as a whole, the value of goods carried by steamer has increased in the last ten years by 40 per cent., as against 50 per cent. in the case of goods carried by boat.

53. Full details of the imports into, and exports from, Assam to foreign countries and to the neighbouring province of Bengal will be found in Part IIB of the General Administration Report. In 1892-93, the total value of the imports from foreign countries amounted to Rs. 7,92,189, and that of the exports amounted to Rs. 2,54,192. The total value of the trans-frontier trade was therefore Rs. 10,46,381. Considerably more than half the imports were from Hill Tippera, and consisted mainly of timber, canes, and other forest produce. Next in value were the imports from Bhutan and Towang, amongst which blankets and ponies formed the most important items. Of the exports, the largest were those to Bhutan and Towang (chiefly rice and raw silk), and to Hill Tippera (salt).

Turning to the inter-provincial trade, it may be noted that the imports aggregated Rs. 3,17,81,690, and the exports Rs. 6,30,48,969. In the following table, statistics are given showing the imports and exports from each valley separately, and the form of carriage used :

II

Section 7.

Trade and Commerce.

Valley.	Exports.				Imports.				Total.			
	Total.	Steamer.	Boat.	Road.	Total.	Steamer.	Boat.	Road.	Total.	Steamer.	Boat.	Road.
	Rs.	Rs.	Rs.	Rs.	Rs.	Rs.	Rs.	Rs.	Rs.	Rs.	Rs.	Rs.
Brahmaputra Valley.	3,76,58,416	3,05,34,451	70,51,958	72,007	1,71,59,212	1,44,23,663	23,72,616	3,62,933	5,48,17,626	4,49,58,114	94,24,574	4,34,940
Surma Valley.	2,53,90,553	1,77,05,957	76,84,596	Not recorded.	1,46,22,478	70,59,375	75,63,103	...	4,00,13,031	2,47,65,332	1,52,47,690	...
Total for the province.	6,30,48,969	4,82,40,408	1,47,36,554	72,007	3,17,81,690	2,14,83,038	99,35,779	3,62,933	9,48,30,6?0	6,97,23,416	2,46,72,273	4,34,940

The principal imports into the Brahmaputra Valley were rice, salt, gram and pulse, kerosine-oil, iron and sugar, while salt, gram, kerosine-oil and pulse, sugar, tobacco, and coal and coke figured most largely amongst the Surma Valley imports. Of the exports from the Brahmaputra Valley, coal and coke, rape and mustard-seed, timber, tea, raw jute, and rice in the husk, were the most important, and rice in the husk, lime, bamboo, and tea from the Surma Valley. Rice in the husk (paddy) is exported from the Brahmaputra Valley, and husked rice is imported. Lime forms one of the most important articles of export from the Surma Valley, while in the Brahmaputra Valley a considerable quantity of the same commodity is imported from Bengal.

54. The classes who conduct the trade of the province are different in the two valleys. In both, tea, the great export of Assam, is consigned straight from the gardens where it is produced to Calcutta, either to be sold there or shipped to England for sale. But almost all the rest of the export traffic, and nearly the whole of the import traffic, of the Assam Valley is in the hands of Marwari traders, commonly called Kaiyas, who not only manage the wholesale, but to a very large extent the retail, trade of the valley. Besides these, there are a few Muhammadan merchants from Dacca, who have settlements in the chief centres; but their transactions are small compared with those of the Kaiyas. It is very remarkable to notice the complete mastery of the internal commerce of the valley which these strangers possess. The native Assamese hardly ever engages in anything more extensive than petty shopkeeping, and this only in the western portion of the valley. But the Marwari is found, keen to buy and sell, wherever money is to be made; he settles himself not only in the populous villages of the inhabited region, but in the midst of the jungle, on the paths leading to the mountains from which the wild tribes come; and it is exclusively with him that these visitors do business.

Trading classes.

In the Surma Valley the conditions are different. Here there are comparatively few Marwaris, though they are not altogether absent. The native population contains a large trading element, and merchants from Dacca are more numerous than in Assam.

SECTION 7.

Trade and Commerce.

In the hill districts there are considerable differences in the extent to which the people themselves engage in trade. In most of these tracts, traffic is a necessary of life, the hills not producing sufficient food for the people to live upon; but in most also it takes the simple form of barter, the exports consisting chiefly of cotton, wax, ivory, and forest produce, and the imports of rice, salt, dried fish, and cloth. But in the Khási and Jaintia Hills there is a much more active commerce. The valuable staples of this tract have already been mentioned, and the trade in them is kept by the people almost entirely in their own hands. Many of them are adventurous merchants, travelling as far as Dacca, or even Calcutta, during the cold season. In the Nága Hills, too, the Angámi Nágas, who occupy the central region, though producing nothing of commercial importance themselves, do a thriving business as carriers between Manipur and Assam, and spend much money in the markets of the plains in the purchase of articles of use or luxury for themselves.

55. All over the province there are weekly *háts*, or markets, on

Trading centres.

stated dates, where buyers and sellers meet, and most of the business is done. Except at a few places, there are no permanent *bázárs*. During the cold weather, fairs are held along the foot of the hills which mark the frontier, and to these the hillmen come down with their produce. The most important permanent centres of commerce are Goálpára, Barpeta, Rangia, Gauháti, Kalaigaon, Tezpur, Nowgong, Chapparmukh, Bishnáth, Golághát, Jorhát, Lakhimpur, Dibrugarh, and Sadiya, in the Assam Valley; and Habiganj, Ajmiriganj, Sunámganj, Chhátak, Báláganj, Sylhet, and Silchar in the Surma Valley. The cold-weather fairs for frontier trade are held at Udalguri, Kherkheria, and Daimára in the Darrang district for the Bhutias; and at Sadiya in the Lakhimpur district for the Abors, Mishmis, Khámptis, and Singphos. Besides these places, the Bhutias resort largely to various marts in North Kámrúp, the Akás and Daflas to Tezpur, the Daflas and Miris to Lakhimpur, and the southern Nágas to Jaipur and Golághát. In the Surma Valley, Barkhola is the chief mart for North Cachar, Jaintiapur for the Jaintia Hills, and Lakhát, Bholáganj, and several other smaller markets to the

east for the Khási Hills. The Lushais are mainly served by a
bázár at Changsil, where there are a few shops kept by Bengalis
from Silchar. The Manipur trade is chiefly carried on at Lakhipur,
and that with Hill Tippera down the rivers which emerge from
that country into Sylhet.

SECTION 8.—MINES AND MINERALS.

56. In the section dealing with the geology of the province
some account has been given of the most
General remarks.   important minerals found in Assam, *viz.*, coal
and limestone. Iron occurs in the metamorphic and sub-metamorphic rocks of the Shillong plateau, and is found in small quantities,
in the form of nodular masses of clay ironstone, in the neighbourhood of the coal of the Makum field. Petroleum springs exist in
the same locality. Gold was anciently washed in the rivers of
Upper Assam, but the industry is not now found to be worth
pursuing. Salt springs exist in several parts of the Barúil-Pátkoi
section of the Assam Range.

57. The mineral of the first economic importance to Assam is
undoubtedly the coal which is found on the
Coal.   north-western face of the Eastern Nága Hills.
Upper Assam.   Situated as these fields are, near the upper
terminus of steam navigation on the Brahmaputra, it had long
been recognised that their successful exploitation would effect a
revolution in the carrying trade by steamers on that river, which
formerly depended on Raniganj for their fuel supply. The existence of coal here has been known since 1825. The question of
opening out the fields was reported on by a coal committee, assembled at Calcutta in 1840 and 1845. The localities were summarily
examined by Mr. Medlicott, of the Geological Survey, in 1865, and
in the seasons 1874-75 and 1875-76 Mr. Mallet, of the same Survey,
made a careful inspection of all the coal outcrops from the Tiráp
to the Desoi river. His report, which contains a detailed description of the several fields, will be found in Volume XII of the
Memoirs of the Geological Survey. The coal measures extend
along a distance of about 110 miles, but are exposed only where

the river valleys have cut into them. Five coal-fields have been described and named by Mr. Mallet, *viz.*, the Makum, Jaipur, Nazira (Dikhu and Safrai), Jhanzi, and Desoi fields. Besides these, in the further extension of the Nága Hills up the Dihing Valley to the frontiers of Burma, there are other known, but not regularly-explored, localities where coal occurs. The most important is the Makum field on the Dihing river, where the seams reach an immense thickness. Several desultory attempts had, from time to time, been made to work the coal there, but, owing to difficulties of labour and transport due to the uninhabited character of the country, and the difficult navigation of the Dihing river, no large quantity had, at any time, been brought out, until some ten years ago, when the mine was leased to the Assam Railways and Trading Company, and a railway was constructed from the Brahmaputra at Dibrugarh to the coal measures on the Dihing. Since

Year.		Output in tons.
1889	...	116,676
1890	...	145,708
1891	...	154,208
1892	...	164,015

that time the mines have been vigorously worked, and the output of coal has risen steadily. The coal, which is of excellent quality, not surpassed by any and equalled by few coals in India, is now exclusively used by the steamers navigating the Brahmaputra. Local requirements in the Brahmaputra Valley are entirely met by it, and in addition large quantities are exported for consumption in ocean-going steamers and other purposes.

A portion of the Dikhu or Nazira field, situated a short distance within the hills south of Sibságar, whence that river issues, is held on lease by the Assam Company, but, except for the needs of the lessees, has not yet been worked to any extent. In fact, since 1888 no coal at all has been extracted from this field. The other outcrops, the Jaipur field in the Dihing, which is very favourably situated for working, and the Jhanzi and Desoi fields, which are less accessible from the plains, have not yet been exploited.

58. The only other localities where coal has been found in the province are situated in the Gáro and the Khási and Jaintia Hills. As already noticed, this coal is of two very distinct kinds, the older or cretaceous

Gáro and Khási Hills.

coal, and the newer or nummulitic coal. The greatest deposits are those of the former in the coal-field of Darranggiri, on the Someswari river, in the Gáro Hills. This field (which has been described in the " Records of the Geological Survey," Volume XV, page 175) is situated north of the main axis of the Gáro Hills, on either side of the gorge through which the river makes its way to the plains. It has been estimated to contain 76 million tons of good workable coal. At the exit of the Jadukata river, near the western boundary of the Khási Hills, cretaceous coal is found almost at the level of the plains, and the coal-bearing rocks are exposed over an area of 30 square miles, so that there is a large amount of coal available here in a very accessible situation. A tramway might be laid from the Darranggiri field to the plains of Mymensingh without much difficulty, and would bring within reach of a market a very large supply of coal. With these exceptions, both the cretaceous and the nummulitic coal in the Khási Hills are found in small confined areas, which may be described as pockets, representing original depressions in the surface where the forests grew or woody matter accumulated. The seams soon thin out, and no very extensive supply from any one place can be reckoned on. The largest of these minor fields are those at Cherra Punji and Lakadong. The last estimate of the available coal (nummulitic) in the Cherra coal-field places it from 1,200,000 to 1,370,000 tons (" Records of the Geological Survey," Volume XXII, page 167), so that it would be exhausted in less than ten years if extracted at the rate now attained at Makum. Another obstacle in the way of working it is the elevation at which the coal is found, and the consequent cost and difficulty which would be involved in transporting it to the plains. The coal, however, is of excellent quality, and is one of the few Indian coals which can be used with absolute safety on board ocean-going steamers. The Lakadong coal-field is situated near the southern edge of the Jaintia Hills, about 7 miles from the plains, at Barghat on the Hari river. It was last visited in 1890 by Mr. T. D. LaTouche, whose report will be found in the " Records of the Geological Survey," Volume XXIII, page 14. The

SECTION 3. field is calculated to contain about 1,164,000 tons of coal, which,
Mines and like that of Cherra Punji, belongs to the nummulitic or lower
Minerals. eocene division of the tertiary formation. The elevation of this
field is 2,200 feet, or about half of that at Cherra Punji.

59. Iron exists in Assam, as in most other parts of India, in

Iron. great quantity and in various forms; but the
competition of English iron, with the exhaus-
tion of the supplies of fuel which supported the native furnaces,
has almost extinguished the indigenous industry in the Khási
Hills; while in Sibságar, where in the days of the Assam Rajas
iron-smelting was extensively practised, and the great iron cannon
for which Assam was once famous were forged, the art has
completely ceased to exist. The Khási Hills iron, which is still
made in small quantities and exported to the submontane bázárs,
is derived from the minute crystals of titaniferous iron ore, which
are found in the decomposed granite on the surface of the central
dyke of that rock, near the highest portion of the plateau. The
decomposed granite is rolled down into a stream, where it is
washed to separate the iron-sand, which is collected in wooden
troughs, dried, and reduced with charcoal in small furnaces. The
quality of the iron is excellent, and it is still sought after to some
extent for manufacture into hoes and *dhaos*; but it cannot be
doubted that the industry must soon die out. Its great extension
in former times is evidenced by the remains of smelting furnaces
which cover the surface for many miles, from the brow of the
hill below Cherra Punji as far north as Molim and beyond. The
slag from these workings supplied a considerable portion of the
metal for the cart road between Cherra and Shillong.

In Upper Assam, clay ironstone occurs in nodules of various
sizes, and sometimes in thin beds, interstratified with shales and
sandstones, in the coal measures of the Nága Hills; but it is
believed that the ore is not in sufficient abundance to afford a
supply for a blast furnace on the English principle; while the
scarcity of limestone required to form a flux would, even if the ore
were in greater quantity, probably form an insuperable obstacle
to operations on a large scale. The company who have the

concession of the Makum coal-field have also the monopoly of the *Section 8.*
iron of that region, but have hitherto made no attempt to work *Mines and*
it. The iron ore formerly smelted in Sibságar was derived both *Minerals.*
from the clay ironstones in the coal measures (chiefly those of the
Nazira field), and from the impure limonite which occurs in great
abundance in the Tipám rocks south of the Dhodar Ali ; the
former was the source most used.

60. Pyritous shales are also found associated with the coal

Alum.   measures of Upper Assam; and it may,
perhaps, hereafter be found profitable to use
them for the manufacture of alum and copperas.

61. Petroleum is found in the neighbourhood of the coal of

Petroleum.   Upper Assam. It is a heavy oil, containing
a comparatively small proportion of the light
illuminating hydro-carbons, in which respect it could not compete
with the imported oils. For lubricating purposes, however, and
for yielding solid paraffine, it is believed that it will prove valuable.
The earliest experiments in working it were made at Nahor Pung,
in the Jaipur field (where they were a failure) and near Makum,
when a considerable amount of oil was extracted in 1868. A
concession for working petroleum in the Makum field was granted
to the Assam Railways and Trading Company in 1882-83, and two
similar concessions in the same neighbourhood have recently been
granted—one to the company already mentioned, and the other
to a syndicate. Borings have been made by both concessionaires,
and petroleum has been extracted, but their operations have not
yet resulted in any considerable extraction of oil. In fact, the
only field which has been at all properly worked up to date is the
second concession of the Assam Railways and Trading Company,
the output from which in 1892 amounted to slightly over 19,000
gallons.

Besides the petroleum of Upper Assam, this mineral is also
found in Cachar. It occurs on the banks of the Barák, at Másim-
pur, where the Tilain range crosses the river, and near Badarpur,
where the Sirispur hills run up to the stream from the south ; it has
besides been detected at various places along these ridges, which

I

are part of the prolongation into the Surma Valley of the Arakan meridional ranges. It has also been found north of the Barák, on the Lárang, a small stream issuing from the Baráil range north of Kalain, and joining the Surma near Lebharpota. Specimens of petroleum from these localities have been sent for examination to Calcutta, but no active steps have been taken to utilise it.

62. Salt-springs are found in conjunction with petroleum in Salt. the Upper Assam coal area, at Borhat, Jaipur, and other places. In former times their brine was largely used for conversion into merchantable salt ; and to this day a small quantity of salt so made (the brine being boiled down in joints of bamboo) is imported by the Nágas into Jaipur. Salt-springs exist in Cachar, both in the southern ranges (Sirispur and Bhuban hills) and in the Baráil. Those in the Hailákándi Valley, in mauzas Bánsbari and Chandipur, are the only ones which are now worked, though formerly the industry was more extensive. The springs are leased annually for a trifling sum ; the brine is not boiled down, the water being disposed of in *gharas* to the people of the neighbouring villages. Several salt-springs are worked in Manipur, where they are highly valued.

63. Next in importance to coal in this province are the vast Lime. stores of limestone which exist on the southern face of the Khási and Jaintia Hills, where the downward bending strata of the nummulitic rocks have been worked as a lime-supply from a period long anterior to British rule. "Sylhet lime" was a monopoly of the Mogul Governors of Bengal, and, as such, figures in the early *sanads*, *farmans*, and treaties by which the East India Company acquired command over that province. The limestone is found from the exit of the Someswari river in the Gáro Hills to that of the Hari river in Jaintia ; but it can only be economically quarried in the neighbourhood of the small State Railway which runs from Tharia to Companyganj, or where facilities for water carriage exist, that is, where rivers navigable by boats in the rains adjoin the rock faces whence the stone is hewn. The most important of these quarries are those situated on the Jádukáta and Púnatirth rivers, which

debouch near Laur in Sylhet ; the Dwára quarries to the east of these ; the Cheyla or Shella quarries, on the Bogapáni ; the Máolong, Byrang, Sohbar, and Borpunji quarries, which lie immediately under Cherrapunji ; and the Utma quarries a little to the east on an affluent of the Piyáin. Those beyond have rarely been worked, the advantages possessed by the quarries nearer the great limestone marts of Chhátak and Sunámganj enabling the latter to undersell them. Altogether, there are 34 limestone tracts which are separately treated as quarries in the Khási and Jaintia Hills, one in Sylhet, and one in the Gáro Hills. The Government is the sole proprietor of all the quarries in the Jaintia and Gáro Hills and the one in Sylhet, as well as of four in the Khási Hills ; the remainder (with one exception) are the joint property of the Khási rulers or communities and the British Government, the latter administering the estates and reaping half the profits.

Owing to the depression in the lime trade, and the consequent decline in the Government revenue from the quarries, a special enquiry was made in 1889 by the Director of Land Records, as the result of which all the small quarries in the Khási Hills were closed for five years, and the five principal quarries only (Sohbar, Borpunji, and Shella under the permit system, and Langrin and Nongstoin under lease) were kept open for work. In consequence of this step, the revenue from the quarries rose from Rs. 13,580 in 1889-90 to Rs. 17,646 in 1890-91. In 1892-93, the revenue amounted to Rs. 15,536.

The stone is quarried chiefly during the dry months, and either carried by rail to Companyganj, whence it is taken by boat to Chhátak, or rolled down to the river banks and conveyed over the rapids, which occur before the rivers issue on the plains, in small boats when the hill streams are in flood during the rains. Below the rapids it is generally reloaded on larger boats, and carried down to the Surma river, on the banks of which it is burnt into lime during the cold weather. The kilns are of a primitive description, being mere excavations in the river bank, faced and roofed with clay. The fuel used consists of the reeds and grasses of the swampy tract which stretches along the foot of the hills. This industry gives employment to a great number of people, the quarriers being generally Khásis, and the boatmen and lime-burners Bengalis of Sylhet. For the last three years the exports of lime from Sylhet to Bengal (all of which is derived from this source) have been as follows:

			Maunds.
1890-91	...	...	18,04,197
1891-92	...	...	18,26,675
1892-93	...	...	13,14,161

Limestone is also found exposed in the Doigrung, a tributary of the Dhansiri, a few miles south of Golághát. A description of this formation, which still remains unworked, will be found in the "Records of the Geological Survey," Volume XVII, page 31.

64. The rivers of Assam which have yielded gold are those of
Gold.
the Darrang and Lakhimpur districts north of the Brahmaputra, the Brahmaputra itself in its upper course, the Noa and Buri Dihings, and a small stream called the Jaglo, which rises in the Tipám Hills and falls into the Buri Dihing. In the Sibságar district the Dhansiri, Disoi, and Jhanzi rivers are said to have been auriferous. Of these streams, the Bhoroli, Dikrang, and Subansiri in Darrang and Lakhimpur appear to have formerly given the largest quantities. The gold in these rivers is probably doubly derivative, being washed out of the tertiary sandstones of the sub-Himalayan formations, themselves the result of the denudation of the crystalline rocks in the interior of the chain. The industry was maintained in the time of the Assam Rajas by the peculiar system of taxation which then prevailed, each class of the population being bound to contribute in kind or labour to the State. The *Sonwals*, or gold-washers, were taxed at four annas' weight, or four rupees' worth, of gold per annum. Since the British occupation of the country, the pursuit of the precious metal has dwindled almost to nothing, and the lease of the gold-washings in North Lakhimpur has of late years been sold for Rs. 5 or Rs. 6 a year. In 1882, a European speculator obtained

a monopoly for ten years of the right of seeking gold in the Subansiri and its tributaries, but his operations were not attended with
success. This concession has recently again been granted to other
persons, and it is hoped that the work will be more vigorously
prosecuted than on previous occasions.

65. Platinum has been noticed with samples of gold obtained

Platinum. from washings in the Noa Dihing river, and
it is possible that, if specially searched for, it
might be found in large quantities (" Records of the Geological
Survey," Volume XV, page 54).

CHAPTER II.

Historical Summary.

66. The different portions of territory included in the province

Introductory.

of Assam were formerly quite distinct, and have different histories; they were brought under British Administration at different times and in different ways, and it is, therefore, necessary to treat them separately before proceeding to describe the present organization of the province. This chapter is accordingly divided into sections, summarising the history of the following areas :

I. Assam Proper, that is, the five districts of Kámrúp, Darrang, Nowgong, Sibságar, and Lakhimpur.

II. Goálpára, including the Eastern Duárs.

III. Cachar.

IV. Sylhet, including Jaintia.

V. The hill districts, *viz.,*—

  (1) The Garo Hills.   (3) North Cachar.
  (2) The Khási „   (4) The Nága Hills.

SECTION I.—ASSAM PROPER.

67. The history of so much of the valley of the Brahmaputra

The ancient Kámarúpa.

as belongs to the modern province of Assam may be said to begin with the growth of the Koch power upon its western frontier, and the invasion of the Ahoms in the east. From such hints and glimpses of the country as can be gathered from the *Tantras* and *Purans,* and other ancient writings, it appears certain that, while the bulk of the inhabitants have always been of non-Aryan origin, the colonisation or conquest of parts of the valley by Aryan settlers began at an early date. Krishna is said to have carried away his bride

Rukmini from her father Bhismaka, king of Kundilya, the name of whose kingdom survives in the Kundil river to the east of Sadiya, while the memory of the monarch is still preserved in Upper Assam. Krishna's son, Anirudha, captured Sronitpur, now called Tezpur, the capital of Raja Ban, and carried off his daughter Usha.[*] Still more famous than Raja Ban was his contemporary, Narak, who ruled in Gauháti, and is famed in Hindu mythology as the guardian of Kámákhyá and the conqueror of Ghatak, the king of the Kirats. He is said to have been the son of the earth by Vishnu, and for a long time enjoyed the favour of his celestial progenitor. But success turned his head, and his pride and waywardness at length gave such offence to Vishnu, that he was slain by him in the incarnation of Krishna. His son Bhogdatta is renowned for his zeal in propagating the Hindu religion, and is said to have given his daughter in marriage to Duryodhana and to have fallen in the battle of Kuruk-shetra, fighting on the Kauravas' side. Later on, we find a king of Kámarupa sending a present of elephants to the hero of the *Raghuvansa*, and again when Hiouen Thsang visited India, Kámarupa is mentioned as a country famous for these animals. Kámarupa is described in the *Jogini Tantra* as extending from the Karatuya to the eastern boundary of the Brahmaputra Valley.[†] Its ancient divisions were Kampith, from the Karatuya to the Sankosh, Ratnapith, from the Sankosh to the Rupohi in the present district of Kámrúp, Suvarnapith from the Rupohi to the Bhoroli, and Saumarpith, from the latter river to the eastern end of the valley. The name Kámarupa, however, varied greatly in its territorial signification from time to time. Between these legendary notices of Assam and the beginnings of what may be called history, a gap of about a thousand years intervenes ; but the Hindu religion would seem to have existed uninterruptedly during this interval at various points in the valley, whether professed by pure Aryans, or, as is more likely, by communities of mixed descent, or by converted non-Aryan tribes. A Sudra king,

---

[*] The adventures of Krishna and the life of Narak are described in Chapters 36-42 of the *Kalika Puran*, and on page 81 of the *Jogini Tantra*. *Raghuvansa*, IV—81.

[†] *Jogini Tantra*, page 76.

named Debeswar, reigned in Gauháti, a place which the proximity of the sacred hill Nilachal has always rendered notable. The temple of Kámákhyá on its summit is of comparatively modern origin, but rests on foundations reputed to be as old as the first introduction of the Hindu religion into the valley of the Brahmaputra. In Tezpur we find Rája Nágasankar, who built the temple of Biswanath, and whose descendant, Jongal Balahu, was defeated in battle by the Kachári Rája, near Roha on the Kopili.*

When Hiouen Thsang visited the country in 640 A.D., a prince, named Kumár Bháskara Barman, was on the throne. The people are described as being of small stature, with dark yellow complexions; they were fierce in appearance, but upright and studious. Hinduism was the State religion, and the number of Buddhists was very small. The soil was deep and fertile, and the towns were surrounded by moats with water brought from rivers or banked up lakes.†

68. Subsequently, we read of Pál rulers in Assam. It is supposed that these kings were Buddhist, and belonged to the Pál dynasty of Bengal. The latter supposition is strengthened by the recent discovery at Benares of a copper plate, on which is inscribed a deed of gift of some land in the neighbourhood of Pragjyotisha (Gauháti) by Kumára Pál, son of Ráma Pál and grandson of Vigraha Pál, the name of the two latter being synonymous with those of two of the later kings of the Bengal line of Páls.‡ The fact that Deva Pál (who ruled from about 895 to 915 A.D.) conquered Kámarúpa§ furnishes another reason for supposing that the Assam Páls were a branch of the royal family ruling in Bengal, even if they were not lineal descendants of that dynasty. It should, however, be noted that "Pál" was not an uncommon title at the period under discussion; it was the designation of many of the Báro Bhuiyás, and was also

Pál rulers.

---

* Gunabhiram's Asam Buranji, page 48.

† Beal's "Buddhist Records of the Western World," Volume II, page 196.

‡ This copper plate, which bears a date equivalent to 1105 A.D., was deciphered by Professor Venis of the Government Sanskrit College at Benares.

§ "Journal of the Asiatic Society of Bengal," 1878, page 407.

borne by an Aryan dynasty reigning over Kundilya, or the country about Sadiya.

69. After the fall of the Pál dynasty, the Khyen tribe under

Khyen dynasty.

Niladhwaj rose to power, and thus became worthy of the attention of the Brahmans.[*] Niladhwaj became a Hindu, and ordered that his caste should thenceforth be known as "High Sudra." He was succeeded by his son Chakradhwaj, who was followed by Nilámbar, the last king of this line. Nilámbar quarrelled with his councillor, a Brahman named Suchi Patra, and the latter fled to the Nawab of Gaur, and persuaded him to invade the country. The result was Husan Shah's invasion, and the fall of the capital, Kamatápur, in 1498 A.D.[†] The remains of this old city are still traceable, near the Dharlá, in the State of Koch Bihar.[‡]

70. Although the whole of Kámarúpa appears from time to

Báro Bhuiyás.

time to have been united into one kingdom under some unusually powerful monarch, it was more often split up into numerous petty States, each of which, under its own chief, was practically independent of the rest, and this was once more the condition of the country after the defeat of Nilámbar. About this time, two brothers, Chandan and Madan, ruled for a few years at Marálávas, some miles north of Kamatápur,[§] and the twelve chiefs, known as the Báro Bhuiyás, were exercising sovereign rights in Kámrúp and Goálpára.

The settlement of the Bhuiyás in Assam is detailed in the *Guru Charitra*, in which work it is said that they were introduced by a king named Durlabh Náráyan, who appears to have held sway in Goálpára and Kámrúp, but whose lineage is still uncertain. This king engaged in war with a Hindu prince, who called himself Gaureswar, or "the ruler of Gaur." Durlabh was victorious, and,

* Gunabhiram's *Asam Buranji*, pages 52-54.

† The Musalman accounts of the fall of Kamatápur have been reproduced by Blochmann in the "Journal of the Asiatic Society of Bengal" for 1872, pages 79 and 336, and 1874, page 281.

‡ The ruins are described by Buchanan Hamilton, whose account is reproduced in Dr. Hunter's "Statistical Account of Koch Bihar," page 362.

§ Hunter's "Statistical Account of Koch Bihar," page 407.

K

on the conclusion of hostilities, obtained seven families of Bráhmans and seven of Káyasthas under twelve acknowledged heads, the chief of whom was a Káyastha, named Chandibar, *alias* Debidás. These people were settled by Durlabh Náráyan in the country between Hájo and the Bornadi, and soon became powerful feudatories. The date assigned to their advent in Assam corresponds to the year 1220 A.D.* Their leader Chandibar was the lineal ancestor of the celebrated Assamese religious reformer Sankar Deb.

71. Nearly three centuries before the fall of Kamatápur, an event occurred at the eastern extremity of the valley, which was destined to change the whole course of Assam history.† This was the invasion of the Ahoms. The Ahoms were Shans, from the ancient Shan kingdom of Pong, whose capital, Mogaung, still exists in the upper portion of the valley of the Irrawaddy. A quarrel as to the right of succession to the throne is said to have been the cause of the secession of Chukapha, one of the rival claimants, who, after wandering about the country between the Irrawaddy and the Pátkoi mountains for some years, at length crossed the range and entered Assam with a small following. This was in the year 1228 A.D. The Ahoms found the country into which they descended peopled by small settlements of Moráns and Boráhis, people of the Bodo race, whom they had no difficulty in subduing. There was, however, a Chutia kingdom of considerable power in the background, which had absorbed the ancient Pál dynasty of Sadiya,

The Ahoms.

---

* This seems too early. Chandibar was Sankar Deb's great-great-grandfather, and we have every reason for believing that the tradition that Sankar Deb was born in 1449A.D. is approximately correct. Allowing twenty-five years a generation, it would seem that Chandibar could not well have come to Assam before 1300A.D. at the earliest.

† The above account of the Ahoms is taken from Kásinath Tamuli Phukan's *Assam Buranji*, which was compiled about 1840 A.D., under the orders of Raja Purandar Singh. The Ahoms appear to have possessed the historical faculty to a very considerable extent, and many of their leading families maintained chronicles of important events. Our information regarding Ahom history would have been much fuller than it is but for an act of literary iconoclasm in the reign of Rajeswar Singh (1751-1768), when many of these family histories were destroyed, owing to some remarks adverse to the Prime Minister having been made in a history produced by Numali Bar Phukan.

and in so doing had adopted the Hindu religion, and imported an
Aryan strain into the royal blood by the marriage of the Pal king's
daughter with the Chutia prince who succeeded him. The Chutia
dynasty at that time reigned at Sadiya and at Rangpur in the
Sibságar district, but their dominions did not extend uninterruptedly between the two places, nor did they reach very far back towards the southern hills, and the Ahoms consequently had room
in which to develop themselves, for a considerable time, before
coming into collision with the actual possessors of Upper Assam.
Within the narrow limits of a territory corresponding to the
south-eastern portion of Lakhimpur and part of the Sibságar
districts, the Ahom kings succeeded each other with great regula-
rity, governing through the means of their chief officers of State,
whose names and the dates of their appointments are duly
chronicled in the native histories of Assam, together with the
names of the kings and their dates of accession. We read that
in 1350 A.D. the Chutia king invited his Ahom neighbour to a
boat race on the Safrai river, and there treacherously captured
and murdered him; but the final struggle between Ahom and
Chutia for the supremacy of Upper Assam did not take place until
a century and a half later. Meanwhile, the Ahoms, extending
their power along the south bank of the Brahmaputra, drove the
Kacharis back to the Kopili and Dhansiri Valleys, and thus touched
the Koch power on the west, as they touched the Chutia power on
the south-east. The three powers between which the contest for
the Assam Valley lay were the Koch, the Ahom, and the Chutia.

72. We have seen that, after the fall of Nilámbar, the eastern
portion of Kámarúpa was split up into
The Koch kings.   numerous petty States, each of which was
ruled by its own chief. Amongst these, the Koch kings rapidly
forced their way to the front.* The legend runs that Hájo Koch

---

* The story as related here follows the *Bangsábali* of Rája Lakshmi Narayan Kuar
of Howli Mohanpur. This *Bangsábali* is inscribed on oblong strips of *sadi* bark, each
strip being illustrated. It is supposed to have been written under the orders of Rája
Sumudra Narayan about 1806 A.D. This version differs in some respects from accounts
given elsewhere, but seems, on the whole, to be the most trustworthy narrative
available.

had two daughters, Hira and Jira, whom he married to Haria Mandal, a Mech. Hira was an incarnation of Bhagavati, and was visited by Siva in the guise of Haria Mandal. The offspring of this intercourse was a son, Bisu, who consolidated the power of his tribe, and defeated the Báro Bhuiyás, who had become powerful during the reign of Nilámbar. He became a Hindu, taking the name of Biswa Singh, and imported Baidik Brahmans from Sylhet in the place of the Kálitas, who were previously the priests of his tribe. He made an abortive attempt to invade the country of the Ahoms, but was more successful in the internal management of his kingdom. He settled the different offices of State, and established his army on a secure basis. During his reign, the Ahoms attacked the Chutias, and, after several campaigns of varied fortune, defeated and slew the Chutia king, seized his capital, and overthrew the Chutia dominion in Upper Assam for ever. His son, Nar Náráyan, succeeded him about 1528 A.D., and at once commenced a series of expeditions against the neighbouring powers. He defeated the Ahoms, and made them tributary to him; and his brother Sukladhwaj, *alias* Silarai, subsequently conquered the kings of Hiramba (Cachar), Jaintia, and Sylhet, but was defeated and made prisoner by the Musalman ruler of Gaur. Silarai's son, Raghu, was adopted by Nar Náráyan as his successor. Then Silarai died, and Nar Náráyan begat a son of his own, named Lakshmi, whereupon Raghu, fearing that he would lose the succession, broke out in rebellion. The armies met, but a peace was concluded without bloodshed; the kingdom was divided into two parts, Raghu taking the portion east of the Sankosh, while the part west of that river was reserved for Nar Náráyan's son Lakshmi. This division of the kingdom took place about 1581 A.D.

Raghu was succeeded by his son Parikshit, who fought with and defeated Lakshmi. The latter then invoked the aid of the Emperor of Delhi, by whose troops the former was in his turn defeated and made prisoner. His brother, Balit Náráyan, fled to the Ahom Rája Swarga Náráyan, who sent an army against the Musalmans, and drove them across the Karatuya. From that time, the independent rule of the Koch kings ceased. Balit

Náráyan became a tributary of the Ahoms, and the western branch

succumbed to the Musalmans.

73. The Musalman invasions of the Brahmaputra Valley all
bear the character of temporary success due

Musalman invasions.
to superior arms and discipline, and ultimate failure induced by the unfavourable nature of the climate, ignorance of the country, want of communications, and the impossibility of repairing losses by reinforcements.* The first expedition of the kind was despatched after the overthrow of the kingdom of Kamatápur, under a leader recorded in Assamese history as Turbuk, who fought his way as far as Koliabar, and was then defeated and destroyed. A second invasion occurred about the middle of the sixteenth century. The leader of this expedition was Kála Páhár, an apostate from Hinduism, whose chief object appears to have been the destruction of Hindu temples, and to him is ascribed the spoliation of the old temples at Hájo and Kámákhyá. The next invasion was that, already referred to, in which Parikshit was overthrown, and this was followed later by another (in 1637) in which Balit Náráyan was slain, and the rule of the Musalmans was extended as far as Gauháti. The last and greatest invasion was that undertaken by Mir Jumla in 1660-62. He captured the capital of the Ahoms, and is said to have sent word to the Emperor that the next campaign would carry him to the confines of China; but his force melted away in the rains, and he was obliged to retreat with the loss of all his guns. The ultimate result of this disastrous invasion was to strengthen the hold of the Ahoms on Lower Assam, and their rule was shortly afterwards extended to Gauháti, at which place an Ahom Governor was stationed, until near the end of the eighteenth century, when it became the headquarters of the Ahom kings.

74. Before the last Muhammadan invasion, the Ahoms had
been largely converted to the Hindu religion.

*Fall of the Ahom
kingdom.*
The reigning monarch became a convert in 1655 A.D., and adopted the name of Jayadwaja Singh, and henceforward all the Ahom kings bear both

* The accounts of these invasions, furnished by Musalman historians, have been collected by Blochmann in an article in the "Journal of the Asiatic Society of Bengal" for 1872.

Ahom and Hindu names. There were now no rivals to the Ahoms in the Assam Valley. The Kachâris had been defeated just before Mir Jumla's invasion, and the Râjas of Darrang and Bijni had become tributary to the Ahom power on the fall of the Koch monarchy. In 1695, Rudra Singh, the greatest of the Ahom kings, ascended the throne. His dominions comprised the whole of the Brahmaputra Valley, so far as it was inhabited, except a strip of submontane territory claimed by the Bhutias. In 1780, Gaurinâth Singh succeeded to the throne. His reign was marked chiefly by a formidable rising of the Moamarias, a powerful religious sect. Gaurinâth, being hard-pressed, applied in his extremity to Mr. Rausch, a salt farmer at Goâlpâra. Mr. Rausch, it is said, sent a body of 700 sipahis to Gaurinâth's aid, but these sipahis were cut to pieces by the Moamarias. The Râja of Manipur also sent an armed force to Gaurinâth's assistance, but the Manipuris were likewise defeated. At this juncture, the king of Darrang, Krishna Nârâyan, taking advantage of Gaurinâth's distress, made an attack upon Gauhâti, whither Gaurinâth had retired. Gaurinâth again applied to Mr. Rausch for help, and also sent a deputation to Calcutta. At the close of 1792 the British Government sent a detachment, under the command of Captain Welsh, to assist Gaurinâth.* Captain Welsh defeated Krishna Nârâyan, put down the Moamaria insurrection, and reduced the whole valley to obedience. He was, however, recalled in 1794. A few months later Gaurinâth died. He was succeeded by Kamaleswar Singh, who was a mere puppet in the hands of his minister. He died in 1809, and was succeeded by his brother, Chandra Kânta Singh. The reign of this prince was marked by the appearance of the Burmese in Assam. Chandra Kânta, having quarrelled with his minister, the Bura Gohain, applied for aid to the Burmese. The Burmese entered Assam with a force with which the Assamese were utterly unable to cope. Shortly afterwards, however, the Burmese retired, when the Bura Gohain deposed Chandra Kânta and set up Purandar Singh. Chandra Kânta again applied to the Burmese, who sent an army and reinstated him. In 1819,

---

* A full account of Captain Welsh's expedition has been given by Sir J. Johnston in a pamphlet published by the Foreign Department some years ago.

Purandar Singh applied for aid to the British Government, but was refused. Chandra Kánta, however, quarrelled with the Burmese, who finally expelled him from Assam, and he sought refuge with the British officers at Goálpára. But at this juncture matters had come to a crisis between the British and the Burmese, and on the 5th March 1824 war was declared against Burma.* A British force, advancing with a gunboat flotilla, conquered the valley as far as Koliabar, and during the next cold season completed the subjugation of the rest. Finally, on the 24th February 1826, the Burmese, by the treaty of Yandaboo, ceded Assam to the East India Company.

75. For some time after the conquest, it was still doubtful whether the Company would retain in their hands or not the province they had won. Mr. Scott, the Commissioner of North-East Rangpur, administered the country, Captain White being appointed in 1827 to assist him in Lower Assam, and Captain Neufville in 1828 to have charge under him of Upper Assam. The Moamarias, who had contributed so largely to the downfall of the Ahom power, and whose country (known as Matak) was the present district of Dibrugarh south of the Brahmaputra, were left under their own ruler, styled the Bor Senapati, who in May 1826 executed an agreement of allegiance to the British Government. And the Khámpti chief of Sadiya, called the Sadiya-khoa, on the 15th of the same month, was confirmed as the Company's feudatory in possession of that district.

Commencement of British rule.

At first, the civil and criminal duties of Assam Proper were performed by councils of the Assamese gentry, called *panchǎyats*, of which there were two or three in each district of the province. In judicial cases Captains White and Neufville were both Magistrates and Judges, trying the accused with the assistance of a *panchǎyat*, but referring all heinous cases, with their opinions, to Mr. Scott for final judgment.†

---

* A full account of the Burmese war, so far as Assam is concerned, will be found in Robinson's "Descriptive Account of Assam," published in 1841, pages 180-188.

† The information in this and the next paragraph is taken from Robinson's "Descriptive Account of Assam," pages 207-211.

76. In 1833 the districts of Sibságar and Lakhimpur north of the Brahmaputra were placed under the administration of Rája Purandar Singh, who executed a treaty binding himself to adminis-ter the country upon the principles of justice established in their territories by the East India Company, to act according to the advice of the Political Agent stationed in his principality, and to pay an annual tribute of Rs. 50,000. Thus, of Assam Proper there remained British in 1833 only the districts of Kámrúp, Nowgong, and Darrang (which then only extended to and included Bishnáth, beyond which was Lakhimpur, subject to Purandar Singh).

*Rule of Purandar Singh
in Upper Assam.*

77. In 1835, Act II of that year was passed, which placed all functionaries in British Assam under the control and superintendence, in civil and criminal cases, of the Sadr Court, and in revenue cases under that of the Board of Revenue, Lower Provinces, and further declared that such superintendence should be exercised in conformity with the instructions which these functionaries might receive from the Government of Fort William in Bengal. Under this Act, rules for the administration of Assam were framed by the Commis-sioner, revised by the Sadr Court, and finally issued by that Court with the sanction of Government in 1837. They applied not only to Assam Proper, but also (*vide* the next section) to Goálpára. These rules consisted of extracts from the Bengal Regulations of all that was considered at that time suitable to the circumstances and necessary for the proper administration of Assam. They were, however, merely rules of judicial procedure. They declared what courts, civil and criminal, should be established, and the mode of appointing officers thereto ; they declared the jurisdiction of these courts, and provided for appeals ; they prescribed a period of limitation for the institution of civil suits and a procedure to be followed in mortgage cases ; they provided also for the appoint-ment of *vakils*, the establishment and remuneration of process-servers, and the keeping of judicial registers and records. They established in each district a summary suit court, to be presided over generally by the Assistant in charge of the district (now called the Deputy Commissioner) in his capacity of Collector ; they also

The Assam Code.

established an office for the registry of deeds. Lastly, in all cases not specially provided for in the rules, officers were directed to conform, as nearly as the circumstances of the province would permit, to the provisions of the Bengal Regulations, and in all doubtful matters of a judicial nature to refer for instructions to the Sadr Court. The Police Law of Assam was at the same time declared to be Regulation XX of 1817, with certain modifications.

In 1839, a few supplementary civil rules were issued by the Sadr Court with the sanction of Government, the effect of which was to give to Junior Assistants (now called Assistant Commissioners) and Sub-Assistants (now called Extra Assistant Commissioners) a greater share in the judicial administration of the country than was allowed to them by the rules of 1837; and in the same year an officer, styled Deputy Commissioner (whose designation was in 1861 changed to that of Judicial Commissioner), was appointed to relieve the Commissioner of his duties as Civil and Sessions Judge.

78. In October 1838, the territories which had been placed in charge of Purandar Singh were resumed by the Government of India. The Rája had fallen deeply into arrears with his tribute, and declared himself unable any longer to carry on the administration. At first, the officers placed in charge of this tract acted under the direct orders of the Government of India in the Foreign Department; but in July 1839 a proclamation was issued by the Governor General in Council annexing the territory to Bengal, dividing it into two districts, Sibságar and Lakhimpur, and directing that these two districts should be administered in the same manner as the districts of Lower Assam. In August 1842 another proclamation was issued, annexing the territory of the Bor Senapati, who had died in 1839, and whose son refused to accept the management of the country on the terms offered to him. Sadiya, the district of the Khámpti chief, was, by the same proclamation, incorporated with the rest of the province. This place had been the scene of a rising of the Khámptis in 1839. They treacherously attacked the station of Sadiya, and killed the

Resumption of Upper Assam.

L

Political Agent, Colonel White. The combination was not broken up and dispersed till many lives had been lost. The son of the Sadiya-khoa, for his complicity in this rebellion, was exiled with his followers to Náráyanpur, on the Dikrang, in the west of the Lakhimpur district, where the colony still exists.

Thus, from 1842, the whole of Assam Proper was under the same system of administration, save that in Lakhimpur, including Matak and Sadiya, an establishment of *panchâyat* courts was, for special reasons, maintained, to which persons of rank and influence in the district were appointed, without much regard to their judicial qualifications. This special *panchâyat* system was abolished in 1860.

79. In that year, Act VIII of 1859 (the Civil Procedure Code) and the Limitation Act (XIV of 1859) were extended to the whole of Assam Proper and Goálpára. In 1861 the Criminal Procedure Code of that year was extended to the province, and in 1862 the Police Act (V of 1861). In 1862, also, the Penal Code came into force in the province without special extension. By these measures the Assam Code of 1837 (which had been meanwhile revised in 1847) was superseded. In 1861 the designations of the officers serving in the province under the Commissioner were changed, with the sanction of the Government of India, as follows: the Deputy Commissioner became Judicial Commissioner, the Senior or Principal Assistants Deputy Commissioners, the Junior Assistants Assistant Commissioners, and the Sub-Assistants Extra Assistant Commissioners. Side by side with these officers, there existed in the province a separate judicial establishment, consisting of one Principal Sadr Amin, two Sadr Amins, and ten Munsifs. In March 1872 this branch of the service was entirely abolished; several of the Munsifs were created Extra Assistant Commissioners, and the ordinary district staff were invested with civil judicial powers, the Deputy Commissioner becoming Subordinate Judge and the Assistant and Extra Assistant Commissioners Munsifs This arrangement is substantially that which now exists.

SECTION 2.—GOÁLPÁRA.

80. This district consists of two very distinct portions: the permanently settled part, comprising the three thánas of Goálpára, Dhubri, and Karaibari; and the temporarily settled part, called the Eastern Duárs.

Early history.

The first tract was originally a portion of the district of Rangpur, and, as such, was included in the province of Bengal, which, by the Mogul Emperor's *farmán* of the 12th August 1765, became part of the dominions of the East India Company. Like the neighbouring district of Kámrúp, this tract was inhabited chiefly by Koches, Meches, or Kacháris. It formed part of the dominions of the Koch dynasty, the rise and fall of which have already been described, and passed out of their hands on the defeat of Parikshit, when it became a Musalman province.

On its southern border, the Goálpára district marches with the Gáro Hills, and the thána of Karaibari, which stretches southwards from Dhubri, is almost wholly composed of hilly country inhabited by Gáros. These mountaineers were, in the early period of our rule, a terror to the people of the plains; and the chiefs of the border country, who had to restrain their incursions, were allowed in return for this duty to hold their estates at a very light revenue. Thus, it happened that when the decennial settlement of Bengal was made, the few great zamindárs among whom the permanently-settled portion of Goálpára was divided were assessed at an almost nominal amount. It is somewhat doubtful whether this assessment was ever formally converted into a permanent charge; but these estates have uniformly been treated as covered by the permanent settlement of Bengal.

81. Shortly after this settlement, however, it became manifest that the zamindárs of the plains country, instead of proving guardians of the peace of the border, were rather likely, by their oppressions and exactions, to foster strife with the Gáros of the hills, whose raids were constantly provoked by the treatment they received from the landholders to whose markets they resorted. In order to check these

Regulation X of 1822.

L 2

SECTION 2. exactions, and to promote the growth of order and civilisation
Goálpára. amongst the hill people, it was deemed necessary to place this tract
under a special form of administration. Then in 1822, a Regulation (No. X) was passed by the Governor General in Council,
exempting the three thánas of north-eastern Rangpur from the
operation of the General Regulations, and placing them under the
control of a Special Civil Commissioner. Mr. David Scott was the
first official entrusted with the charge ; and he took into his own
hands the collection of the rents claimed by the zamindárs from
the Gáro villages, paying over to them the proceeds, after deducting the costs of collection and administration. At the same time,
the duties levied by the zamindárs on the hill produce (chiefly
cotton) were commuted to an annual payment by Government, and
abolished, Government recouping itself by imposing a special house
assessment upon the Gáro villages.

82. When Assam Proper was conquered from the Burmese in
1826, Mr. Scott became Commissioner of the
Incorporation in Assam new province, with which Goálpára was
Proper.
incorporated as a separate district ; and from
that date until 1866 it remained a portion of Assam, and was
administered on the same system as the rest of the province.

83. In 1866, the Eastern Duárs, a thinly peopled but extensive
tract along the base of the Himalayas north
Transfer to Koch Bihar.
of permanently-settled Goálpára, which had
previously been under the rule of the Deb Rája of Bhutan, was
annexed by the British Government on the conclusion of the
Bhutan war. For some little time these Duárs were a separate
district ; but in 1867 the Bengal Commissionership of Koch Bihar
was formed, and from the 1st January of that year the Eastern
Duárs were joined to Goálpára, and the entire district was included
in that Commissionership, the Commissioner having the powers of
a Civil and Sessions Judge within his jurisdiction. In October
1868, the judicial administration of Goálpára and the Gáro Hills
was taken away from the Commissioner of Koch Bihar, because of
the inconvenient distance of this tract of country from his headquarters, and placed in the hands of the Judicial Commissioner of

Assam. The executive control, however, remained, as before, with the Commissioner of Koch Bihar. In 1869, the Gáro Hills were formed into a separate district by Act XXII of that year, which repealed Regulation X of 1822, but still exempted the hills from the operation of the General Regulations. In the same year the Eastern Duárs were similarly deregulationised by Act XVI of 1869.

Finally, when the Chief Commissionership of Assam was formed in February 1874, the district of Goálpára and the Eastern Duárs, and the district of the Gáro Hills were retransferred to Assam.

SECTION 3.—CACHAR.

84. The early history of Cachar, or Hiramba, is extremely obscure. Although it bears the same name

Early history.

as a section of the Bodo population of Assam, the part of the district south of the Baráil was not until some two hundred years ago in the possession of the race now called Kacháris. It would appear that it belonged to the kingdom of Tippera, or Tripura, since it is stated to have been acquired by the Kachári king, who had his capital at Maibong, as a dowry upon his marriage with a Tippera princess. The Tipperas, however, are undoubtedly, as is proved by their language, themselves of the Bodo stock, and very near kinsmen, not only of the Kacháris of North Cachar, but also of those of the Brahmaputra Valley and of the Gáros of the Gáro Hills. Their true history, like that of the Kachári kings of Dimapur, Maibong, and Kháspur, has been lost in the fugitive memory of a barbarous people, unacquainted with letters, and has been further darkened by the fictitious genealogies which have been invented for them by Brahman priests on their reception within the pale of Hinduism.

It is, however, certain that the last native king of Cachar was the descendant of a line of princes who came originally from the Assam Valley. Their deserted capital, Dimapur, on the Dhansiri river, beneath the Angámi Nága Hills, contains some very striking monuments, the meaning and purpose of which have much perplexed explorers, and a number of large and fine tanks. From this site, now buried in dense jungle, the Kachári kings were forced, by the aggressions of the Ahoms on the north and of the Angámi Nágas on the south, to remove into the interior of the hills, and took up their abode at Maibong, on the Máhur river. While settled there, about the beginning or middle of the seventeenth century, the Kachári king married a daughter of the Tippera Rája, and received the valley of Cachar as her dowry. And some time between 1700 and 1750 the court was transferred from the hills, across the Baráil, to Kháspur, on the Madhura river in the plains. Here the Kachári rulers found themselves in presence of an already settled population of Hindus and Musalmans from Sylhet, who had over-flowed from that district into the valley. The process of Hindui-sation had probably already commenced at Maibong, at least among the royal family and the court, if not among the Kachári population. At Kháspur it proceeded rapidly; and in 1790 the formal act of conversion took place, the Rája Krishna Chandra and his brother, Govind Chandra, entering the body of a copper image of a cow, and emerging therefrom as Hindus and Kshatriyas. A genealogy of a hundred generations, reaching to Bhima, the hero of the *Mahábhárata*, was composed for them by the Brahmans, only the last nine or ten names in which have probably any claim to represent real personages.

85. In the beginning of the present century the valley of Cachar became the scene of a struggle for supremacy between the Manipuri brothers, Márjit, Chaurjit, and Gambhír Singh, who had been driven from their own country by the Burmese. Krishna Chandra had died in 1813, and Govind Chandra succeeded him. The Manipuri invaders speedily overran the country, and set at naught the feeble authority of the Kachári king. In 1823 Márjit held the Hailákándi valley, and Gambhír Singh the rest of South Cachar. The Burmese were then in Assam, and, as lords of Manipur (which they had conquered from Márjit in 1819), threat-ened to annex Cachar. This the British Government, seeing the danger which it would cause to Sylhet, decided to prevent. Negotiations were first entered on with a view to an alliance with

Taken under British protection.

the Manipuri brothers. These overtures fell through, and it was

resolved to take up the cause of Govind Chandra, who was, with
the Rája of Jaintia, taken under British protection. The Burmese
armies, which had advanced both from Assam and Manipur, were
driven out, and Govind Chandra was replaced on the throne. A
treaty was executed on the 6th March 1824, by which the Rája
placed himself under British protection, and agreed to pay a tribute
of Rs. 10,000.* Govind Chandra's reign after his restoration was
very short; he was assassinated in 1830, and, as he left no heir,
either natural or adopted, the country was annexed by proclamation on the 14th August 1832.

86. In its subsequent history Cachar much resembles Assam.
British rule. Act VI of 1835 (like Act II of that year in
the Assam Valley) placed it under the
control of the Sadr Court and Board of Revenue. It was administered from the first by a Superintendent, who in 1833 was vested
with the powers of a Magistrate and Collector; and in the same
year it was transferred from the supervision of the Commissioner
of Assam to that of the Commissioner of Dacca. It differs from
Assam in never having had any special code of administrative
rules drawn up for it; the officers in charge applied "the spirit of
the Regulations" in sacrifi...g with judicial matters. The Civil
Procedure Code and Limped ion Act were formally extended to the
district in 1859; in 1862 the Criminal Procedure Code was
extended, and the Penal Code came into force. A special peculiarity of the Cachar revenue system, which is a survival from
native rule, will be noticed in Chapter IV, section 1.

Since Cachar became British territory, the only important
political events which have marked its history have been the
Lushai raids of 1849 and subsequent years, which will be discussed
in the section dealing with the Lushais. In the Mutiny of 1857 the
sepoys of the 34th Native Infantry, who mutinied in Chittagong in
November of that year, were met in Cachar, and were defeated
and dispersed by the Sylhet Light Infantry.

* It is commonly asserted that the Burmese were driven out of Cachar in the course
of the first Burmese war. These events, however, occurred before the formal declaration
of war (5th March 1824).

SECTION 4—SYLHET AND JAINTIA.

87. Of Sylhet under its early Hindu rulers hardly anything is
known. It is believed that its native popula-

Sylhet.

tion is largely made up of non-Aryan tribes,
probably of the same race as the Bodo Tipperas who now inhabit
the hills on its southern margin. The Rájas who held the country
at the date of the Musalman conquest, the chief of whom was
Gaur Govind, who ruled the south and centre, while the Rája of
Laur, under the Khási Hills, governed the north, had evidently,
from their names, been taken up into Hinduism, and the country
colonised by Brahmans, who gradually extended their proselytising
operations. The district was conquered by the Muhammadan
kings of Bengal in 1384 A.D., the invaders being led by a spiritual
chief named Sháh Jalál, whose shrine at Sylhet is still famous.
Laur and Jaintia, under the hills, retained their independence
during the rule of the Bengal kings. After the absorption of that
province in the Mogul Empire under Akbar, Laur became a dependent principality. The last Hindu Rája of Laur embraced Muhammadanism at Delhi in Aurangzeb's reign. Todar Mal assessed
Sylhet (excluding Jaintia, which was ~~~~ conquered by the
Moguls, and Laur) at Rs. 1,67,040, and was ruled continuously
from that date, until it passed into the hands of the East India
Company with the rest of Bengal in 1765, by a succession of *Amils*
subordinate to the Nawab of Dacca.

The district was included in the decennial settlement of Bengal,
which afterwards became permanent in 1793, but the operation
of assessment was conducted in an exceptional manner, each holding being separately measured and settled upon fixed rates. Thus,
in Sylhet, the permanent settlement assumed a form which it bears
nowhere else, except perhaps in Chittagong. It was the policy of
the Collector, Mr. J. Willes, to put aside the *chaudhuris*, or zamindárs, who elsewhere obtained settlement, and to deal direct with
the better class of raiyats or *mirasdárs*. The result is that the settlement is in great part a permanent *raiyatwari* one, the area which
each holding should contain being (so far as the records have been

preserved and can be trusted) accurately known. All land not included in the permanent settlement, or not subsequently settled in perpetuity, is held on temporary leases.

The history of Sylhet since the permanent settlement has not been eventful. The depredations of the Khásis on the north were brought to a close by the occupation of the station of Cherra Punji in 1828; and those of the Lushais on the south were stopped, so far as Sylhet is concerned, by the expedition of 1871-72.

88. The Rája of Jaintia, a Chief of Khási lineage, was found by us, on the annexation of the district, in possession of a tract of plains country lying between the town of Sylhet and the Cachar border, and measuring about 450 square miles, in addition to his hill territory stretching from the foot of the hills overlooking the Surma Valley to the Kalang river in Nowgong. At the same time that Cachar was taken under British protection, in March 1824, a treaty was made with Ram Singh, the Rája of Jaintia, by which he acknowledged allegiance to the Company, and promised to aid in the military operations then commenced against the Burmese in Assam. In 1832 four British subjects were seized by Chattar Singh, chief of Gobha, under the orders of the heir-apparent, Rajendra Singh, and three of them were sacrificed to Káli, the tutelary goddess of the Rája's family. One escaped, and gave information of the outrage, which led to a demand by the British Government for the surrender of the culprits. Negotiations went on for two years without any result. In November 1832 Ram Singh died, and Rajendra Singh succeeded him; and it was finally resolved to punish this atrocious crime (which had been preceded by similar outrages in 1821, 1827, and 1832) by dispossessing the Rája of his territory in the plains, and confining him thenceforth to the hilly tract. On the 15th March 1835 formal possession was taken of Jaintiapur, and the annexation of the plains territory proclaimed by Colonel Lister; in April the district of Gobha was similarly annexed to Nowgong in Assam. Upon this, the Rája declared himself unwilling to continue in possession of his hill territory, over which he had but little control, and it thus also became included in the Company's

Jaintia.

dominions. The population of the plains of Jaintia, like that of Cachar, is made up of Sylhet raiyats, with but a slight leaven of settlers from the hills.

SECTION 5.—THE HILL DISTRICTS.

89. The history of the Gáro Hills has already been partly touched

I. Gáro Hills.

upon in the account given of the Goálpára district, in which, up to 1866, they were, so far as British administration extended, included. These hills, peopled by a wild race nearly akin to the Meches or Kacharis of the plains, were surrounded on all sides except the east by the estates of the great frontier zamindárs or *chaudhuris* of Rangpur and Mymensingh. The Gáros were in the habit of resorting to the markets in the plains estates of these zamindars for the sale of their cotton and the purchase of the supplies they needed ; and the police of the border was maintained, and taxation levied on the hill produce, by the zamindárs by means of *barkandázes* whom they established at these marts. The chief of these *chaudhuris* were those of Mechpára, Kálumálupára, and Karaibári in Rangpur, and Sherpur and Shushang in Mymensingh. The Gáros, like most of the wild tribes of the north-east frontier, lived in a state of constant internecine warfare, and it was a necessary ceremony at the funeral of a great chief to bury with him as many human heads as could be procured for the purpose, and, if possible, to put to death on the occasion living captives. The border was thus vexed by constant raids for the purpose of obtaining heads or prisoners ; and the exactions of the plains zamindárs at the submontane *háts* likewise furnished frequent occasions for quarrel.

Under the Moguls, the *chaudhuris* of the border paid their assessment in elephants, cotton, and *agar* wood to the *faujdár* of Rangamati, midway between Goálpára and Dhubri. After the Company obtained the *Diwáni*, a *sazáwal*, or contractor, was annually appointed, who took the place of the *faujdár*, and made his own arrangements with the *chaudhuris*. Until 1787 the revenue of these landlords continued to be paid, as before, in kind. Cash

payments were introduced in 1788, and the permanent settlement
shortly afterwards followed.

90. In 1775, the *chaudhuris* of Mechpára and Karaibári, to avenge some Gáro raids of more than usual severity, invaded the hills bordering on their respective estates, and entered on a career of
Part of the Gáros brought within zamindárs' estates.
conquest. They remained two or three years in the hills, and brought the tribes of a large tract entirely under their control. The zamindár of Karaibári, Mahendra Náráyan, was especially successful in establishing his influence over the south-western portion of the hills, and when the Company called his proceedings in question, defied them from his fastnesses. After a long course of warfare with other *chaudhuris* and with the chiefs of the interior, Mahendra Náráyan's estates were at last sold by the Company for arrears of revenue, and his influence gradually dwindled.

91. Meantime the raids of the Gáros on the plains continued, and in 1816 Mr. David Scott was deputed to report on the best means of preserving the peace of the frontier. He found that at that
Mr. Scott's proposals, 1816.
time the frontier zamindárs had for the most part succeeded in reducing a greater or smaller area on their borders to a state of subjection, the largest conquests being those made by Karaibári and Mechpára; beyond these areas thus incorporated in their zamindáris, the *chaudhuris* had so far established their influence that several villages in the interior paid them tribute. Beyond these, again, in the heart of the hills, were the independent or *bemalica* Gáros. Mr. Scott proposed to separate all the tributary Gáros (from whom, and from the independent villages beyond, the raids proceeded) from the zamindár's control, and take them under Government management, compensating the zamindárs for any losses which they might show that they had sustained; to appoint the chiefs of the villages thus brought under our jurisdiction to be responsible for the peace and the collection of revenue; and to bring the submontane *háts* under Government control, all duties being abolished there, except upon independent Gáros frequenting them. These proposals were approved by Government, and after-

wards embodied in Regulation X of 1822, which gave Mr. Scott, who was appointed Special Commissioner, authority to extend British administration over other Gáro communities which might be still independent, and exempted the whole tract (together with the district of Goálpára) from the operation of the General Regulations. After the passing of the Regulation, Mr. Scott proceeded to conclude engagements with the independent chiefs, and no fewer than 121 of those living west of the Someswari are said to have entered into terms with him.

92. Mr. Scott was shortly afterwards called away from his work among the Gáros to assume the administration of Assam and the Eastern Frontier generally, and his place was taken by the Principal Assistant of Goálpára, who was aided by a Gáro Sarbaráh-kár with his headquarters at Singhimári, situated nearly opposite the middle of the western face of the hills. For many years the British Government maintained a policy of non-interference with the interior of the hills. The tributary Gáros within paid with great irregularity the tribute which they had agreed upon. Raids were frequent, and were followed either by expeditions or by blockade of the submontane markets—measures which were found to be quite ineffectual to stop them. Some little influence was occasionally brought to bear upon the tributary Gáros through visits paid to them by the Principal Assistant of Goálpára; but these annual tours were not regularly carried out, as designed by Mr. Scott, and any intermission in them was followed by an increase in the number of raids.

Affairs subsequent to Regulation X of 1822.

93. For all these years it was believed that the climate of the hills was so deadly that no European could survive within them, and that it was impracticable to attempt any establishment of a permanent post in their midst. At last, in 1866, after two expeditions to punish raids on the side of Mymensingh of more than usual atrocity, the Government for the first time resolved to appoint a special officer to the charge of the hills. Lieutenant Williamson was selected for this purpose, and was established on

Establishment of a Deputy Commissioner within the hills.

a spur of the Tura mountain, with a special armed police force.
Shortly after, in 1869, Act XXII of that year was passed, which
enabled the Lieutenant-Governor to make special provision for the
administration of the district, and to prevent the collection by
zamindárs or other persons of tributes, cesses, or other exactions
in the hills. By this Act, Regulation X of 1822 was repealed.
That Regulation had applied only to North-East Rangpur, afterwards the Goálpára district. The Act of 1869 included Mymensingh, on which side also zamindári influence had been pushed into
the hills, and had provoked retaliation by the hillmen.

This experiment proved completely successful. The Deputy
Commissioner of the Gáro Hills and his police force brought almost
instant quiet to the district. Hearty aid was given to him by the
Gáros, and the headmen, relieved from the dread of retaliatory
feuds, at once began to perform their duty, to deliver up offenders,
and to enforce the payment of revenue. Raids ceased, and numerous villages, theretofore independent, voluntarily became tributary.

94. In 1870 the survey, which had been carried through the
neighbouring Khási Hills, entered the district,
Subjection of the last independent Gáros.
and it was resolved to explore as much of
the independent Gáro country as was possible
in the course of surveying that which acknowledged British
authority. During that year no opposition whatever was offered
by the independent villages, of which about 60 still remained in
the heart of the district; but in March 1871 a survey coolie, who
had been sent to clear a station on the top of a hill, was seized
by some Gáros of Rongmagiri, and was tortured and murdered.
This put a stop to survey operations for the time, and in the
ensuing cold weather (1871-72) an expedition was led against the
offending village. In the summer of 1872 some independent
villages raided upon protected Gáro villages which had afforded
assistance to the expedition against Rongmagiri, and were attacked
and occupied by the Deputy Commissioner. It was eventually
resolved that the whole of the country which had hitherto been
left to its independence should be brought under the same management as the rest; and in the cold weather of 1872-73 three detach-

ments of police, from Mymensingh on the south, from Tura on the west, and from Goálpára on the north, marched through the country which it had been decided to annex. All resistance was easily overpowered, *lashkars* or headmen were appointed, the heads taken in recent raids were surrendered, and peaceful administration was established.

95. Since the expedition of 1872-73, the history of the district

Recent history.

has been one of profound peace. In February and March 1881, a slight disturbance took place near Bangálkháta, at the north-western corner of the hills, in consequence of the construction of a road through that tract ; but it was speedily suppressed without bloodshed. The whole of the district, with the exception of a small tract of plains land on the north, is now under the exclusive management of the Deputy Commissioner, and is free from the exactions of zamindárs, the greater part of whose interests in the area formerly included in their zamindáris or tributary to them have been bought out and extinguished.

96. The Khási Hills were first brought into direct relations

II. The Khási Hills.

with the British Government in 1826, after the conquest of Assam.* The chiefs of the Khási States on the northern border of the hills had gradually, since the decay of the Ahom power in the year 1794, established themselves in the plains of Kámrúp in the tracts known as Duárs, and were accustomed to pay only a nominal allegiance to the Assam kings. When Assam was acquired by the East India Company, it became an object with Mr. Scott to establish communication through the hills with Sylhet, and while the new administration of Kámrúp refused to recognise the right of the Khási rulers to encroach on the plains of Assam, Mr. Scott was able, by agreeing to allow Tírat Singh, Seim of Nongkhláo, to rent some lands in Borduár, to induce that chief, and to persuade the

---

* The Khásis had previously been known only as troublesome marauders upon the plains of Sylhet, where they were much dreaded. During the last century their ravages between 1780 and 1790 are specially mentioned as severe. A line of forts was kept up under the hills to check these incursions.

other Seims, to permit a road to be made through the hills *viá* Cherra Punji, Máophláng, and Nongkhláo to Gauháti.

In 1829, the insolent talk of some native servants belonging to the surveying party who were making the road led to an attack upon the party at the village of Nongkhláo, and Lieutenants Burlton and Bedingfield, with about fifty or sixty natives, were massacred. This event was followed by a general confederacy of most of the neighbouring chiefs to resist the British, and led to a long and harassing war, in which troops from Assam and Sylhet co-operated. Eventually, Tirat Singh submitted in 1833, and was confined as a prisoner for life in the Dacca Jail. The other chiefs had either before made terms with the British Government, or did so immediately after; and since that date the establishment of a British officer with an adequate military force in the midst of the people, at Cherra Punji, which was abandoned in 1866 for Shillong, has sufficed to maintain the most absolute tranquillity.

The greater part of the Khási Hills consists of the territories of native chiefs in subsidiary alliance with the British Government; only a few scattered villages have remained British since the conquest of 1833, or have been ceded since then under special circumstances. The people govern themselves through their elected rulers, who are bound to follow the advice of their *darbárs*. They pay no revenue to the British Government, but the Seims are required on investiture to confirm the cession to the paramount power of the mines and minerals, elephants, forests, and other natural products of their States, on the condition of receiving half the profits from these sources. All petty crime committed by their subjects is dealt with by the chiefs and their *darbárs*, only heinous offences, or those cases in which subjects of different States are concerned, being tried by the district authorities. The people are extremely well-to-do, and make much money by trade with the plains in the valuable staples which the hills produce.

97. It has already been related how, on the annexation of the plains country of Jaintia in 1835, Rája Rájendra Singh declined to retain the hilly portion of his principality, which thus lapsed to the British Govern-

The Jaintia Hills.

SECTION 5.
The Hill Districts.

ment. This tract, inhabited by the same race of mountaineers as the neighbouring Khási territory, was thereupon placed under the administration of the Political Agent at Cherra Punji. The Jaintia Hills were (and still are) divided into 23 petty districts, 19 of which are in charge of headmen, chosen by the people themselves, called Dollois, and the remaining 4 in that of hereditary Sardárs. From 1835 to 1855 the people were left very much to themselves. The Dollois heard all civil cases, at first without exception, and after 1841 up to a certain limit, and all criminal complaints not of a heinous character in which only people of their own villages were concerned. No taxes of any kind were levied throughout the hills, the only contribution required being the annual offering of a he-goat from each village, which had been exacted by the Jaintia Rája. In 1853 Mr. Mills, of the Sadr Court, reported on the district and drew attention to the absence of administrative control in this portion of it. He suggested that a house-tax (which had been proposed by the Political Officer in 1849, and then negatived by Government) should be imposed, and a police thána posted in the hills with a view to check the lawless proceedings of the Dollois. The latter recommendation was carried out, and a thána established at Jowai; but the former, though approved by Lord Dalhousie, remained without effect. In 1858, Mr. Allen, of the Board of Revenue, again reported on the district, and strongly urged Mr. Mills' recommendation that a moderate house-tax should be imposed, but he added that a European civil officer should be stationed in the midst of the tract, to be to the people a visible representative of British authority. The latter of these proposals was neglected, the former was adopted. In 1860 the house-tax was imposed, and within a few months the people were in open rebellion. Fortunately, a large force of troops was close at hand; and before the revolt could make any head, it was stamped out and the villages were awed into apparent submission. After this rising, measures were taken to improve the administration of the Dollois, who were notoriously corrupt, but still no officer was posted to the subdivision.

In January 1862, the people of the Jaintia Hills were again in fierce rebellion. The occasion was the imposition, only a year after the house tax had been introduced, of the income tax, to which 310 persons in the hills were subjected. This new impost, quickly succeeding the former, roused the deepest resentment among a people who had paid nothing for generations, either to their own Rája or to the British Government, and had been left since annexation entirely to themselves. The suppression of the revolt was long and tedious. Crushed apparently in four months after its outbreak, it again almost immediately burst out afresh; and it was not till November 1863 that the last of the rebel leaders surrendered, and the pacification of Jaintia could be said to be complete.

An English officer has since those events been stationed at Jowai. He is required to make himself acquainted with the Khási language, and to be able to dispense with interpreters; the administration of the Dollois has been reformed, education (by the agency of the Welsh Mission, established in the Khási Hills since 1842) has been encouraged, and the country has been thoroughly opened up by roads. The Jaintia Hills are now as secure and peaceable as the neighbouring Khási States.

98. North Cachar, the tract of thinly-peopled, low undulating hills, divided from the valley of the Barák by the range of the Baráil, and interposed

III. North Cachar.

between the Jaintia and the Nága Hills, has already been briefly referred to in the section dealing with Cachar. When the district was under native rule, during the last years of the reign of Govind Chandra, this portion of it was the scene of a struggle between that prince and one of his officers, named Kacha Dín,[*] who rebelled and endeavoured to establish an independent government in the hills. He was captured and put to death by Govind Chandra, but his son, Tularám, a _chaprási_ in the Rája's service, immediately revived the rebellion, and in 1824 joined the Burmese in their attack on Cachar. After a series of years, during which Tularám successfully held his own, Mr. Scott induced Govind Chandra in 1829 to assign to him a tract of country in the hills, and bind himself not to molest him within these limits. After the assassina-

[*] Called " Kohee Dan " by Colonel Butler, Mills' "Assam Report," page clxiii. " Kacha Din " is the name given by Pemberton, "Eastern Frontier," page 191.

tion of the Rája of Cachar, Tularám was a candidate for the vacant throne, but failed to establish his title. In 1835, he entered into an agreement with the British Government, in which he resigned all the western portion of the tract ceded by Govind Chandra, retaining the tract on the east, bounded on the south by the Máhur river and the Nága Hills, on the west by the Diyung, on the east by the Dhansiri, and on the north by the Jamuna and Diyung. For this he was to pay a tribute of four pairs of elephants' tusks annually, receiving a monthly pension of Rs. 50. Tularám died in October 1850. His sons, Nakulrám and Braja Náth, held the country for two and half years more, when the former was killed in the Nága Hills, whither he had led an expedition to avenge an attack on his village of Semkhor; and in 1854 the tract was resumed by the British Government, the surviving members of Tularám's family receiving pensions.

In 1839, the portion of North Cachar, not included in Tularám's dominions, was annexed to Nowgong; and in 1853 a separate officer was placed in charge of the subdivision, with his headquarters at Asálu, near the northern skirts of the Baráil, whose business it was to keep order among the Kukis and Arung Nágas dwelling in this neighbourhood, and to protect them against the Angámi Nágas to the east, who were constantly making raids into this country and that held by Tularám. In 1854, that officer's charge was augmented by the addition of Tularám's principality.

99. The defence of North Cachar and the Mikir Hills in
Nowgong, lying to the north of that sub-

IV. Nága Hills. Early
history.
division, from the attacks of the Angámi Nágas was a task, however, which experience proved could not be successfully effected from Asálu. These turbulent neighbours led yearly expeditions into the hills and the valleys of the Jamuna, Diyung, and Dhansiri rivers. Outposts throughout the hills held only the ground they covered, and the Nágas were able to creep by them with impunity. Ten military expeditions were led into the Nága Hills between 1835 and 1851, the greater number of which were to punish raids. In 1846, a police post, under Bhogchand Darogha, was established at Sama-

guting on a hill overlooking the Dhansiri Valley south of Dimapur. In 1849, Bhogchand was killed at Piphima in the hills by the men of Khonoma and Mezuma. In 1850, Lieutenant Vincent led a force to Mezuma to avenge Bhogchand's death, and remained there for six months, burning Khonoma during his stay. In the winter of 1850-51, the tenth expedition, the greatest British force which had entered the hills, advanced to complete the work of punishment; and on the 10th and 11th December 1850, the strong fort of Khonoma was taken under almost the same circumstances as attended its capture twenty-nine years later, in November 1879. Paplongmai was burnt, and the Nágas of Kekrima, who challenged our troops, lost 300 killed in a hand-to-hand fight which was long remembered in the hills.

After this successful expedition the Government of India decided upon a complete withdrawal from interference with the internal concerns of the Angámi Nágas. The Governor General, Lord Dalhousie, wrote in his minute of the 20th February 1851:

Hereafter we should confine ourselves to our own ground; protect it as it can and must be protected; not meddle in the feuds or fights of these savages; encourage trade with them as long as they are peaceful towards us; and rigidly exclude them from all communication, either to sell what they have got or to buy what they want, if they should become turbulent or troublesome.

These are the measures which are calculated to allay their natural fears of our aggression upon them, and to repel their aggression on our people. These will make them feel our power both to repel their attacks, and to exclude them from advantages they desire, far better, at less cost, and with more justice, than by annexing their country openly by a declaration, or virtually by a partial occupation.

In March 1851, our troops were withdrawn, and in that year twenty-two Nága raids were reported, in which 55 persons were killed, 10 were wounded, and 113 were taken captive. In 1853, as already related, an officer was stationed in the North Cachar Hills at Asálu; but he was instructed to regard the Angámis as persons living beyond the jurisdiction of the British Government, although in 1841 the watershed of the Baráil range to the south of

N

the Angámi country had been authoritatively laid down as the boundary of jurisdiction between Manipur and Assam. A line of outposts, with regular patrols, was established between Asálu and Barpathár, in the Nambar forest; but in 1857 these outposts were reduced and gradually withdrawn.

100. Raids continued to be numerous between 1853 and 1865,

Formation of the Nága
Hills district.
during which years 19 occurred, in which 232 British subjects were killed, wounded, or carried off. In 1864 and 1865 the policy to be followed towards the Angámi Nágas again came under review, and the concurrent opinion of the local officers, of the Commissioner, Colonel Hopkinson, and of the Lieutenant-Governor, Sir Cecil Beadon, was that it was necessary for the credit of our administration to advance into the hills, " to re-assert our authority over the Nágas, and bring them under a system of administration suited to their circumstances, and gradually to reclaim them from habits of lawlessness to those of order and civilisation. "

The Government of India, in 1866, agreed to the proposal that a new district should be formed, with its headquarters at Samaguting, Asálu being abolished as a subdivision, and North Cachar being divided between the Khási and Jaintia Hills, South Cachar, and Nowgong, that portion lying to the west of the Dhansiri and the country on both banks of the Doyong forming, with the Angámi Nága Hills, the new district. But they desired that the main object to be kept in view should be not to extend our rule into the interior, but to protect the lowlands from the incursion of the Nágas.

Captain Gregory, the first officer in charge of the new district, was succeeded in 1869 by Captain J. Butler, whose energetic administration did much to consolidate our power in the hills. Acting in the spirit of his instructions, he received the allegiance of those villages which freely tendered it, but made no effort to include those who were not willing to become British subjects. Much of his time was given to exploration with survey parties ; and in 1876 he met his death in a fight with the Lhota Nágas of Pángti, a village in the hills east of the Doyong river.

101. In February 1877, the Angámi Nágas of Mezuma raided

Advance to Kohima.

upon the Arung Nága village of Gumaigaju, in the heart of North Cachar, killing 6 and wounding 2 persons. The cause of the attack was a feud thirty years old. With this exception, no raid had been committed by Angámi Nágas within British territory since 1866, although there were numerous complaints of their depredations in Manipur ; and their internal feuds were, as always, incessant. The village of Mezuma refused to give up the raiders, and in the cold weather of 1877-78 an expedition was sent against it, by which the village was burned. Mr. Carnegy, the Political Officer, was accidentally killed by a sentry of his own party while occupying Mezuma. These events led to a review of the position which we occupied in the hills ; and in 1878, it was determined by Colonel Keatinge, after a visit to the country, to abandon Samaguting, a low and unhealthy site on the extreme edge of the Angámi country, and to fix the future head-quarters of the Political Officer at Kohima in the midst of the group of powerful villages which it was specially necessary to control. This selection was approved by the Government of India in March 1878, and by the end of the next cold weather the transfer from Samaguting to Kohima was completed.

In the course of the rains of 1879, indications of coming trouble began to present themselves, but no serious apprehensions were entertained by the Political Officer, Mr. Damant, who had planned an expedition during the cold weather into the Hatigoria country to the east of the Doyong. Before starting on this, however, he resolved to visit the powerful villages of Jotsoma, Khonoma, and Mezuma, to ascertain their disposition, and whether he might safely leave Kohima. On the 14th October he arrived at Khonoma, and leaving half his escort of 21 sepoys and 65 police with his baggage at the foot of the hill, he advanced with the other half up the narrow path leading to the strongly-fortified village site. The gate of the village was found closed, and as Mr. Damant stood before it, he was shot dead. A volley was then poured into his escort, who turned and fled down the hill. The Nágas followed, and dispersed the troops and police, who endeavoured by twos and threes to escape to Kohima. Of the military accompanying Mr. Damant, 10 were killed and 5 were wounded; of the police, 25 were killed and 14 were wounded.

When this news reached Kohima, preparations were made to resist the attack. The subdivisional officer was summoned from Wokha, 57 miles distant, and arrived with his force of sepoys and police on the 19th October. The stockade was besieged by the Nágas from the 16th to the 27th, when the garrison, who were reduced to great straits for want of food and water, were relieved, and the siege was raised, by the arrival of Colonel Johnstone, Political Agent of Manipur, with a force of 2,000 Manipuri troops, and his own escort of 30 sepoys and a few police.

A campaign against the Nágas then ensued, in which the 42nd and 44th Regiments, with a wing of the 18th Native Infantry and a detachment of the 43rd Native Infantry, took part, and which lasted till March 1880. Khonoma was taken on the 22nd November 1879, but the defenders retreated to a very strong position above the village on a spur of Jápvo, where they maintained themselves until the end of the campaign. Jotsoma was captured on the 27th November, and every one of the 13 villages which had entered into the coalition against us was either occupied or destroyed. The most notable event of the war, however, was the daring raid made in January 1880, by a party of Khonoma men from the fort above the village, at the time beleaguered by our troops, upon the tea garden of Báládhan in Cachar, more than 80 miles distant, where they killed the manager, Mr. Blyth, and 16 coolies, plundered what they could, and burned everything in the place.

On the 27th March, the fort above Khonoma submitted, and the war was at an end. Fines in grain, cash, and labour were imposed upon those villages which took part against us. The Nágas were made to surrender the firearms they were known to possess, and in some instances the removal of a village from a fortified and inaccessible crest to a site below was directed. Khonoma was razed to the ground, and its site occupied by an outpost. From all villages an agreement was taken to pay revenue in the shape of 1 maund of rice and 1 rupee per house, to provide a certain

amount of labour annually for State purposes, and to appoint
a headman who should be responsible for good order and for
carrying out the wishes of Government.

After the close of this, the twelfth and last expedition, the
question of the policy to be adopted in dealing with the Nágas
was submitted by the Chief Commissioner to the Government of
India, who in February 1881 finally decided that our position at
Kohima should be retained, that a regiment should be permanently
stationed in the hills, and that the district should be administered as British territory. Since that date the history of the
district has been one of the progressive establishment of peace
and good order, and the quiet submission of the Nágas to our
rule.

102. In 1875, a subdivision was opened at Wokha, which is
situated in the country of the Lhota Nágas,
Wokha subdivision.
who are separated from the Angámis by the
Rengmas and Semas. The village of Wokha had on several occasions attacked survey parties sent into the hills, and it was determined to occupy the site to secure our position there. The Lhotas
have no connection with the Angámis, who do not pass through
their country in visiting the plains. This tract has been in charge
of a tahsildár since 1889, when the Mokokchang subdivision was
formed, as the Lhotas had by that time become so amenable to
authority that it was considered unnecessary any longer to retain
a European officer in their midst.

103. The boundaries of the Nága Hills district were gazetted
in 1882, and the only change since that date
Mokokchang subdivision.
has been the inclusion, in 1889, of the cis-
Dikhu tract of country inhabited by the Ao Nágas. The reasons
for this step were the difficulty of protecting the Aos from raids by
trans-Dikhu tribes unless a garrison was permanently established
in their midst, and the fact that the leading Ao villages had peti-
tioned the Deputy Commissioner for their incorporation in British
territory. The necessary measures were successfully carried out,
and the tract in question is now known as the Mokokchang subdivision of the Nága Hills district.

Re-establishment of the North Cachar subdivision.

104. At the close of the Nága war of 1879-80, Sir Steuart Bayley recommended, and the Government of India approved, the re-establishment of the subdivisional charge of North Cachar, where, since 1866, no officer had been located, the hillmen being left, save for the rare cold-weather tours of the Deputy Commissioner, entirely to themselves. The subdivision was opened in December 1880, and placed in charge of an Assistant Superintendent of Police, who was stationed at Gunjong, in the centre of the tract, a point connected by easy hill paths with Nowgong to the north, Silchar to the south, and Jowai to the west. A bridle path to Kohima, *viâ* the Kacha or Arung Nága country, has since been constructed. In this hitherto isolated and thinly-peopled region, in the cold weather of 1881-82, an event occurred which cost the life of a valued officer, Major Boyd, the Deputy Commissioner of Cachar. A Kachári, named Sambhudán, declared himself inspired, claimed to work miraculous cures, and with his followers, who, like himself, took the title of *deo*, or god, levied contributions on the villagers about Maibong, the old capital of the Kachári kings, where he took up his abode. The matter came under the notice of the subdivisional officer, who reported it, and the Deputy Commissioner, Major Boyd, immediately started for Gunjong with 30 police, and reached that place without impediment. On the 15th January he left Gunjong with Mr. Soppitt, the subdivisional officer, for Maibong, which is six or eight hours' march distant; Maibong was reached and found deserted, and the party encamped in the huts of the *deos*. On the same day Sambhudán and his party, some 20 men, countermarched him, and about noon fell upon Gunjong, where only a weak police guard, composed mainly of Kachári constables, who shared in the superstitions of their people, had been left. They were panic-stricken, and fled without firing a shot; and the *deos* burned down all the houses at Gunjong, killed two servants and a sick policeman, and left precipitately for Maibong. On the morning of the 16th, soon after dawn, Major Boyd was awakened by the shouts and drums of Sambhudán and his followers, who had passed the night in the jungle. The police formed up in line with bayonets fixed, but did not fire at first. The enemy advanced right up to them, and struck at them with their *daos*; one man was wounded on the shoulder with a *dao*, and Major Boyd received a deep cut between the forefinger and thumb. The police then fired a volley, and killed eight of their assailants; two or three more were afterwards found dead in the jungle. Sambhudán escaped for the time, but the insurrection completely collapsed at once. Major Boyd was carried into Silchar; his wound brought on tetanus, from which he died on the 30th January 1882. Sambhudán evaded capture till the end of the year, when he was surrounded by the police, who had received information of his hiding place. In endeavouring to escape, he received a wound, from which he quickly bled to death. Four of his gang were arrested, of whom two died in jail, and two were tried at the sessions; one was acquitted, and the other was sentenced to transportation for life.

During the last ten years the history of this subdivision has been peaceful and uneventful, and nothing has transpired worthy of permanent record.

SECTION 6.—FORMATION OF THE CHIEF COMMISSIONER-SHIP.

105. In 1873 it was determined by the Government of India to separate the districts now forming the Assam Province from the administration of the Government of Bengal, and to form them into a Chief Commissionership. By a proclamation dated the 6th February 1874, the districts of Goálpára, Kámrúp, Darrang, Nowgong, Sibságar, Lakhimpur, the three hill districts, and the district of Cachar were taken under the immediate authority and management of the Governor General in Council; and by a notification of the same date they were formed into a Chief Commissionership, and Lieutenant-Colonel R. H. Keatinge, V.C., C.S.I., was appointed the first Chief Commissioner. On the 12th September of the same year, by another proclamation and notification, Sylhet was added, and the province, as it now exists, was completed.

O

SECTION 6.

Formation of the Chief Commissionership.

The following statement shows the officers who have filled the post of Chief Commissioner since the formation of the Chief Commissionership :

Name.	From	To	Remarks.
Colonel R. H. Keatinge, V.C., C S.I.	7th February 1874	21st June 1878.	
Sir S. C. Bayley, K.C.S.I....	22nd June 1878 .	1st March 1881.	
Mr. C. A. Elliott, C.S.I. ...	2nd March 1881 .	7th July 1883.	
Mr. W. E. Ward ...	7th July 1883 ...	7th October 1883	Officiating.
Mr. C. A. Elliott, C.S.I. ...	7th October 1883	23rd February 1885.	
Mr. W. E. Ward ...	23rd February 1885.	31st October 1887	Officiating.
Mr. D. Fitzpatrick, C.S.I.	31st October 1887	15th July 1889.	
Mr. J. Westland, C.S.I. ...	15th July 1889	22nd October 1889.	
Mr. J. W. Quinton, C.S I.	22nd October 1889	24th March 1891.	
Brigadier-General Sir H. Collett, K.C.B.	24th March 1891	27th May 1891...	Officiating.
Mr. W. E. Ward, C.S.I. ...	27th May 1891.		

CHAPTER III.

Form of Administration.

106. The province of Assam, excluding Sylhet, as already mentioned, was taken under the immediate authority and management of the Governor General in Council, and constituted a separate Administration, by a proclamation, dated the 6th February 1874. A Chief Commissioner having been appointed, Act VIII of 1874 was passed to provide for the exercise by him of executive powers. In September of the same year, on the addition of the district of Sylhet to the Chief Commissionership, Act XII of that year made the same provision in regard to that district. By these Acts the powers which, on the date of the formation of the Chief Commissionership, and on that of the transfer to it of the district of Sylhet, were, by virtue of any law or regulation vested in, or exercisable by, the Lieutenant Governor of Bengal or the Board of Revenue, Lower Provinces, were transferred to, and vested in, the Governor General in Council; and it was enacted that the Governor General in Council might, from time to time, delegate to the Chief Commissioner all or any of the said powers, and withdraw any powers so delegated.

. By notification, dated the 16th April 1874, the Government of India delegated to the Chief Commissioner all powers which were vested in the Lieutenant Governor of Bengal by the direct operation of any Act of the Governor General in Council, which also conferred the same powers on the Chief Commissioners of Oudh, the Central Provinces, and British Burma. By Act I of 1868, section 2, clause 10, all powers conferred upon a Local Government by any Act of the Governor General in Council in force in

Powers of the Chief Commissioner.

Assam, and passed subsequently to the constitution of the Chief Commissionership, vest in the Chief Commissioner. By the operation of this clause and the notification of the 16th April (and, in regard to Sylhet, a similar notification of the 12th September 1874), the Chief Commissioner has, in respect to all the general Acts of the Governor General in Council, the powers of a Local Government.

Other powers have from time to time been delegated to the Chief Commissioner under Acts VIII and XII of 1874 [or assumed under section 6(c) of Act XIV of the same year], which, generally speaking, place him in the position of a Local Government in regard to most of the Regulations and Acts, whether of the Legislative Council of India or that of Bengal, in practical operation in the province.

The Chief Commissioner is assisted by a Secretary and an Assistant Secretary.

107. From the constitution of the province in 1874 down to 1880 there were no Commissioners in Assam.

But in June of the latter year one was appointed for the six districts of the Assam Valley, the office being combined with that of Judge in these districts, and the Commissioner being invested generally with the powers of a Commissioner of Division in Bengal. In the other districts of the province, that is, in the Surma Valley and Hill districts, the Chief Commissioner continues to perform himself the duties of a Commissioner of Division.

Each of the eleven districts of the province has a Deputy Commissioner as its chief executive officer, who is aided by a staff of Assistant Commissioners and Extra Assistant Commissioners. The functions of these officers are similar to those exercised by officers of the same name in other provinces.

In addition to the above, there is the Director, Department of Land Records and Agriculture, whose main duty it is to supervise all survey and settlement operations, but who is also entrusted with the collection of trade and agricultural statistics, the management of survey schools, and other similar matters.

108. The judicial organisation of the province is at present in much the same condition as at its constitution in 1874. The six districts of the Brahmaputra Valley, and the districts of Sylhet and Cachar, are subordinate to the High Court of Fort William in Bengal. For the whole of the Brahmaputra Valley there is one District and Sessions Judge (who is also the Commissioner), whose headquarters are at Gauhátí, but who holds sessions at the various district headquarters when required. The Deputy Commissioners of the six districts have the civil powers of Subordinate Judges, and the special powers conferred by sections 30 and 34 of the Criminal Procedure Code of trying all offences not punishable with death and awarding a sentence of seven years' imprisonment. The Assistant and Extra Assistant Commissioners have the ordinary powers of Magistrates of the first, second, and third classes, and have also generally the civil powers of a Munsif, though only the senior Extra Assistant Commissioner or, where there is no Extra Assistant Commissioner, the senior Assistant Commissioner at a headquarters station, and the subdivisional officer at a subdivisional station ordinarily exercises the latter powers.

Judicial staff.

In the Surma Valley a different system prevails. In Sylhet there is a separate judicial service, at the head of which is the District and Sessions Judge, aided by a Subordinate Judge and a staff of Munsifs for the disposal of civil cases. The Deputy Commissioner, Assistant Commissioners, and Extra Assistant Commissioners have here no civil powers, and exercise only the ordinary magisterial powers in criminal matters. In Cachar the Sessions Judge is the Judge of Sylhet, who holds sessions at Silchar when necessary; but the Deputy Commissioner has the special criminal powers mentioned in sections 30 and 34 of the Criminal Procedure Code. The Deputy Commissioner, however, and not the Judge of Sylhet, is the District Civil Judge; there is no Subordinate Judge, and the Assistant and Extra Assistant Commissioners exercise the powers of Munsifs in addition to their functions as Magistrates and executive officers.

In the hill districts and certain frontier tracts (the North

Cachar subdivision, the Mikir Hills tract in Nowgong, and the Dibrugarh frontier tract in Lakhimpur), the High Court possesses no jurisdiction except over European British subjects. The Hill districts were formerly under the operation of the Deregulationizing Act, XXII of 1869, which was repealed by the Scheduled Districts Act, XIV of 1874. Subsequently, the Frontier Tracts Regulation, II of 1880, was passed, under which power is given to the Chief Commissioner, with the previous sanction of the Governor General in Council, to direct that any enactment in force in any frontier tract shall cease to be in force therein, and this Regulation (with the additional power of extension conferred by Regulation III of 1884) has been brought into force in all the hill districts and frontier tracts referred to above. Under its provisions, the operation of the enactments relating to Civil and Criminal Procedure, Court-fees, Stamps, Transfer of Property, and Registration, has been barred,* and a simpler system of administering justice in civil and criminal matters has been prescribed by rules framed under section 6 of the Scheduled Districts Act, XIV of 1874. By these rules the Chief Commissioner is himself the chief appellate authority in civil and criminal cases. The Deputy Commissioner exercises the combined powers of District and Sessions Judge and Magistrate of a district, and the Assistant Commissioners and Extra Assistant Commissioners the powers of Magistrates and Munsifs. The judicial administration in all petty civil and criminal cases is carried on by village tribunals, presided over by headmen chosen from among the people themselves, whose procedure is completely free from legal technicalities, and whose proceedings are not reduced to writing. The Criminal Procedure Code is in force in the Eastern Duárs in Goálpára, and that tract is, therefore, on the same footing as the plains districts so far as the administration of criminal justice is concerned. The Civil Procedure Code, however, is not in force; its place is taken by rules under section 6 of Act XIV of 1874, which con-

---

* Except in cases when such enactments never were in force. The Civil Procedure Code, for instance, was never extended to the hill districts, and it was, therefore, unnecessary to include this in the declarations under Regulation II of 1880, which were issued in regard to these districts.

tain much the same provisions as the corresponding rules framed

for the tracts which are under the operation of Regulation II of 1880.

Besides the judicial officers named above, there are a few Honorary Magistrates in nearly every district. The latter in all cases, however, sit singly, no benches of Honorary Magistrates having yet been formed in any district except Sylhet.

109. Up to the year 1886, Sylhet Proper was under the

Revenue administration.

operation of the old Bengal Regulations and the other land revenue enactments in force in Bengal. In Jaintia and Cachar, and also, though to a less extent, in Goálpára, these enactments were generally followed, but they were not treated as actually in force. In the Brahmaputra Valley Proper, the settlement rules of the Board of Revenue had been replaced by local rules, which were revised and recast in 1883. In other respects the revenue law of Bengal was followed, so far as the local officers considered it to be applicable, but it was not treated as legally in force. All doubt and uncertainty have now been removed by the enactment of the Assam Land and Revenue Regulation, I of 1886, which has been brought into force in all the plains districts of the province. It contains all the necessary provisions of the revenue law of Bengal, the whole of which it repeals, so far as Assam is concerned. The Regulation was amended in some respects as regards the recovery of arrears of revenue by Regulation II of 1889, and its provisions regarding settlements, mutations, partitions, the recovery of arrears, &c., have been supplemented by rules issued under it and deriving from it the force of law. The superior authorities entrusted with the revenue administration have already been stated. They are the Chief Commissioner (as Local Government and Board of Revenue, and, in the Surma Valley and hill districts, as Commissioner), the Commissioner (in the Brahmaputra Valley), the Director, Department of Land Records and Agriculture, and an assistant for supervising the preparation and maintenance of land records in cadastrally surveyed tracts in the Assam Valley districts, the Deputy Commissioners in each district, and the Assistant and Extra Assistant Commissioners. Below these there are different subordinate officers in different districts. Each subdivision in the plains districts, except South Sylhet and Goálpára, has an officer called a Sub-Deputy Collector, who is employed mainly upon supervision of the revenue establishments, upon surveying waste and cultivated lands (the extent and importance of this work in Assam will be seen from the following chapter), and the compilation of the revenue records and returns.

Goálpára, except the Eastern Duárs, is, for all practical purposes, a permanently-settled tract, and there are no *mufassal* revenue establishments; in the other districts of the Brahmaputra Valley the whole of the revenue was formerly collected by contractors, called *mauzadárs*, holding charge of the revenue assessment and collection within definite areas, called *mauzas*, into which these districts are divided. On the conclusion of the annual assessment (which will be described in a subsequent section*), the *mauzadár* entered into a contract to pay into the treasury the revenue assessed, together with any additional revenue which might be assessed on lands subsequently taken up within the year for cold weather cultivation, irrespective of whether he succeeded in realising the full amount from the cultivators or not, and was remunerated by a commission calculated at 10 per cent. on the first Rs. 6,000 of revenue and 5 per cent. on any amount above that sum. This system is still largely in vogue, but is being rapidly superseded by the formation of *tahsils*, whereby from 3 to 11 *mauzas* are amalgamated and placed in charge of an official called a *tahsildár*, who is paid by a regular salary, and not by commission. The first *tahsils* were started in 1883-84 during which year four were formed in the Kámrúp district, and from that date the extension of the system has progressed rapidly. There were at the close of 1892-93, 23 *tahsils* in the Brahmaputra Valley, absorbing in all 125 *mauzas*.

The chief argument in favour of the *tahsildári* as opposed to the *mauzadári* system is the great saving which is thereby effected in the cost of collection, the percentage in 1892-93 of collection

* See *post*, Chapter IV, Section 3, System of Survey and Settlement.

charges in *tahsils* being only 2·38, against 3·71 in *mauzas*.* The amount thus saved is devoted to increasing the efficiency of the assessment operations, as will be described in the paragraphs dealing with the system of survey and settlement. Where *tahsils* have not yet been introduced, the cost of collection has been reduced as far as possible by amalgamating *mauzas*, thereby reducing the number of *mauzadárs*, and saving to that extent the higher rate of commission which is payable on the first Rs. 6,000 of a *mauzadár's* collections. Ten years ago, the collection charges amounted to 11·87 per cent. of the total revenue collected, while in the present year the corresponding percentage is only 3·53.

It should be mentioned here that there are certain estates, the revenue on which is paid direct into the treasury, and not through the local revenue collector. This privilege is conceded in the cases of waste land grants, all *nisf-khiráj* estates in Nowgong and Darrang and many of those in Kámrúp, and a few other special tenures. Certain communities of Miris in North Lakhimpur also pay their revenue direct into the treasury, through their own headmen or *gams*.

At each subdivisional headquarters in Sylhet there is a collecting office, where the revenue is paid in and the accounts are made up. There are also *mufassal* establishments, *viz.*, in Kanairghát in Jaintia, and at Hakaluki and Pratabgarh in Karimganj. Proceedings for the realisation of arrears (which are here generally recovered by means of the Sale Law) are taken at the subdivisions.

In the plains portion of Cachar also, there are three collecting or *tahsil* establishments for receipt of the revenue, which is here settled for a term. Two of these are located at the sadr and subdivisional headquarters, and the third at a point close to the Sylhet boundary.

In the hill districts, the general rule is that house tax, and not land revenue, properly so called, is paid; but in the Gáro Hills and a small area in the Jaintia and Nága Hills, there are tracts where land revenue is taken, and *mauzadárs* are the agency employed for collection. The house tax is, in the Gáro, Jaintia, Nága

* In this calculation the Bijni tahsil has not been included, as the circumstances of that tahsil are somewhat exceptional.

P

Section 1.

General
Administra-
tion System
and S. P.

Hills, and North Cachar, and the few villages in the Khási Hills which are British territory, collected and paid in by headmen, who, like the *mauzadárs* of the Assam Valley are remunerated by a commission. These officers are called *Lashkars* and *Lakmas* in the Gáro Hills, *Dollois* and *Sardárs* in the Jaintia and Khási Hills, *Lambardárs* in the Nága Hills, and *Mauzadárs* in North Cachar.

110. The province of Assam is a general police district under

Police.

Act V of 1861, and the police are under the control of an Inspector General, who is on the graded list of Deputy Commissioners. In each of the plains districts there is an officer, either a District Superintendent or an Assistant Superintendent, who has charge of the Civil Police work. These officers are borne on the Bengal staff of police officers, and receive promotion in that list. In addition to these officers, whose work is to superintend the prevention and detection of crime, there is a small staff consisting of one Civil and three Military Police officers, who, under the designation of Command-ants of Military Police, control that division of the Assam Police Force which performs semi-military duties in manning the frontier outposts, and in holding as a garrison the Gáro, Nága, and North Lushai Hills. This division of the force, besides being subject to Act V of 1861, is under a special Regulation (The Assam Military Police Regulation, 1890), which makes provision for the enforce-ment of due discipline, and assimilates generally the terms of service to those prevailing in the Native Army. The four divisions of the Military Police are located as follows : (1) in the Brahma-putra Valley, with headquarters at Dibrugarh; (2) in the Surma Valley, with headquarters at Silchar; (3) in the Nága Hills, with headquarters at Kohima; and (4) in the Gáro Hills, with head-quarters at Tura. The Surma Valley battalion also holds the North Lushai Hills, but a proposal has recently been sanctioned to form a separate battalion for that purpose. In the meantime, the Commandant is assisted by a second military officer, who is called an Assistant Commandant. At the close of 1892 the sanctioned strength of the Civil and Armed Civil Police in Assam was 2,178 officers and men, and of the Military Police 2,535 officers and men.

Besides the regular Civil Police, there are a few municipal police entertained in towns which have been constituted "Unions" *General Administra- tion Section and Staff.* under the Bengal Municipal Act (these numbered 15 officers and men at the close of 1892), and there is a force of *chaukidárs*, or rural police, in the districts of Sylhet, Cachar, and Goálpára. Except in the last-named district, there are no village police in the Brahmaputra Valley. The *mauzadárs* and *mandals* are re- quired to give information and aid in detection of crime, and in each village, or group of hamlets, there is a *gaonbura*, or village elder, who is the recognised representative of the villagers in police matters, but receives no remuneration from Government. The *chaukidárs* in Goálpára are governed by the Bengal Chauki- dári Act [VI (B.C.) of 1870 as amended by Act I (B.C.) of 1871], and those in the Surma Valley by the Sylhet and Cachar Rural Police Regulation, I of 1883. On the last day of 1892 there were 6,812 village police in the province, of whom 5,616 were in Sylhet, 480 in Cachar, and 716 in Goálpára. Their cost was Rs. 2,93,960 for the year, the whole of which was paid by the villagers.

111. The jails in Assam are divided into three *jails*, large es-

Jails.

tablishments at Gauháti, Tezpur, and Sylhet; six *subsidiary jails*, smaller places of con- finement, at Dhubri, Nowgong, Sibságar, Dibrugarh, Silchar, and Shillong; and thirteen *lock-ups*, at the headquarters stations of Tura and Kohima, and the subdivisional stations of Goálpára, Barpeta, Mangaldai, Jorhát, Golághát, Lakhimpur, Sunámganj, Karimganj, Habiganj, Maulvi Bázár, and Hailákándi. Besides these, temporary jails are also opened, from time to time as necessary, for the accommodation of prisoners employed upon public works at a distance from the permanent jails.

Where a civil medical officer is employed (as is generally the case at Gauháti, Tezpur, and Sylhet), he is the Superintendent of the Jail. The department is supervised by an Inspector General, who is also Inspector General of Police.

The Jail Law of the province is Act XXVI of 1870, which was brought into force in supersession of the Jail Acts, II of 1864 and V of 1865, of the Bengal Council, by Regulation No. II of 1875.

The Bengal Jail Manual, consisting of rules and orders issued by the Government and the Inspector General of Jails in that province, is followed in Assam so far as it does not conflict with the provisions of Act XXVI of 1870.

112. Excise is managed (under the Excise Laws of Bengal, which have been extended to Assam) by
Excise, Stamps, Registration.
the Commissioner of Excise, an office which is held by the Inspector General of Police and Jails in addition to his other duties. The same officer is also Superintendent of Stamps and Inspector General of Registration, as well as Registrar of Joint Stock Companies under the Companies' Act, and Registrar General of Births, Deaths, and Marriages under Act VI of 1886. All Deputy Commissioners are Registrars in their respective districts; the Sub-Registrars at headquarters are either Extra Assistant Commissioners, who do this work in addition to their other work, or special Sub-Registrars (at Sylhet and Silchar); at subdivisions either the subdivisional officer, or a second officer (generally an Extra Assistant Commissioner), if there is one, is Sub-Registrar. But in all the subdivisions of Sylhet there are special Sub-Registrars, and at Balaganj, Hingajia, and Madhabpur in the same district there are rural Sub-Registrars.

113. The Educational Department is supervised by a Director
Educational Department.
of Public Instruction, who is borne on the graded list of Bengal. He is assisted by four Deputy Inspectors (one for the Surma Valley and three for the Brahmaputra Valley, *i.e.*, one each for Upper, Central, and Lower Assam) and 24 Sub-Inspectors, *viz.*, one for each subdivision in the plains districts, with an extra man for Gauháti, one for the Gáro Hills, and two for the Khási and Jaintia Hills. Besides these departmental officers, who directly control the Government high and middle schools and the higher normal school at Gauháti, all classes of aided schools in the eight plains districts are under the supervision of the several Local Boards established under the Assam Local Rates Regulation, 1879. These authorities receive applications and make allotments of grants-in-aid without reference

to the Director, but subject to the rules prescribed for such grants.

The aided schools are still generally under the control of the Director of Public Instruction, and are, of course, subject to inspection by him, the Deputy Inspectors, and the Sub-Inspectors.

114. The Forest Department is under the control of a Con-

Forest Department. servator, who is assisted by a staff of Deputy and Assistant and Extra Assistant Conservators. These officers are now borne on a separate Provincial list, and their standing in the department depends on their places in that list. At the time of writing this report, the sanctioned list consists of six Deputy Conservators, three Assistant and three Extra Assistant Conservators, but two of the three appointments of Assistant Conservators are vacant.

The remaining ten officers are posted respectively to Lakhimpur, Sibságar, and the Nága Hills, Darrang, Nowgong, Kámrúp, and the Khási Hills, Goálpára, the Gáro Hills, Cachar, Sylhet, and the Working Plans Division.

115. The staff of direction of the Public Works Department in

Public Works Department. Assam consists of a Chief or Superintending Engineer, who is also Secretary to the Chief Commissioner in that Department, aided by an Assistant Secretary, and, as regards the accounts of Provincial and Imperial works, by an Examiner and the usual staff. Excluding the above, as also the special establishment sanctioned for the Nichuguard-Manipur road (an Imperial work), the present sanctioned scale of executive staff provides seven Executive and five Assistant Engineers. Besides the foregoing, the following special staff is at present employed in the province :—Attached to the Assam-Bengal Railway, a Consulting Engineer, a Deputy Consulting Engineer, and an Examiner of Accounts ; for the Nichuguard-Manipur road, one Superintendent of Works, two Executive and two Assistant Engineers.

116. The medical institutions of the province are supervised

Medical and sanitary establishments. by the Principal Medical Officer, Assam District, who, in addition to his military duties, is the Sanitary Commissioner of the province, and is the Chief Commissioner's adviser on sanitary and medical matters generally. Each district has a Civil Surgeon, one of whom, assisted by an Assistant Surgeon (at Kohima), holds that post in addition to his duties as Regimental Surgeon. The Civil Surgeon of Tezpur, besides holding charge of the jail there, is also Superintendent of the only Lunatic Asylum which the province possesses, and which receives lunatics from the Assam Valley and Hill districts; lunatics from the Surma Valley are treated in the Dacca Asylum. The Civil Surgeons of Sylhet and Gauháti are Superintendents of the jails there. The Civil Surgeon of Dhubri is Embarkation Agent for emigrants recruited for the labour districts of the Brahmaputra Valley. A medical officer is stationed at Aijal as Civil Surgeon, North Lushai Hills, and the Regimental Surgeon at Manipur is in civil medical charge of that station.

117. The only Government Chaplain in the province is the
Ecclesiastical officers.
Minister of Shillong, who also visits Sylhet, Dhubri, and Gauháti at intervals during the course of the year. Small allowances are, besides, given to clergymen provided by the Additional Clergy Society or by the Society for the Propagation of the Gospel, for the spiritual charge of the European population in other districts. These allowances are drawn by ministers stationed at Tezpur, Dibrugarh, and Silchar.

118. The accounts of the province are in charge of a Comp-
*Imperial departments
in the province.*
troller, who is directly subordinate to the Financial Department of the Government of India. The Post Office Department is in charge of a Deputy Postmaster General, and the Telegraph Department in that of a Superintendent. These officers, as well as the officers of the Survey Department serving in the province, are not subordinate to the Chief Commissioner.

SECTION 2.—LEGISLATIVE AUTHORITY.

119. There are three ways in which measures of legislation are
*Acts of the Governor
General's Council.*
brought into force in this province. The first is the ordinary method, common to the whole of India, of passing Acts in the Council of the Governor General for making Laws and Regulations.

120. The second is the method of passing Regulations in

Regulations under 33 Victoria, Chapter 3, section 1. accordance with the provisions of 33 Victoria, Chapter 3, section 1 (an Act to make better provision for making Laws and Regulations for certain parts of India, and for certain other purposes relating thereto). This Act was, by Resolutions passed by the Secretary of State for India in Council, made applicable to the districts of Kámrúp, Darrang, Nowgong, Sibságar, and Lakhimpur, and the Gáro, Khási and Jaintia, Nága Hills, and Cachar from the 1st January 1873 ; to the district of Goálpára from the 15th December 1873 ; and to the district of Sylhet from the 1st August 1874. Under its provisions, the Chief Commissioner has power to "propose to the Governor General in Council drafts of any Regulations, together with the reasons for proposing the same, for the peace and government of the territories under his administration." Such drafts, when approved by the Governor General in Council, and after they have received the Governor General's assent, are published in the *Gazette of India,* and thereupon have the force of law. This method, which was first used in Assam in 1873, on the passing of Regulation V of that year (the Inner Line Regulation), before the constitution of the Chief Commissionership, has since been frequently resorted to.

121. The third method is to make use of section 5 of Act

Extension under section 5 of the Scheduled Districts Act. XIV of 1874 (The Scheduled Districts Act), which declares that " the Local Government, with the previous sanction of the Governor General in Council, may from time to time, by notification in the *Gazette of India,* and also in the local Gazette (if any), extend to any of the scheduled districts, or to any part of any such district, any enactment which is in force in any part of British India at the date of such extension." By section 6, clause (e), of the same Act, the Chief Commissioner is empowered to direct by what authority any jurisdiction, powers, or duties incident to the operation of any enactment for the time being in force in a scheduled district shall be exercised or performed.

Assam is one of the scheduled districts under this Act (Sche-

Section 3. dule I, Part X); and the Act was declared to be in force in the
Education. province by notification on the 7th November 1877. Since that
date, numerous Acts in force in other parts of India have, under
the powers given by section 5, been brought into force in Assam.

DEPARTMENTAL SYSTEMS.

SECTION 3.—EDUCATION.

122. The inspecting staff of the Educational Department has
already been described. It remains to state
Divisions of schools. here the system of teaching, the kinds of
schools, and the manner in which they are supported.

In the first place, educational institutions in Assam are divided
into those subject to departmental inspection and rules and those
not so subject. The former are either Government institutions,
or receive some kind of assistance from public money, whether
granted direct from Provincial revenues or from Local Funds, and
are classified as follows:

I. Primary, divided into (*a*) Lower primary or *páthshálas*, and
(*b*) Upper primary.

II. Middle, divided into (*a*) Vernacular, and (*b*) English.

III. High schools.

IV. Training and special.

The latter are of two kinds: either wholly unaided and unin-
spected, being for the most part religious in their object; or
schools established with a view to eventually obtaining a Government grant, and carried on entirely on the model of Government
schools. The latter differ in no respect, expect in efficiency, from
the Government schools which they imitate. The former are
chiefly *tols*, or Sanskrit schools, where, in addition to religious
subjects, books on literature, logic, philosophy, &c., in that language are read; and *maktabs*, Muhammadan schools, where the
Koran is learned by rote, and Arabic and Persian reading and
writing are taught. In 1887, however, reward rules for *tols* and
maktabs were framed, and schools competing for three rewards are

liable to inspection. The result of this change is a marked improvement in the method of teaching, and pupils from *tols* in Sylhet have of late years competed with success at the Title Exam- inations held in Bengal. In addition to these, there are Khampti Buddhist schools, which are found in every village of that people, where a monk, or *bápu*, gives instruction to the boys in reading and writing the Shán language, and teaches them the doctrines of Buddha in that language and Páli. Attendance at school is quite optional, but the boys are kindly treated, and nearly all of them avail themselves of the educational opportunities offered to them. The usual course lasts three years, during which time the boys live in the temple. Some of them elect to remain on when the usual course is finished, and qualify themselves for the priesthood. The boys first learn to write with chalk on a piece of dark stained wood, and when more advanced, they are allowed the use of paper of local manufacture. Arithmetic does not apparently enter into the curriculum. The teacher is remunerated by daily offerings of food, and not by money.

123. The lower primary schools or *páthshálas* are institutions

Primary schools.
where an elementary knowledge of the local vernacular is imparted. Beginning at the beginning, they teach up to a course of study which forms the subject of an examination, called the Primary Scholarship Exam- ination. The subjects of this course are—

I. (*a*) Handwriting and dictation.
(*b*) Easy questions in grammar and explanations from vernacular text-books.
II. Arithmetic—the first four rules, simple and compound, after the European method; practice, simple and com- pound, after the native method; and mental arithmetic, native and European methods, on above rules.
III. Zamindári and mahajani accounts and simple mensuration after the native method.
IV. Sanitary Science.

A certain number of primary scholarships, worth Rs. 3 a month, and tenable for two years at any school of a higher status

Q

Section 3. is allotted to each district, and these are awarded to the pupils
Education. who pass best in the Primary Scholarship Examination.

The course in the upper primary schools also works up to a
scholarship examination, the amount and conditions of the scholarship being the same as for the lower primaries. In these
schools a slightly higher degree of acquaintance with literature, a
more extensive knowledge of arithmetic, part of Book I of Euclid
as well as mensuration, the history of Assam or Bengal (according
as the school is in the Assam or the Surma Valley), the geography
of the province (with a general knowledge of the four quarters),
and the elements of sanitation, are the objects aimed at in the
course of study.

124. In Government middle vernacular schools the course of
Middle schools. instruction is altogether in Bengali, but in
aided schools of this class in the Brahma-
putra Valley the option is allowed of imparting instruction through
the medium of Assamese. The following are the subjects taught :

    I. Bengali, or Assamese, comprising literature, grammar, and
        composition.

    II. History of India—Hindu, Muhammadan, and English
         periods.

    III. Geography, a general knowledge of the four quarters,
         with special knowledge of that of India, and map-drawing.

    IV. Arithmetic, general bazar, and zamindári accounts, and
         mental arithmetic.

    V. Euclid (Book I), mensuration of plane surfaces and sur-
       veying.

    VI. Sanitary Science.

The course of study is closed by the Middle Vernacular Scholarship Examination, the successful candidates in which receive
scholarships worth Rs. 4 per mensem, tenable for four years in
any school of a higher class.

The middle English schools take up the full vernacular course,
with English as a second language. The course of instruction is
terminated by the Middle English Examination. The value of

these scholarships is Rs. 5 a month for three years, and they are tenable at any high school.

There are 26 middle vernacular and 15 middle English scholarships for which the candidates at the scholarship examination compete.

125. Under the definition of high schools are included all schools that profess to teach up to the Calcutta University Entrance standard. The course of study here is that prescribed for the University Examination, and needs no further description. Junior scholarships are awarded to students who, after passing the Entrance Examination, go up to study for the F. A. Examination at any college in Bengal. The number of these scholarships is 36 in all, viz., 11 for the Surma Valley, 14 for natives of the Brahmaputra Valley, 3 for natives of the hill districts, and 8 for other than natives of the Brahmaputra Valley or hill districts reading in high schools in those parts. The monthly value of these scholarships is fixed at Rs. 25 for the two best boys, Rs. 20 for natives of the Brahmaputra Valley and hill districts, Rs. 15 for boys passing in the Surma Valley, and Rs. 20, Rs. 15, or Rs. 10 for boys other than natives who pass from schools in the Brahmaputra Valley and hill districts according as they pass in the first, second, or third division at the Entrance Examination. Junior scholars, who pass the F. A. Examination within two years of matriculating, are awarded senior scholarships of an amount equal to that of the junior scholarship previously granted to them.

There is no Government institution in the province which imparts instruction in the University course beyond the Entrance Examination ; a lower grade college formerly existed in Gauháti, but it was reduced in 1876 to the status of a Government high school, on account of the excessive expense of its maintenance and the small number of students who read at it. It is considered more desirable that the natives of the province (aided, if necessary, by scholarships under the scheme mentioned above) should resort to Bengal to prosecute their studies, and thus enlarge their minds by contact with a higher civilisation, than that an

Section 3.
Education.

expensive Government college should be maintained for them in Assam. It should, however, be mentioned that a private college teaching up to the F. A. standard was started in the town of Sylhet in 1892, at which twelve junior scholarships may be held. In all these schools, whether middle or high, it must be understood that the lower classes include mere beginners, and that the courses of study actually pursued by the boys in each kind of schools very largely overlap.

126. The fourth class of schools consists of the training and special schools. The first are the normal schools and training classes in which lads are taught with a view to becoming teachers. There are fifteen institutions or classes for the training of *gurus*, or teachers for primary schools, two of which (Gauháti and Shillong) also prepare teachers for middle schools. The second or special schools include an artizan school at Jorhát maintained by a special bequest made by Mr. Williamson, a tea-planter in Upper Assam, and some survey schools. The latter are under the control of the Director, Department of Land Records and Agriculture.

Training and special schools.

127. With the exception of a few schools which teach up to the middle standard, female education in Assam is confined to elementary instruction in primary schools. There are *páthshálas*, exclusively for females, managed on the same principle as boys' primary schools, and, in addition, a considerable number of girls read in boys' *páthshálas*. The Khási and Jaintia Hills is the only district in which female education has made any considerable progress. The census returns for that district show that, out of every 1,000 females, 13·7 are learning and 10·5 are literate, the corresponding figures for the province as a whole being 1·3 and 2·2 respectively.

Female education.

128. The only school in the province for the education of Europeans and Eurasians is the aided school at Shillong. The number of scholars in this school in 1892-93 was 23, of whom 11 were boys and 12 were girls. The Government grant-in-aid is Rs. 140 per month, and the use of the school house and furniture (which

European and Eurasian education.

belong to Government) is allowed at a rent of Rs. 50 a month. A mixed school was opened at Gauháti in 1882 and a boys' school at Shillong in 1883, but neither of these proved a success, and they were closed in 1886. The girls' school which had been started at Shillong in 1884 was closed in 1887 for the same reason. Two scholarships of Rs. 15 a month are given annually to sons of indigent European or Eurasian parents who are *bonâ fide* residents of Assam. These scholarships are tenable for three years at any European hill school approved by the Director of Public Instruction.

129. Schools under inspection are, as already stated, divided into (1) Government, the salaries of the teachers being borne entirely by public funds and the fees credited in the treasury; (2) aided, a fixed contribution being made to meet the expenses of the school; and (3) unaided. The following list shows how many schools there were of each class in the year 1892-93; the three classes of religious unaided schools mentioned in paragraph 120 are not included:

Division into Government, aided, and unaided schools.

Class of institution.	Government.		Aided.		Unaided.	
	Number of institutions.	Number of pupils.	Number of institutions.	Number of pupils.	Number of institutions.	Number of pupils.
ARTS COLLEGES.						
University Education—English ...	......	......			1	18
For Boys—						
High Schools ...	11	1,991	3	664	5	818
Middle Schools { English	2	146	35	2,849	19	931
{ Vernacular	15	1,195	23	1,701	2	101
For Girls—						
Middle Schools—Vernacular ...	......	......	2	49		
Primary Schools—						
For Boys	1,173	32,748	1,026	30,995	150	4,479
,, Girls	123	1,711	27	671	27	350
SCHOOLS FOR SPECIAL INSTRUCTION.						
Training Schools and Classes ...	13	230	3	134	......	......
Law Schools	......	......	......	......	3	43
Industrial Schools	1	9	......	......	......	......
Other Schools	1	22	1	23	1	35

School Education, General.

School Education, Special.

130. Except in the case of high schools, the grants-in-aid for which are now given by the Education Department, all grants-in-aid are given from funds administered by Local Boards and Municipalities, but before making any grant, the local authority must satisfy itself that there is a probability that the school will be kept up, that it meets a recognised want, that the education provided is likely to be good, and that local subscriptions are forthcoming. The principles on which they are awarded are the following :

Principle of grants-in-aid.

(1) *Middle and Upper Primary Schools.*

(*a*) The grants must be given on the principle of strict religious neutrality.

(*b*) The schools receiving them must require some fee from their scholars, unless in special cases exemption is recommended by the Local Board and allowed by the Director of Public Instruction, Assam.

(*c*) Grants to middle schools at sadr and subdivisional headquarters may not exceed two-thirds of the income expended from private sources; at other places they may not exceed the total sum so expended. Grants to upper primary schools in Sylhet may not exceed the local income, elsewhere they may not exceed three-fifths of the total monthly expenditure ; in no case must the grant exceed Rs. 10 a month.

Such schools must have a responsible committee of management and a Secretary to conduct their correspondence ; they must submit the prescribed returns, and be always open to inspection by the inspecting officers ; and they must keep strict accounts of receipts and disbursements. If the school becomes inefficient, the grant is liable to be reduced or withdrawn.

(2) *Lower Primary Schools.*

In these schools the *gurus* are paid—

(*a*) by a fixed monthly salary combined with rewards for pupils who pass an examination, (*b*) by rewards alone, or

(*c*) under special rules.

Under (*a*) the maximum fixed salary is Rs. 48, and the maximum reward at the rate of Rs. 48, a year. Under (*b*) the maximum reward is at the rate of Rs. 96 a year. Under (*c*) fixed salaries are given not exceeding Rs. 6 a month for one teacher or Rs. 10 for two in the case of girls' schools and schools for backward races. For municipal schools and schools in hill districts, the limit of pay for a teacher is fixed at Rs. 10 a month.

In addition to the above, small rewards are paid for each pupil passing the Lower Primary Scholarship Examination, provided that the Deputy or Sub-Inspector certifies that the junior classes of the school have not been neglected.

131. In the Gáro, Nága, and Khási and Jaintia Hills, and among the Kachari population of Darrang and the Mikirs of Nowgong, the control of education is in the hands of different missionary bodies, who receive grants from the Local Boards concerned (or from Government where there are no Local Boards), and themselves make considerable contributions to the work. The most important of these is the Welsh Mission in the Khási and Jaintia Hills, who receive a grant of Rs. 6,000 a year from Government, the Mission themselves contributing (in 1892-93) Rs. 29,085 towards primary education. In the Gáro Hills the yearly grant to the American Baptist Mission is Rs. 2,600, and in Goálpára a grant of Rs. 400 is made to the same Mission for the furtherance of education amongst the Gáros resident in that district. In Darrang, the Kachari S. P. G. Mission receive Rs. 1,500 a year towards the support of Kachari schools. A grant of Rs. 1,500 a year is similarly made to the American Baptist Mission in Nowgong for Mikir schools and of Rs. 780 a year to the same Mission at Amguri to assist them in keeping up schools in the Ao Nága country. It has long been recognised that among these primitive races, destitute of any settled form of religion, there is not the same objection to the subsidising of missionary schools by the State as exists in the case of Hindus and Muhammadans.

Special arrangements with missionary bodies.

Fees.

132. It only remains to notice the scale of fees levied from the pupils attending these different classes of schools. In primary schools or *páthshálas* there are no fixed rules for fees; no pupil is prevented from reading by his inability to pay a fee: those who can pay, do so, and those who cannot, do not. Often the fees are given in kind, the *guru* being supplied with food and other necessaries by the parents of the pupils. In upper primary schools, the rate of fees varies from one pice in the lowest to four annas in the highest class per month. In middle schools the fees vary in different schools and in different districts: the highest taken are 8 annas in the lowest, and Re. 1 in the highest class; the lowest 1 anna in the lowest class and 2 annas in the highest. The scale of fees has to be approved, if the school is an aided one, at the time the grant-in-aid is settled. In high schools the fees vary from 12 annas in the lowest to Rs. 3 in the highest class. In the normal schools and training classes, on the other hand, the pupils, instead of paying fees, receive small stipends, generally Rs. 3 or Rs. 4 a month.

Total expenditure on education.

133. The total expenditure on education in the province (including the school at Manipur) in schools under Government inspection varies from year to year. The following figures are the most recent, *viz.*, those for 1892-93:

				Rs.
From Provincial	...	...	...	1,79,506
„ Local Boards' Funds	...	...	...	1,64,673
„ Municipal Funds	...	...	...	4,058
„ Fees	...	...	...	1,09,420
„ Subscriptions	...	...	...	21,936
„ Endowments and other sources	...	...	...	60,427
Total	...	...	...	5,40,020

SECTION 4.—IMMIGRATION AND LABOUR INSPECTION.

Policy of Government.

134. The principal recruiting areas are either densely inhabited districts, where the means of subsistence are not sufficient for the support of the entire population in tolerable comfort, or such tracts as Chota Nagpur, where, though the population in proportion to the area does not appear excessive, wages are extremely low, and the labouring classes are unable, without some relief by emigration, to obtain an adequate livelihood. It has, therefore, been the settled policy of Government to promote emigration from such areas to others enjoying more favourable conditions; and the importation of coolies to Assam, at the expense of persons interested in the tea industry, has done much towards opening out and colonising the fertile, but sparsely peopled, districts of Assam.

135. The necessity for legislation on the subject of labour immigration into Assam is of the same charac-

*Necessity for legisla-
tion.*

ter as, though less in degree than, that which exists in respect of emigration from India to colonies beyond the seas. The classes which furnish emigrants in both cases are extremely ignorant, and the interference of Government is required to secure that they are not imposed upon; the transport between their homes and the place of labour, notwithstanding the improvements of recent years, is still long and tedious, and supervision is necessary to prevent overcrowding, disease, and consequent mortality; and under the changed conditions of life, and especially of climate and food, which the new country imposes, the immigrant is peculiarly liable to sickness, often fatal in its results, and it is thus needful that the provision of the requisite comforts, medical attendance, and other appliances for his well-being should be enforced by law. Of these reasons, the first is yearly becoming less and less operative, as returned immigrants settle again in their homes, and form a centre of information as to work and residence in the tea districts for their neighbours. It is hoped that the second will also become less cogent as communications continue to improve.

On the other hand, some regulation of the contract between the labourer and his employer, and some more effectual means of enforcing it than a civil action, is demanded by justice. It costs a large sum to import a coolie into Assam; and the provisions for his comfort, which the law requires, are also expensive. The employer is compelled by law to guarantee to the coolie a minimum wage ; and it is only equitable that the law should provide him with the means of obtaining the due fulfilment of the contract by the coolie, whose only capital is his labour, and who ought not to be allowed capriciously to withdraw himself from the service of the employer who has paid for his introduction.

A penal labour law and Government protection to the labourer are thus correlative terms ; and both have been provided together in the series of enactments which have from time to time been passed on the subject, and of which a sketch is given in the following paragraphs.

136. The first of the labour Acts was Act III (B.C.) of 1863.

History of legislation on the subject. This was an Act to regulate the transport of native labourers emigrating to Assam, Cachar, and Sylhet. In 1865, Act VI (B.C.) of that year was passed to provide for the protection of the labourers after their arrival in the labour districts and for the enforcement of the contracts entered into by them. Act II (B.C.) of 1870 consolidated and amended the law relating to the transport of labourers to the labour districts and their employment therein, and repealed the two previous Acts. Then came Act VII (B.C.) of 1873, which repealed Act II (B.C.) of 1870, and was the labour law of the province for nine years. During the last three years of this period the amendment of the law regulating immigration and the relations between employers and labourers in the tea districts was under discussion.

In April 1880, in consequence of a memorial by the Indian Tea Districts Association (an Association formed in London of persons interested in the Indian tea industry), praying that some measures might be taken to improve the position of the tea industry by the amendment of Act VII (B.C.) of 1873, a Commission was appointed to enquire into the working of Act VII (B.C.) of 1873. The opinions of district officers and of the managers of tea gardens consulted by them were laid before the Commission, as well as the recommendations of the Lieutenant Governor of Bengal and those of the Chief Commissioner, and, after successive meetings, the Commission submitted its final report, with a draft

Bill embodying the amendments proposed in the law, in January 1881.

This draft Bill was eventually passed into law as Act I of 1882. In giving his assent to this Act, the Secretary of State for India desired that at the end of three years he might receive a special report on the working of the Act, with a view to considering the possibility of abandoning all exceptional legislation respecting contracts of labour in the Indian tea districts. On receipt of the first special report, which was submitted in 1886, the Secretary of State agreed that the time had not yet arrived when special legislation might be abandoned, but added that such legislation should be regarded as temporary only, and desired that a further special report should be submitted after the lapse of another period of three years. This report was submitted in 1890. It was again admitted that exceptional legislation was still necessary, but as experience had shown that Act I of 1882 was defective in certain respects, it was decided to amend it. The draft amending Bill was introduced into Council in January 1893, and was eventually passed as Act VII of that year.

137. Act VII (B.C.) of 1873 had been passed in the expectation *Object of Act VII (B.C.) of 1873 and its principal provisions.* that it would give a great impetus to free immigration, and that such immigration would gradually establish itself and eventually render the existence of a special law unnecessary. Among the changes made by the Act which were looked upon as most important, were those by which time-expired labourers were, on re-engagement, freed from the ordinary provisions of the law, and by which a new class of free labourers, those under contract for a term not exceeding one year, was recognised. The collection of labourers by means of garden sardars, without the intervention of contractors, was provided for; and the opportunity was taken, in amending the law, to render more definite than before the provisions regarding the closing of gardens declared unfit for the habitation of labourers.

138. The Commissioners appointed to enquire into the working of Act VII (B.C.) of 1873 reported that they found that the law was defective in respect chiefly of the following points :

Alleged defects in Act VII (B.C.) of 1873.

(1) That it did not afford sufficient encouragement to free emigration.

(2) That it imposed unnecessary restrictions upon sardari recruiting.

(3) That it failed to provide for the enforcement of contracts made otherwise than under the provisions of the Act itself, even in the case of imported labourers.

(4) That the remedies provided for employers in the event of the unlawful absence, idleness, or desertion of their contract labourers, were insufficient.

139. Act II (B.C.) of 1870 did not recognise free recruiting, but made it penal to engage or convey an immigrant to the labour districts except in accordance with its provisions. Act VII (B.C.) of 1873, which repealed the Act of 1870, contained no penal clauses forbidding free recruiting, and section 7 allowed contracts between an intending immigrant and an employer for a term not exceeding one year, although not made under the provisions of the Act. Under the present Act, I of 1882, a labourer may now proceed to the labour districts as a free immigrant, and on arrival he may take work on an ordinary contract not under the Act ; or, having gone to the labour districts as a free immigrant, he may on arrival enter into a contract under the Act ; or, lastly, he may go to the labour districts as an immigrant recruited and registered under the Act, and having executed a contract to labour before arrival in the labour districts. In the first case he is in no way subject to the Act ; in the second case he is subject only to such of its provisions as refer to the carrying out of the labour contract ; and in the third he is completely under the Act from the date of his recruitment until the expiration of his engagement.

Free immigration and free recruiting.

140. As to the second point, under the old law a garden
sardar's certificate was only allowed to run
Sardari recruiting.   for six months ; he was not allowed to travel
with another garden sardar if the total number of their united
band of immigrants exceeded twenty ; and if he recruited more than
twenty immigrants himself, he was obliged to take them to a contractor's depôt. Under the present Act, a garden sardar's certificate may be given for a period of one year, and, on the application
of the employer by whom the certificate was granted, an Inspector
or Magistrate may, without requiring the reappearance of the
garden sardar before him, countersign and forward, for delivery
to the garden sardar by the Magistrate of the district in which the
sardar is employed, a fresh certificate in renewal of a former
certificate. All connection between garden sardars and contractors'
depôts has been severed, and a garden sardar may now recruit any
number of persons. Moreover, the employment of local agents to
supervise the operations of garden sardars, or, under special
license, to recruit emigrants themselves and despatch them to the
labour districts without the assistance of certificated sardars, has
been authorised.

141. With respect to the third point, labour contracts could not
be made under Act VII (B.C.) of 1873 in a
Labour contracts made in the labour districts.   labour district. Labour contracts entered
into in the tea districts, before the passing of
Act I of 1882, were made under the ordinary law. Act XIII of
1859 (*an Act to provide for the punishment of breaches of contract by
artificers, workmen, and labourers in certain cases*) has been applied,
and is still applied, in these districts to locally-made contracts ;
but, as was remarked in the Statement of Objects and Reasons
published with the Bill which afterwards became the present Act
I of 1882, " its provisions were obviously never intended to meet
such cases." Act I of 1882, as originally enacted, permitted local
labour contracts to be made in labour districts by any natives of
India, whether immigrants to, or residing in, Assam on the same
conditions and subject to the same penalties for breach of the
conditions, as labour contracts made outside the province by

Section 4. intending immigrants. As now amended, the Act distinguishes
Immigration between contracts made in the presence of a Magistrate or
and Labour Inspector and contracts not so made, and permits contracts of the
Inspection. latter class to be entered into for a term of one year only.

142. With regard to the fourth point as to which the Commission considered that the law was defective,
Penalty for unlawful the present Act provides for a system of
absence from labour. monthly lists of defaulters from work to be
forwarded by the employer to the Inspector, who, on enquiry, may
punish any such defaulter by entering the days of absence on his
contract and adding them to the term thereof, unless the labourer
consents to forfeit to his employer the sum of 4 annas for each
day of absence. Prolonged and repeated absence, or desertion, may
be punished criminally by the Magistrate as under the former law.

143. The only other points in which the provisions of Act VII
(B.C.) of 1873 were altered by Act I of 1882,
Other changes in Act which need be noticed, are the extension of
VII (B.C.) of 1873. the term, for which a labourer may contract
to labour, from three years under the old law to five years under
Act I of 1882 as originally enacted, and its subsequent reduction
to four years by the recent amending Act; the provision in the
present Act that the maximum annual capitation fee leviable from
employers for each labourer on contract under the Act shall not
exceed one rupee (one rupee eight annas was the rate levied under
the old law); and the provisions making it compulsory for all
employers to keep up registers and submit returns of vital statistics
of the labour force employed by them, whether on contract under
the Act or not.

144. Two important changes effected by Act VII of 1893, *viz.*,
the reduction of the general term of contract
Alterations effected by to four years, and of local contracts not made
Act VII of 1893. in the presence of a Magistrate or Inspector
to one year, have already been referred to. Another important
feature of the recent enactment is that it recognises what is known
as the " Dhubri system." As already stated, one of the main features of Act I of 1882 was that, while imposing careful restrictions

on recruitment by contractors and garden sardars, it aimed at encouraging and facilitating free emigration. The result was that both contractors and garden sardars evaded the restrictions intended for them by refusing to register in the district of recruitment, and by bringing their coolies as free labourers to Dhubri and putting them under a local contract there. Although unforeseen, this system has, in practice, been found, on the whole, to work well, and Act VII of 1893 accordingly places it on a legal footing by bringing contracts so executed within the scope of section 112 of the Act and by empowering the Chief Commissioner to make rules having the force of law for regulating the procedure for the execution of these contracts.

The other provisions of the amending Act are framed to prevent and remedy abuses in recruitment, and to strengthen the control of the Local Administration over unhealthy gardens. The cancellation of contracts in certain cases and the repatriation of coolies are provided for in greater detail, and the option of a fine is allowed in some cases in which imprisonment was formerly the only legal penalty.

Government supervision of the immigrant labourer. 145. The whole subject of the Government supervision of the immigrant labourer falls into three parts :

    I. The recruitment of the labourer.

    II. His journey to the labour districts.

    III. His status while labouring under contract.

The immigrant labour force of the tea gardens of the province is recruited by free immigrants (that is, by immigrants who go to the tea districts without having been registered and without having made contracts under the Immigration Law) and by labourers who have been registered and who have executed contracts under Act I of 1882, imported through garden sardars authorised by employers to recruit, or through contractors and recruiters licensed by Government.

146. The extent to which free immigration exists will be apparent from the fact that out of 41,802 adult *The free immigrant.* immigrants who came to the tea gardens of

the province during the year 1892, 13,347, or 31·9 per cent., were " non-Act " or free. Ten years ago the percentage of free immigrants was only 13·5. In this respect the reversal of the policy which framed the penal clauses of Act II (B.C.) of 1870 has been complete. Section 7 of Act I of 1882 provides that nothing in that Act is to be taken to prevent natives of India from emigrating otherwise than under its provisions, and the only restriction is that allowed by section 5, under which power is reserved to Local Governments (with the sanction of the Governor General in Council) to prohibit natives of India, or any specified class of natives, from emigrating from any particular tract to any specified labour district or portion of a labour district. As, however, great sickness and mortality were found to exist amongst these free immigrants, an Act was passed by the Bengal Council in 1889 (No. I of that year), enabling the Local Government to exercise control over the routes by which they should travel and to make such sanitary rules as might seem to be needed. This Act was extended to Assam by Notification No. 1211J., dated the 2nd April 1890; and rules under it have been framed for the regulation of the transit of free immigrants to gardens in the Surma Valley, where the mode of travelling very frequently adopted is by country boats carrying less than twenty passengers. In the Brahmaputra Valley the Act is not needed. Almost all the coolies to gardens in that valley travel by steamer ; and as these steamers carry more than twenty passengers, they require to be licensed, and, in accordance with the rules framed under Act I of 1882, they must carry a medical officer and also medical stores and provisions. On board these steamers the free immigrant is subject to the same supervision as the Act labourer. When the transport is by boats carrying less than twenty passengers, which do not require to be licensed under Act I of 1882, the rules framed under Act I (B.C.) of 1889 provide that the supply of food and water shall be similar to that prescribed for licensed vessels, and lay down that not more than one passenger shall be carried for every 5 maunds of the capacity of the boat. They also empower any magistrate to detain any immigrant who is certified by a medical officer to be unfit to proceed on the journey.

147. The subject of recruitment by garden sardars has been noticed above. A garden sardar must appear with the intending immigrant whom he wishes to engage before the registering officer of the area within which he has been authorised to recruit. Particulars of the intending immigrant are registered by the registering officer, and the labour contract is executed before him. The garden sardar is bound to provide proper food and lodging throughout their journey for the labourers and dependents whom he engages. If the garden sardar's employer has specified in the garden sardar's certificate that he wishes a medical examination to be made of labourers engaged, such an examination is required to be made with reference to the labourer's fitness to travel to, *and to labour in*, the labour district; or if it appears to the registering officer or to any Magistrate or Embarkation Agent to be necessary that a medical examination should be made of any person about to emigrate under the Act, a medical inspection of the labourer's fitness *to travel* is made before he is allowed to proceed. It has already been explained that these provisions have to a great extent become a dead letter, and that the general procedure now followed is for the sardars to recruit coolies and bring them as free immigrants to Dhubri or to the garden for which they are recruited, and to place them under the Act at one or other of these places.

Recruitment by garden sardars.

Section 4. Immigration and Labour Inspection.

148. Contractors and recruiters are licensed by other Governments than that of this province, and their supervision is only to a very small degree the care of this Administration. Contractors are bound to establish suitable depôts for the reception and lodging of labourers engaged by them or by their recruiters, previous to their despatch to the labour districts, and they are bound to provide food, clothing, and medical treatment for such labourers during their stay at the depôt.

Recruitment by contractors and recruiters.

An intending immigrant, who is engaged by a contractor or recruiter, must be brought before the registering officer of the area in which he is recruited, and he must also be examined by a

Section 4.
Immigration
and Labour
Inspection.
medical officer, who must certify to his fitness to travel before he is allowed to proceed. When the labourer reaches the depôt, he undergoes another medical examination by the medical inspector of the depôt, and he executes his labour contract after it has been explained to him by the Superintendent of Emigration. Here also the restrictions imposed by the Act are, as a general rule, avoided by recruiting outside the provisions of the Act and only placing the labourers under contract after their arrival in the labour districts.

149. Practically, the whole of the immigration into the districts of the Brahmaputra Valley is by steamer, while that into the Surma Valley, which was formerly almost entirely confined to boats, is now divided between boats and steamers in very nearly equal proportions. The provisions of the law with regard to Government supervision of the transport by river steamers and boats and the food and medical comforts which they are required to carry have already been touched on. Licensed vessels containing immigrants are inspected at the port of embarkation, which is generally Dhubri or Goalundo for the Brahmaputra Valley districts, and Goalundo for the Surma Valley districts, by the Embarkation Agent and by a Government medical officer if the Embarkation Agent be not himself a medical officer. They are also inspected by Government officers at all ports touched during the voyage where civil officers are stationed. At debarkation ports, where the number of labourers annually landed is large, there are Government depôts under the charge of hospital assistants, to which all Act labourers and their dependents must go for the purpose of being registered. They are also open to the admission of all free immigrants who choose to avail themselves of their accommodation. Sick persons are, if necessary, detained in the depôts for medical treatment.

Transport.

150. Every employer is bound to provide for the labourers employed on his estate proper house accommodation, water-supply, and sanitary arrangements. He must supply Act labourers with rice at a reasonable price, and he must provide hospital accommo-

Care of labourers on the garden.

dation, medicines, and medical attendance. If an estate be declared by Government after enquiry to be unfit for the residence of labourers by reason of climate, situation, or condition, labour contracts to labour on the estate cannot be enforced against the labourer.

151. The duty of inspecting tea gardens upon which immigrant labourers are employed is performed by Inspectors and Assistant Inspectors of Labourers, most of whom are the officers of the Commission, and medical officers. Every garden employing imported Act labourers must be inspected at least once every year, and every garden in which the mortality shown in the return of the last calendar year has exceeded 7 per cent. (the number of deaths having exceeded 9) must be inspected by the Civil Surgeon of the district. The inspection reports state what house accommodation, water-supply, medical attendance, hospital accommodation, and sanitary arrangements have been provided, and what the food-supply is. They also notice the general treatment and condition of the labourers, and record their vital statistics. In the case of unhealthy gardens a special form of inspection report has been prescribed.

Inspection of estates.

152. Contracts under the Act cannot be made for a term exceeding four years, and the minimum monthly wage which can be stipulated for is Rs. 5 for a man and Rs. 4 for a woman for the first three years of the term of contract, and Rs. 6 for a man and Rs. 5 for a woman for the fourth year of the term of contract. They must also state the price at which rice is to be supplied to the labourer. Schedules of tasks must be kept by employers, and if found to be unreasonable, may be revised by an Inspector of Labourers. Weakly labourers may be allowed subsistence allowance or diet by order of an Inspector of Labourers, and labourers permanently incapacitated for labour may be released from their contracts by an Inspector. A labourer so released is entitled to receive from his employer such sum, not exceeding three months' wages, as the Inspector may award, or, if the labourer desires to return to his country, such sum, whether in excess of three months' wages or

Labour contracts under Act I of 1882.

not, as will suffice to defray the expenses of the journey. A labourer may redeem his contract by payment of a sum of Re. 1 for every month of the unexpired portion of the first year, of Rs. 3 for every month of the second year, and of Rs. 5 for every month of the third and fourth years of the term of contract. A contract may be cancelled if ill-usage by the employer is proved, or if the labourer's wages are in arrear for more than four months. When the contracts of husband and wife expire at different times, the Magistrate may equalise the terms of their contracts by adding to the one and deducting from the other in such proportions as may appear to him to be equitable. Labourers who, without reasonable cause, absent themselves from labour during their terms of contract, or who desert, are punishable with fine and imprisonment. In the case of a first conviction for the offence of desertion, the imprisonment may extend to the term of one month ; for a second conviction the term may extend to two months, and for a third conviction to three months. When a labourer has suffered imprisonment for terms amounting altogether to six months for desertion, his labour contract must be cancelled.

153. The fund raised from fees, fines, and rates levied under the provisions of the Act is called the Inland *The Labour Transport* Labour Transport Fund. The law directs that *Fund.* the fund so raised in a province shall be at the disposal of the Local Government, who must apply it, under the control of the Government of India, for defraying the expenses of carrying out the purposes of the Act, including the cost of sending labourers and other persons back to their native districts.

The income of the fund in the year 1892-93 amounted to Rs. 78,763-10-0, of which Rs. 64,043-4-6 were raised in Assam and Rs. 14,720-5-6 in Bengal. The expenditure during the same year amounted to Rs. 71,994-2-7, of which the Assam share was Rs. 47,682-7-10. The principal local heads of receipts were Capitation fees under section 109 (now levied at the rate of 8 annas per head) Rs. 54,975-3-0, Depôt receipts Rs. 5,460-2-9, and Contractors' license fees Rs. 3,148. The heaviest items on the other side of the account were Depôt charges Rs. 8,680-10-4, Supplies and Services Rs. 8,625-9-4, Clerks and servants Rs. 8,453-10-8, Inspectors, Embarkation Agents, etc., Rs. 5,782-6-1, Grants to dispensaries Rs. 5,530, Travelling allowances Rs. 5,081-1-0, and Miscellaneous Rs. 3,774-15-10. In addition to the above, Rs. 9,591-5-3 were transferred to the Bengal portion of the fund, which showed a deficit to that extent.

SECTION 5.—PUBLIC WORKS.

154. For the more efficient administration of the Public Works Department in Assam, it was found necessary, as far back as 1868, to vest the Commissioner with the powers of a Local Administration, subordinate to the Government of Bengal. But his authority to sanction expenditure was then limited to works the cost of which did not exceed Rs. 5,000. The Superintending Engineer was at the same time invested locally with the powers of a Chief Engineer, and was appointed Secretary to the Commissioner in the Public Works Department. On the formation of the Chief Commissionership, therefore, the organisation of the Public Works Department was already in some measure adapted for a separate Administration. The transfer of Sylhet and Cachar to Assam added an executive charge to the three already existing in the Brahmaputra Valley; and a fifth was created on the transfer of the headquarters of the Administration to Shillong, when important public works in the public buildings which had to be erected, and the roads which had to be made, were thereby rendered necessary.

Organisation of the department.

Until the end of the official year 1881-82, the organisation of the Public Works Department in the province underwent little change. The districts of Sylhet and Cachar constituted the Sylhet Division; Goálpára, the Gáro Hills,* and a portion of Kámrúp the Lower Assam Division; the remainder of Kámrúp with the Khási Hills the Shillong Division; Darrang, Nowgong, and part of Sibságar the Central Assam Division; and Lakhimpur and the remainder of

* In the Gáro Hills, public works are directly under the Deputy Commissioner, who is assisted in carrying them out by an upper subordinate of the Public Works Department.

Sibságar the Upper Assam Division. After the close of the Nága Hills expedition of 1879-80, these hills were made into a separate division. In 1882 the Public Works executive divisions were made conterminous with the civil districts of the province, and the Engineer establishment was increased accordingly. These changes were synchronous in their effect with a large transfer to the charge of Local Boards of works which had theretofore been classed as Provincial; and it was at the same time ruled that the officers of the Public Works Department in each district were not only responsible for the due execution of Imperial and Provincial Works, but were also (except in the hill districts, where Local Boards do not exist) to act as assistants to the Chairmen of Local Boards for carrying out works under the Local Boards' control. It will be explained in the next section that many of the works made over to Local Boards in 1882 were afterwards found to be less effectively administered than they were when classed as Provincial, and that they were consequently again made over to the direct control of the Public Works Department. Experience also showed that the position assigned to Executive Engineers in the arrangements of 1882 was not altogether satisfactory. It was therefore decided to sever their connection with local works, except as regards works definitely made over to them for execution by the Boards and the duty of assisting the Boards with their advice on professional matters when called upon to do so; and as the sphere of their duties was thus considerably restricted, it was decided to revert in part to the distribution of Public Works charges which obtained prior to 1882. Kámrúp and Goálpára were combined into one charge under the name of the Lower Assam Division, and Darrang and Nowgong were amalgamated to form the Central Assam Division. The other districts remained, as previously, in charge of separate Engineers. These orders took effect in 1889-90.

The only changes that have since been made are the formation of a new division in the North Lushai Hills, and the temporary appointment of a special officer, as Superintendent of Works, with a sanctioned staff of Executive and Assistant

Engineers, to supervise the construction of the Kohima-Manipur road.

155. The facilities for communication by water which are pro-

Roads.

vided by the river system of the Brahmaputra and Surma Valleys have been already alluded to. Communication by land is less easy. When the British occupied the province, roads were practically unknown, for, although the remains of ancient embankments (chief amongst which is the Gosain Kamala Ali, which stretches from Rangpur to Sadiya) bear witness to the existence of numerous roads at some period of the past, the anarchy which preceded the annexation of the country by the Company had been so great and so prolonged, that they had been allowed to fall into utter disrepair, and were of little or no use to travellers. During the early period of British rule very little was done to improve matters; but since 1861 a more active policy has found favour, and considerable sums are now spent annually on the construction of new roads and the maintenance of those already in existence. The mileage under roads in each district of the province is detailed below :

District.	Imperial roads.		Provincial roads.		Local roads.	
	Metalled.	Unmetalled.	Metalled.	Unmetalled.	Metalled.	Unmetalled.
	Miles.	Miles.	Miles.	Miles.	Miles.	Miles.
Cachar ..	1½	½	......	144	......	142
Sylhet ..	......	63	......	97	......	508
Lower Assam	......	......	18½	448	......	671½
Central ,,	......	......	......	298	......	878½
Sibságar ..	......	......	......	174	......	470
Lakhimpur ..	6½	6½	6	205	......	329½
Khási and Jaintia Hills ..	3½	......	87½	99½	......	....
Naga Hills	......	76¾	......	382½	......	....
Gáro ,, ...	......	......	......	193½	......	....
Nichuguard-Manipur Road Circle ..	......	165	......	......	......	....
North Lushai Hills	......	......	......	125	......	....
Total	11½	311½	112	2,164½	......	3,099¾

From an administrative standpoint, the most important roads are the new military road from Golághát to Manipur, the Assam

Trunk road, and the hill road which connects Shillong, the head-quarters of the Administration, with the Brahmaputra at Gauháti. For local requirements, the short feeder roads, which connect the centres of trade in the interior with the *mukhs* or stations at which the river steamers stop, are by far the most useful. A notable feature in the statement given above is the very small proportion of metalled as compared with unmetalled roads. Two reasons may be given to account for this, firstly, that the requirements of the province in the matter of communications are still so great that many more miles of road must be constructed before any large amount of money can be spared for improving those already in existence; and, secondly, that the soil is alluvial, and stones for metalling would consequently have, as a rule, to be brought from distances so great as to make the cost involved in doing so prohibitive. The fact that in some parts, particularly in the Surma Valley, communication by water competes with communication by road during the rainy season is, another reason why less money is expended on roads in these tracts than would otherwise be necessary.

156. Owing partly to the excellent water carriage available and partly to the backward nature of the country, railway enterprise has not hitherto made much progress. But signs of a new condition of things are not wanting. Within the last ten years three small lines have been constructed, *viz.*, the Dibrugarh-Sadiya Railway (77·5 miles) in Lakhimpur, the Jorhát-Kokilamukh line (28·40 miles) in Sibságar, and the Theria-Companyganj line (8½ miles) in Sylhet. Of these, the firstmentioned was constructed by the Assam Railways and Trading Company with a State guarantee; the other two are purely State Railways, constructed by Government without the intervention of private capitalists. An attempt to extend the last-mentioned line from Theriaghat at the foot of the Shillong plateau to Cherrapunji at its summit, by means of a series of inclines, was unsuccessful; but the plains portion is still worked. It more than pays for the cost of its upkeep, and it is not unlikely that it will, sooner or later, be extended to Chhátak on the Surma river.

Railways.

But the most important railway project which Assam has yet seen still remains to be mentioned. Between the years 1882 and 1886, a railway survey party was engaged in Assam in making a survey with a view to laying down a line connecting this province with Bengal. The route followed by this survey runs from Chittagong through the south of the Sylhet district to Badarpur in Cachar, thence through the North Cachar Hills to Lumding, near Dimapur, and from Lumding, *viâ* Golághát, to Dibrugarh, with a branch line from Lumding to Gauháti.* A survey of the country between Gauháti and Dhubri had been carried out some years previously, when the Eastern Bengal State Railway was under construction. It was long a matter of discussion whether greater advantages might be expected to ensue from a railway along the route surveyed in 1882-1886, or from a line running laterally along the Brahmaputra Valley between Dibrugarh and a point on the Eastern Bengal State Railway, thus connecting the whole of the northern portion of the province with the existing railway system of Bengal. For some years no practical result supervened, as want of funds prevented the construction of a line at the expense of the State, and negotiations with private capitalists were not successful. During the year 1891-92, however, a company was at last formed to construct a railway along the former of the two routes described above, subject to a guarantee by the State, and work was commenced in November 1891. It is hoped that the line, when finished, will be the means of largely opening out the province; but, as some years must elapse before the construction of the railway can be completed, speculation as to the consequences which may be expected to result from it would be premature.

157. The annual assignment to the province for Imperial Public Works varies from year to year, the grant being fixed according to the requirements

Imperial Works.

---

* A line between Mymensingh and Gauháti through the Gáro Hills was also surveyed, and found to be practicable for a railway, but at a cost so great as to be prohibitive.

of the time.   The grants for the last three years, together with the expenditure, are shown below :

Imperial outlay.	1890-91.		1891-92.		1892-93.	
	Final grant.	Expenditure.	Final grant.	Expenditure.	Final grant.	Expenditure.
	Rs.	Rs.	Rs.	Rs.	Rs.	Rs.
Military Works ..	2,07,600	2,09,586	1,04,100	99,538	1,08,100	96,541
Civil ,, ..	17,100	16,064	3,47,700	3,23,591	8,41,2	7,74,736
Total ..	2,24,700	2,25,650	4,51,800	4,23,130	9,49,600	8,71,277

158. The Provincial assignment for Public Works is fixed annually by the Chief Commissioner.   The grants for the years 1890-91, 1891-92, and 1892-93, as compared with the expenditure, are given below :

Provincial Public Works.

Provincial outlay.	1890-91.		1891-92.		1892-93.	
	Final grant.	Expenditure.	Final grant.	Expenditure.	Final grant.	Expenditure.
	Rs.	Rs.	Rs.	Rs.	Rs.	Rs.
Civil Works	12,16,000	11,43,708	11,58,000	10,49,895	13,76,000	13,01,035
Jorhat State Railway, Capital ..	15,000	11,871	4,000	2,725	30,000	27,315
Cherra-Companyganj State Railway, Capital.	4,670	4,042	—400	25	6,000	4,464
Jorhat State Railway, Revenue ..	57,000	57,971	60,000	60,905	60,000	54,950
Cherra-Companyganj State Railway, Revenue.	19,000	19,171	19,500	19,093	17,000	17,503
Subsidised Railways ..	1,01,000	1,01,135	1,01,000	1,00,700	1,01,000	1,00,494
Total ..	14,12,670	13,37,900	13,22,100	12,33,311	15,90,000	15,15,664

This is exclusive of expenditure on public works by Local Boards, figures for which will be found in the next section.

SECTION 6.—LOCAL SELF-GOVERNMENT.

159. Besides the agency of Government officers, much assistance is given to the administration of the province by local bodies, who administer funds raised under special enactments or placed at

Local bodies in Assam.

their disposal by the Chief Commissioner. These are either municipalities for town areas, or Local Boards for the district at
large.

160. The municipalities are the older institutions. Under

Municipalities. this general name are included—(1) Municipalities properly so called ; (2) Stations, whose
administration is less independent than that of the first named ;
and (3) Unions, or towns where a rate is assessed by a *panchayat*
for the purpose of providing funds for local improvements·
Of these, Sylhet, Gauháti, and Dibrugarh are municipalities
under Act III (B C.) of 1884 ; the others are all constituted
under the provisions of Act V (B.C.) of 1876 ; Silchar, Dhubri,
Goálpára, and Barpeta being second-class Municipalities ; Shillong
and Sibságar, Stations ; and Habiganj, Jorhát, and Golághát,
Unions.

In the municipalities of Sylhet, Gauháti, and Dibrugarh the
elective system is in full force, and rules for the conduct of elections
have been framed under section 15 of Act III (B.C.) of 1884. A
system of election has also been introduced, at the instance of the
ratepayers, for the choice of members to sit on the Committees at
Goálpára and Silchar. The official members of all municipal
institutions are very few in number ; and although the Chairmen are
officials in all cases except that of the Sylhet Municipality, the Vice-
Chairmen are usually non-officials.

161. These bodies derive their income partly from taxation

Municipal income. and partly from other sources. The taxation
levied in municipalities is chiefly in the form
of a tax on persons or buildings, a latrine tax, and a water-rate (in
Gauháti) ; in stations the taxation is a house assessment, and in
unions a chaukidári tax. Other small items of taxation are taxes
on animals and wheeled vehicles. These taxes are levied under
the provisions of the Act under which each municipality, etc., is
constituted. No octroi or other duties are taken anywhere in the
province. Of the other sources of income, the most important are
the receipts from ferries [levied under the provisions of sections
148-156 of Act III (B.C.) of 1884, or sections 139-147 of Act V

(B.C.) of 1876, as the case may be] from municipal pounds, the income from municipal markets, and the assignments from Provincial and Local Funds enjoyed by several municipalities. The last item consists of grants made in commutation of the land revenue of the town areas, which in the early days of the province was allowed to be appropriated to the improvement of the towns. In 1892-93, municipalities enjoyed an income of Rs. 1,76,511-2-0, of which Rs. 8,728-9-0 were derived from taxation and Rs. 89,221-9 from other sources. The total expenditure during the same year amounted to Rs. 1,52,916-3. Some account of the working of municipal bodies will be found in Part II B of the General Administration Report, Chapter III, Section 8.

162. The Local Boards are constituted under the Assam Local Rates Regulation, 1879. They exist in the eight plains districts only, the hill districts not being sufficiently advanced to admit of their establishment. By the Regulation a rate may be levied of one anna on every rupee of annual value of the land in these eight districts, and the rate so levied forms the chief item in the income of the Local Boards. Prior to May 1882, these Boards were charged with the administration of primary education, the district post, and repairs of district roads and general improvements, the funds to meet these heads of expenditure being provided from five-eighths of the local rate, ferries (excluding a few retained as Provincial), rents, and other miscellaneous items of income, and the surplus receipts from pounds.

Local Boards.

In 1882, the functions of the District Committees were enlarged by the transfer to their control of grants-in-aid to all schools except high schools, grants to dispensaries, fairs, rewards for the destruction of wild beasts, the cost of the establishments for collecting the local rate, circuit-houses and staging bungalows, grants to municipalities, and almost all the public works theretofore classed as Provincial. To meet these charges, the Provincial grants, previously allotted for them, were made over to the Local Boards, together with the three-fifths of the local rate which had formerly been credited to provincial funds. The

Public Works establishments were transferred to "Local," and
so also were most of the Sub-Inspectors of Schools in plains
districts.

The effect of these orders was to place under Local Boards
the entire control of all local expenditure, except that immediately
connected with the administration of the province. It was soon
seen that the change was too radical, and the policy of subsequent
years up till 1890 was to reduce in some degree the too extended
functions of the Boards by withdrawing from their control the
management of matters of Provincial, rather than of strictly Local,
interest. In the first place (in 1884), the charges on account of
the professional establishment of Executive and Assistant Engineers
and such of their subordinate officers as were borne on the list of
the Public Works Department, were retransferred to the Provincial
budget. At the same time the construction and repairs of
treasuries, jails, circuit-houses, churches, cemeteries, floating dák
bungalows, and cutcherries at headquarters stations were again
classed as Provincial works.

Three years later the construction and repairs of similar
buildings at subdivisions were made a Provincial charge, and so
also were dák bungalows (as distinguished from rest-houses) and
grants to municipalities. In the same year, the Sub-Inspectors of
Schools, who had been made Local in 1882, were again brought on
to the Provincial list. Finally, in 1890, the principle that Local
Boards should deal only with matters of purely local interest was
extended to that portion of Public Works which comes under
the denomination of "Communications." Trunk roads and their
feeder lines connecting them with the steamer ghâts and with subdivisional stations, together with all ferries and rest-houses on such
roads, were made Provincial. All roads not included in the above
category continued to be "Local," as theretofore; and as these
were of purely local importance, far greater independence was
conferred on Local Boards in respect to their management than
had been found possible when the Boards were entrusted with the
upkeep of roads, the importance of which was not confined to the
area administered by any particular Board.

At the same time, the opportunity was taken to introduce greater continuity in the administration of Local Funds, by allotting to each Board Provincial grants fixed for a term of years, instead of an annually varying amount. On the expiry of the term for which these grants had been made (in 1893), the wants of each Board were carefully considered and new grants were allotted; but, instead of these grants being absolutely fixed, it was arranged that they should be increased annually by 2 per cent. in order to meet growing wants. This arrangement will continue in force until 1898, when the amount of the different grants will again be revised and a fresh allotment will be made. The total income of Local Boards in 1892-93 was Rs. 11,57,920, of which Rs. 7,15,184 represent the receipts from local sources of income, and Rs. 1,89,783 the Provincial grants. The expenditure in the same year amounted to Rs. 9,02,146, of which Rs. 6,13,235 represent the expenditure on local public works. In the following statement the expenditure by the Local Boards on public works for the past three years is shown:

Local Fund outlay.	1890-91.		1891-92.		1892-93.	
	Final grant.	Expenditure.	Final grant.	Expenditure.	Final grant.	Expenditure.
	Rs.	Rs.	Rs.	Rs.	Rs.	Rs.
Original Works—						
Civil Buildings	2,800	3,192	2,905	1,143	1,019	1,065
Communications	2,23,900	1,78,348	2,51,053	2,10,171	3,10,340	2,97,681
Miscellaneous Public Improvements	52,000	32,412	43,316	30,422	45,195	34,685
Total	2,78,700	2,13,952	2,96,968	2,41,736	3,56,535	3,30,435
Repairs—						
Civil Buildings	1,600	1,360	1,727	1,529	2,333	2,238
Communications	2,21,900	2,00,716	2,16,625	2,13,272	2,25,590	2,17,171
Miscellaneous Public Improvements	12,500	12,357	18,157	16,564	19,668	14,537
Total	2,36,000	2,14,433	2,36,509	2,31,365	2,45,591	2,33,946
Tools and Plant	4,500	3,459	223	....	....	....
Establishment	47,800	42,235	49,893	45,945	49,074	45,854
Suspense	....	....	....	....	....	....
Grand total	5,67,000	4,74,062	5,85,000	5,19,046	6,51,000	6,13,235

163. Prior to 1882 the administration of Local Funds within Section 6.
Constitution of Boards. a district had been vested in a District Com- *Local Self-Government.*
mittee, with subordinate branch committees
in each subdivision. In that year the subdivision was made the
unit of administration for Local Boards, each Board being entirely
self-contained and independent. At the same time an attempt was
made to introduce the elective principle for the selection of members, instead of the system of nomination which had previously been
followed.

It was decided that election should be the normal mode of
appointment of representatives of the tea interest, who were to form
half the non-official strength of all Boards in districts where that
interest was important. An attempt was also made to select, by
means of election, the representatives of the native community in
Kámrúp, Sibságar, and Sylhet; but the success met with in these
districts has not been such as to encourage the extension of the
elective system to the other districts in which there are Local
Boards. In the latter, therefore, the native members are still
appointed by the Chief Commissioner on the recommendation
of the Deputy Commissioner. Non-official members, whether
elected or nominated, hold office for two years.

Concurrently with the above changes, the number of officials
on the committees was reduced considerably, and there are now
on the average only three or four official members of each Board.
The Chairmen are still, in all cases, officials, it being considered that
for the present their guidance and supervision can most profitably
be exercised from within, rather than from without, the Boards;
but, although they preside at the Board meetings and are the
executive officers of the committees, they have no vote, except
a casting one when members are equally divided.

164. Local Boards are required to meet not less than four times
Procedure. a year for the purpose of transacting such
business as may be laid before them by their
executive officers, the Chairmen. For the more important branches
of their administration (public works, education, and medical and
sanitation), sub-committees are appointed, who are supposed to

SECTION 7. meet monthly and to refer important matters for the consideration
Finance. of the full Board.

One of the most important duties of the Boards is the preparation of the annual budget, which is submitted in October. The works are entered therein in the order of their importance, but no work can be entered until the administrative sanction of the Chief Commissioner has been accorded to it.

Formerly, the Executive Engineer was the servant of the Board, and was responsible for carrying out its undertakings. But this arrangement was not altogether satisfactory, and in 1890, when the separation of Provincial from Local works was effected, the opportunity was taken to place the relations between the Boards on the one side, and the officers of the Public Works Department on the other, on a more definite basis. Greater independence was given to the Boards as regards the selection of the agency for the execution of works not requiring professional skill; but it was ruled that when a work was once made over to the Executive Engineer, he was to be allowed to carry it out in his own way, subject to the necessity of furnishing the Board with information regarding its progress, and of taking up each work in the order of importance indicated by the Board. It was proposed to make over a subordinate officer of the Public Works Department to each Board for the supervision of such works as it might decide to execute without the aid of the Executive Engineer; but it was subsequently found that the Provincial establishment was not large enough to provide every Board with such an officer, and it was therefore decided (in 1892) that each Board should engage and pay for its own staff. It was afterwards ruled that all appointments to the engineering staff require the sanction of the Chief Commissioner, and a fixed scale was laid down showing the maximum scale of establishment permissible for each Board.

SECTION 7.—FINANCE.

165. The year 1892-93 was the first of a new contract between
Provincial contract. the Provincial and Imperial Governments. The province was formed in 1874, and it

will be convenient to divide the period from that year to the year under review into four sections corresponding with the terms of the different contracts, viz., (1) from 1874 to March 1878, (2) from 1878-79 to 1881-82, (3) from 1882-83 to 1886-87, and (4) from 1887-88 to 1891-92.

(1) When the province was formed, in 1874, it took over its proportional share of the then subsisting Provincial contract of Bengal, the principle of which was that certain heads of expenditure were handed over to the control of the Local Government, together with the resources for meeting them, consisting partly of the receipts under the same heads and partly of a fixed consolidated allotment from the Imperial revenues. Any deficit was to be made good by the Local Government, and any surplus was to be applied to Provincial purposes.

(2) From the beginning of 1878-79 a second contract was made upon a more extended basis. Certain heads of revenue were handed over, with their charges, completely to the control of the Local Administration, and the principle was introduced of Provincial responsibility for works undertaken for Local and Provincial purposes. Under this arrangement, the province received the whole revenues from Excise, Provincial Rates, Stamps, Registration, Law and Justice, Police, Education, and a few minor heads, together with 20 per cent. of the Land Revenue, and undertook the whole responsibility for the charges of these departments, besides those for Administration and Provincial Public Works.

(3) The principle of the contract of 1882-83 differed from that of the previous one, chiefly in the following points :—Instead of Provincial revenues taking the whole receipts and charges under certain heads, these were equally divided between Imperial and Provincial. The only heads formerly Provincial which remained so were Provincial Rates, Post Office (i.e., the District Post only), Law and Justice, Police, Education, Medical, Stationery and Printing ; the revenue yielding Departments of Excise, Stamps, and Registration, formerly entirely Provincial, were shared equally between Provincial and Imperial both under receipts and charges ; and Forests, formerly entirely Imperial, was added to the shared

U

heads. As this left the province in deficit, an equilibrium was re-established by allotting to Provincial Funds, in addition to the above resources, a fixed percentage of the Land Revenue sufficient, in the year of contract, to adjust the account. This proportion was a little over 63 per cent. Land Revenue charges were shared in the same proportion as receipts. There remained wholly Imperial only Opium (cost price) and some small miscellaneous receipts, and, under charges, Interest, Assignments, and Compensation, the Offices of Account, Ecclesiastical and Political charges, a few other miscellaneous heads, and Imperial Public Works.

(4) The year 1887-88 was the first of a new quinquennial contract. This contract differed from the last in several respects, principally as regards revenue. These differences were :—(1) The grant to the Local Administration of the whole of the Land Revenue, instead of only a percentage, as in the last contract, subject to the contribution of a certain fixed sum to Imperial revenues, so that the Local Administration enjoyed the whole of any increase in the land revenue of the province during the currency of the contract ; (2) the percentages of the Stamps and Excise revenues made over for Provincial uses were 75 and 25, respectively, instead of 50 in the last contract ; (3) the grant of a moiety of the revenue from Assessed Taxes for Provincial uses, whereas in the last contract the revenue from this source was reserved for Imperial purposes. Under the expenditure heads, the charges on account of " Survey and settlement " and " Charges on account of land revenue collections " (two heads of account subordinate to the general head of Land Revenue) and those on account of Stamps and Excise were shared between the Imperial and the Provincial Governments to the same extent as the revenues were shared. This was also the principle in the last contract, but the percentages were not the same. A moiety of the expenditure upon " Assessed Taxes " now became a Provincial charge, and the political expenditure in the province, which was formerly an Imperial charge, was transferred to the Provincial side of the account. The new contract provided for a scale of expenditure amounting to Rs. 49,08,572, and the revenues and receipts made

over to the Provincial Government were estimated to cover this
expenditure exactly. In the previous contract the revenues and
receipts made over to Provincial uses were estimated to exceed the
scale of expenditure provided for in the contract by Rs. 1,09,000.

This contract expired on the 31st March 1892. During its
currency several alterations were made, which affected the distribution of revenue and expenditure between Imperial and Provincial, the principal of which were that Marine and Political charges
were transferred from the Imperial to the Provincial budget ; that
Imperial made a grant to the province of Rs. 1,82,500 on account
of Capital expenditure on the Cherra-Companyganj and Jorhàt
State Railways ; and that Assam made a special contribution to
Imperial of one lakh of rupees out of the seventy-four lakhs which
the Imperial Government demanded from Provincial Administrations.

The contract was also considerably affected by the grant to
Provincial revenues of the amount of extra expenditure incurred
by Assam owing to the Lushai outbreaks of 1890 and 1891. The
progress of the revenue and expenditure of the province during
the period of this contract was shown in considerable detail on
pages 119-124 of the Provincial General Administration Report
for 1891-92, and may be thus summarised :

The contract provided for an annual expenditure of Rs.
47,40,000, or a total for the five years of Rs. 2,37,00,000, and
revenue sufficient to meet that sum was provided in the contract, the
estimated annual excess, Rs. 13,12,000, being treated as a contribution from Provincial to Imperial. The actual Provincial receipts
during the five years aggregated Rs. 2,62,40,000, or an excess over
the contract of Rs. 25,40,000. The expenditure exceeded the contract allotment by Rs. 18,65,000. The Provincial opening balance
on the 1st April 1887 was Rs. 6,84,000, and at the close of the
contract, on the 31st March 1892, the balance was Rs. 13,59,000.

The total Civil Receipts surplus over the contract was Rs.
15,96,000, mainly due to increase in the Land Revenue (Rs.
12,50,000) and in Forest Receipts (Rs. 2,81,000). The receipts
under Jails and Police at no time came near the contract estimate.
The increase in Civil expenditure under the heads included in

direct demands on the revenue was almost entirely in the Forest expenditure. The cost of the Civil Departments was Rs. 8,99,000 more than the contract allotment, but much of this was due to the transfer of Marine and Political expenditure to Provincial, and to extra expenditure in the North Lushai Hills, all of which was met by a corresponding reduction in the contribution made to Imperial by Provincial.

A satisfactory feature in the finance of the province during this period was the continually decreasing cost of collecting the land revenue, due to the gradual substitution of tahsildárs, as revenue collecting agents, for the mauzadárs, who were paid by commission on the amounts of their collections.

The amount spent on Public Works out of the profits that accrued to the Local Administration on the terms of the contract, i.e., in addition to the contract allotment, was Rs. 8,01,000.

This contract came to an end on the 31st March 1892. In the estimates for the new contract, the expenditure, which was based on the revised estimates of 1891-92, was taken at Rs. 52,80,000; and as the receipts worked out to Rs. 54.53,000, the Government of India proposed to resume the difference of Rs. 1,73,000 per annum. Subsequently, however, it was decided not to resume this surplus, but to leave the province in the same financial position as under the contract which came to an end on the 31st March 1892. The following figures were, therefore, adopted:

				Rs.
Revenue, excluding adjustments	...			65,36,000
Adjustments through the Land Revenue head				10,83,000
Total Provincial Revenue ...	...		...	54,53,000
Total Provincial Expenditure	...		...	54,53,000

The main features of the new contract were (1) that all interprovincial adjustments ceased; the charges paid by other provinces on account of Assam, and vice versâ, were taken into account in fixing the expenditure, and it was decided that such charges as had been paid during the previous contract by one province on account of

the other should continue to be so paid, but that no claim should
be made by either province for reimbursement; (2) the whole of
the Land Revenue receipts were allowed to remain Provincial,
subject to a lump adjustment in favour of Imperial revenues; (3)
certain changes of classification were made, as shown below,
which slightly altered the figures adopted at first for the contract;
(4) the new contract was a consolidated one, and not a collection
of separate contracts for each Provincial head, and therefore no
separate amounts were stated for each head of Provincial revenue
and expenditure.

The lump contribution to Imperial was finally fixed at Rs.
11,27,000, thus:

	Rs.
Expenditure	54,53,000
Compensation to Provincial for change of classification of charges of the office of the Inspector General of Police, &c., formerly charged to divided heads, but now to be charged to General Administration, a head wholly Provincial	+ 4,000
Compensation to Imperial for Comptroller's office Provincial establishment now to be made Imperial	— 5,000
Compensation to Imperial for charge of plain paper used with court-fee stamps to the divided head " Stamps," instead of to the wholly Provincial head " Stationery and Printing "	— 2,000
Reduction of charges formerly debited inter-provincially to Assam, now to be borne by other provinces	—41,000
Expenditure thus revised ...	54,09,000
Revenue ...	65,36,000
Contribution, Provincial to Imperial ...	11,27,000

Subsequently, a question arose as to the claim to the increase
in Land Revenue, not estimated for in the contract, due to the
re-assessment of the Assam Valley districts, amounting to Rs.

7,59,000 a year. In settling this question, the terms of the contract under which a certain sum was allotted for expenditure in the Lushai Hills were also amended. The actual amount of the expenditure in 1891-92 was taken as the assignment in the contract for Lushai charges, *viz.*, Rs. 3,56,000 per annum, and it was settled that, to meet any excess over that amount of the charges in the portion of the Lushai country now under the control of the Chief Commissioner of Assam, an equivalent portion of the excess of Land Revenue over the amount now to be allotted to Assam should be made wholly Provincial.

Instead, therefore, of the whole of the Land Revenue being Provincial, it was decided that the ordinary increase should be taken at Rs. 66,000 per annum, and that the Provincial claim should be limited in—

				Rs.
1893-94	...	...	...	to 47,74,000
1894-95	...	...	...	„ 48,40,000
1895-96	...	...		„ 49,06,000
1896-97	...	...	...	„ 49,72,000

Of the excess over these amounts, a sum equivalent to the excess of the actual charges in the North Lushai country over Rs. 3,56,000 and of the actual charges in the South Lushai country (when that tract was transferred to Assam) over the assignment which might be transferred from Bengal with the territory, would also be wholly Provincial, and that of the remainder one-fourth would be Provincial.

166. Exclusive of the receipts of purely Imperial Departments (Post Office, Telegraph, Military, and Imperial Public Works), the aggregate revenue now (1892-93) derived from the province is nearly 105 lakhs of rupees. The principal heads are Land Revenue ($47\frac{1}{4}$ lakhs), Opium (4 lakhs), Stamps (8 lakhs), Excise (26 lakhs), Provincial Rates ($5\frac{1}{2}$ lakhs), Assessed Taxes ($2\frac{1}{4}$ lakhs), Forest ($3\frac{3}{4}$ lakhs), Registration ($\frac{1}{2}$ lakh), and Tributes ($\frac{1}{4}$ lakh). The receipts by Civil Departments aggregate about 5 lakhs, and Public Works receipts, including receipts for Ferries, $2\frac{1}{2}$ lakhs. Since 1882-83

Total revenues of the province.

the revenue has risen from $81\frac{1}{2}$ to 105 lakhs, or by nearly 29 per cent. Land Revenue and Excise show the most marked increase, $8\frac{1}{4}$ and 6 lakhs respectively. The item under Tributes is a receipt from the Manipur State, and appears for the first time in the accounts of this province. The receipts under Assessed Taxes, being recoveries under Act II of 1886, also constitute a new feature.

167. The ordinary Civil expenditure is now $47\frac{1}{2}$ lakhs, and the Public Works Provincial and Local expenditure about $21\frac{1}{2}$ lakhs, or about 69 lakhs in all, leaving a surplus of 36 lakhs as the contribution of the province to the general expenses of the Empire. Of the Civil expenditure ($47\frac{1}{2}$ lakhs), about 13 lakhs represent direct demands upon the revenue, such as Cost of Collection, Refunds, Assignments and Compensations, &c., about 32 lakhs represent salaries and expenses of the Civil Departments, including General Administration, and about $2\frac{1}{2}$ lakhs are expended in Pensions, Stationery and Printing, and other miscellaneous charges.

Total expenditure of the province.

168. The receipts and expenditure of the Imperial Departments (Post Office, Telegraph, Military, Marine, and Imperial Public Works) aggregate, in round figures, 42 and 32 lakhs, respectively, as compared with 18 and 20 lakhs, respectively, in 1882-83. The increase in the receipts is almost entirely under Post Office, and is due to expansion of money order and savings banks transactions. The excess expenditure is chiefly under Public Works.

Surplus how disposed of.

The Provincial surplus (36 lakhs), and the net receipts of the Imperial Departments (10 lakhs) aggregate 46 lakhs. This is remitted to Calcutta by means of currency note remittances and supply bills granted on Assam treasuries, to the agents of tea planters and others. Notes of the higher denominations accumulate largely in the Assam treasuries. They are imported by planters and Marwari traders, and find their way into the treasury as revenue either through revenue collectors (mauzadárs) or purchasers of opium and excise license-holders. There are no banking establishments in Assam. Nearly 29 lakhs of these notes were remitted to Calcutta in 1892-93. The supply bill payments amounted during the same year to upwards of 15 lakhs, and about 16 lakhs in coin were placed at the Comptroller General's disposal at Calcutta by means of transfers to currency chests. By this means money which was not required in Assam was placed in currency in Assam, the equivalent required in other provinces being withdrawn from currency and placed at the disposal of Government for treasury purposes, thus saving all charges of remittance. Accommodation was thus offered to the commercial public in Assam and in Calcutta to the extent of 90 lakhs, the amount being made up of the local surplus, 46 lakhs, supplemented by the issue of bills upon other provinces, about 31 lakhs, and by remittances from Calcutta and withdrawals from the currency chests, 13 lakhs, equivalent sums being placed in currency chests in other provinces where coin was not immediately required.

For bills issued upon Assam a premium of $\frac{3}{4}$ per cent. is realised by Government; those issued by Assam are granted at par, except in the case of bills in favour of Messrs. Macneill and Co., the Rivers Steam Navigation Company's Agents at Dhubri, for their earnings paid into that treasury, upon which a premium of a quarter per cent. is levied.

169. Dividing the revenues and expenditure between Imperial, Provincial, and Local in accordance with the terms of the current contract, the annual revenue of Provincial and Local Funds in 1892-93 aggregate, in round figures, about 64¼ lakhs, and the expenditure 66 lakhs. The expenditure exceeds the receipts, in consequence of the permission, granted by the Government of India, to the Local Administration to utilise on Provincial Public Works about five lakhs from the accumulated Provincial balances.

Provincial revenue and expenditure.

The following are the chief heads of expenditure in round numbers :

					Rs.
Direct demand on the revenues (collection, &c.)			...	...	11,20,000
Administration	...	...	...	...	2,48,000
Law and Justice—Courts of law			...	...	5,44,000

					Rs.
Law and Justice – Jails			...	...	85,000
Police	...	...	...	...	11,66,000
Marine	...	...	...	...	99,000
Education	...	...	...	...	3,39,000
Medical	...		...	...	2,76,000
Political	...		...	...	2,68,000
Public Works	...		...	...	21,50,000

Since 1882-83 the Assam portion of the Inland Labour Transport Fund has been transferred from Bengal (in 1884). The Local income and expenditure included in the above figures are Rs. 9,69,000 and Rs. 9,59,000 respectively, of which the portions pertaining to the Inland Labour Transport Fund are Rs. 64,000 and Rs. 57,000 respectively, the remainder representing transactions of the nineteen Local Boards, which exist in the eight plains districts of the province. There has been no change in the heads of receipts and expenditure entrusted to these bodies, but there have been several transfers between Provincial and Local, chiefly in the expenditure upon Public Works, which have resulted in a reduction of the amount of Provincial contribution to the Local Boards and of the Local Boards' expenditure. In 1882-83 each Local Board received from Provincial varying amounts sufficient to cover the difference between the Local income and Local expenditure. Each Board now receives from Provincial a fixed annual contribution, *plus* or *minus* the amount of its closing balance, *i.e.*, of the surplus or deficit of the penultimate year. The balances are taken in the accounts as lapsing to Provincial at the end of the year, and are regranted as contributions.

170. The Local Funds, which are excluded from the general accounts, are the following:

Excluded Local Funds.

(1) Municipal Funds.
(2) Cantonment Funds.

(3) Town Funds.
(4) Williamson Educational Endowment Funds.

Of these, the first has been described in the preceding section, and the last has also been mentioned above in paragraph 124.

X

CHAPTER VI.

Character of Land Tenures and System of Settlement and Survey.

SECTION I.—LAND TENURES.

171. The ordinary land tenures in Assam vary considerably in

Division of the subject.

different parts of the province. Distinct systems of tenure are found in—

(1) Assam Proper,   (3) Sylhet,
(2) Goálpára,   (4) Cachar,
                (5) the hill districts,

while several varieties of special waste land tenures granted by Government at different periods exist in all the plains districts.

172. There are three main classes of ordinary tenure in the Assam Valley exclusive of Goálpára,

Assam Proper raiyat-wári tenure.

viz., *raiyatwári*, *nisf-khiráj*, and *lákhiráj*. The original *raiyatwári* tenure is of the simplest character: the raiyat holds on annual or decennial lease from the Government, being free to relinquish the whole or any part of his holding or to take up new lands, provided that notice is given to the revenue officers at the proper time of the year. In 1870 a set of rules for the encouragement of ten-year (instead of annual) leases was sanctioned by the Bengal Government, expressly declaring that holdings so settled should be heritable and transferable, on condition of the transfer being registered in the Deputy Commissioner's office, while holders on annual *patta* were left without any legal assurance on these points. The principle of these rules was afterwards embodied in the Land and Revenue Regulation of 1886, which confers a permanent, heritable, and transferable right on persons holding land under a decennial lease, but recognizes no rights beyond those expressed in the lease in the case of annual tenants. The Rules of 1870 remained practically inoperative until 1883, when they were recast, and a general system of ten-year settlements was introduced in all parts of the Assam Valley, where the cultivation and occupation of land are of a permanent character.* The large tracts of land, however, consisting chiefly of the *chápori*, or inundated tracts along the rivers, and the thinly-peopled country under the hills, where only shifting cultivation is practised, were left to the system of annual settlements, as the only one adapted to their peculiar circumstances. In the five districts of Assam Proper, the bulk of the more permanently cultivated land is, therefore, now held under a ten-year settlement, during the currency of which the raiyat is guaranteed against enhancement of the revenue rates. He is at liberty to relinquish any portion of his holding that consists of entire fields, and to take up new lands; while he will receive compensation from Government for any lands taken up for a public purpose. The rest of the area, where a fluctuating system of cultivation prevails, is resettled annually on the basis of actual occupation; and if dispossessed by Government for a public purpose, the raiyat is only entitled to compensation for the value of trees, houses, crops, &c., actually standing on the land at the time of its resumption, but not to compensation for the land itself.

173. *Chamuas* are said to have originated in the early days of British administration, when raiyats sometimes made over their leases to some person of standing in the neighbourhood, and paid their revenue to him in order to avoid the exactions of the *mauzadárs*. An estate thus formed was called a *chamua*, and the *chamuadár* was allowed the privilege of paying direct into the Government treasury. The only *chamua* still remaining is situated in the Barpeta subdivision.

Chamuas and khiráj-kháts.

There is one estate called a *khát* in Kámrúp and another in

---

* Although nominally decennial, all such settlements are fixed so as to expire in the same year, so that only those settlements which are made in the first year of the term are actually made for ten years. All decennial leases now being issued will expire in the year 1903, so that leases issued in 1893-94 will be for a term of ten years, those issued in 1894-95 for nine years, and so on.

Nowgong, while in Lakhimpur there are two *khiráj-kháts*. The owners of these estates, like the *chamuadár* of Barpeta, pay their revenue direct into the Government treasury instead of through the *mauzadár*. Except for this privilege, there is nothing to distinguish the holders of these tenures from ordinary raiyats. Their estates are mostly cultivated by sub-tenants, who pay a grain rent of half the produce of their fields (*adhyá*), or, where cash is taken, the Government rates, except in the more densely-peopled parts, where land is specially valuable. Where the Government rates only are paid, the landlord's profit consists in the command of his tenants' services for supplies, carriage, and house-building, and for reaping and harvesting his crops, and in such occasional contributions as he is able to levy.

174. The history of the *nisf-khiráj* tenure in Assam is a curious example of the manner in which rights in land are sometimes allowed to grow up.

Nisf-khiráj and *lákhiráj* estates.

Former rulers of the country had granted certain lands rent free for religious and other purposes (that is, had assigned to persons or institutions the Government right to the revenue, then taken mostly in labour, of these lands). The last Ahom ruler, however, Chandra Kanta Singh, imposed on the lands in question a tax called *kharikátina*, of 6 annas a *pura* (a measure of four *bighas*), which continued to be levied by the Burmese invaders after their conquest of the country. When Assam became British by conquest, all these grants were held to have lapsed; but Mr. Scott retained the moderate assessment which he found in force upon them, adding later on 2 annas a *pura*, so that the whole assessment came, as left by him, to 8 annas a *pura*. In 1834 the Government directed that a full enquiry should be made into all claims to hold land rent free, as *debottar*, *dharmottar*, or on any other plea, throughout the districts of Assam. Captain Bogle was appointed to make this enquiry, subject to the control and orders of the Commissioner, Captain Jenkins. Another officer, Captain Matthie, was also similarly employed. At the same time the following principles were laid down for the guidance of these officers:

(1) All rights to hold land free of assessment founded on grants

by any former Government were to be considered as cancelled; and it was pointed out that all claims for restoration to any such tenures could rest only on the indulgence of Government.

(2) All lands found to be held in excess of what was held and possessed on *bonâ fide* grants prior to the Burmese conquest, or for services still performed, as well as all lands held for services no longer performed, were to be assessed at full rates.

(3) All lands held on *bonâ fide* grants before the Burmese conquest, or for services still performed, were to be reported to Government; on receipt of the report, special orders would be issued on each case.

(4) Captain Jenkins might in his discretion suspend the orders for bringing any particular land on full rates; but he was to submit his reasons for the consideration of Government.

(5) Pending the *lakhiráj* enquiry, Mr. Scott's moderate rates were to be levied as before on all lands claimed as *lakhiráj* (whether as *debottar*, *brahmottar*, *dharmottar*, or on whatever plea) until brought under assessment at full rates, or until orders to the contrary were received from Government.

The work was commenced in 1834, but was not concluded till 1860, and in the lapse of time these orders were altogether forgotten. Instead of referring the cases which came before him for the orders of Government, General Jenkins dealt with them in a manner which was not authorised by his instructions. He drew a distinction between *debottar*, or temple lands, and other grants, such as *brahmottar* (personal grants to Brahmans for religious service), *dharmottar* (grants to religious communities other than temples, or for pious uses), &c. In the case of the first, when he found the grants to be *bonâ fide* and valid, he confirmed them as revenue free, without, as he was ordered, referring the case to superior authority. In all other cases of *bonâ fide* and valid grants, he simply confirmed the grantee in possession, and directed that, as ordered in his instructions, the land should be assessed as before, *i.e.*, at Mr. Scott's favourable rates of 8 annas a *pura*, pending the final orders of

Government on the whole question. Where the land held was not found to be held under a *bona fide* and valid grant, it was resumed and settled at full rates, which in those days were Re. 1 a *pura*. But no reference was ever made to Government on the conclusion of the proceedings ; and thus until 1851, when the revenue rates were raised throughout Assam, the second class of lands continued to be assessed at rates which, though this was not expressly intended, were, as a matter of fact, half the rates prevailing for other lands.

The question what was to be done with these lands was not again stirred till 1872, when a long correspondence began, which was not finally closed till 1879. It was considered by the Government of India that the grantees having so long been suffered to hold at half rates, it would not be judicious to make any alteration in their status ; and so General Jenkins' unauthorised action was condoned. These half-rate holders were at that time called, equally with the revenue-free holders, *lákhirájdárs*. The term *nisf-khirájdár* was adopted in 1871, as a more accurate description of their status as landholders liable to be assessed at only half the current rates of revenue, whatever these may happen to be.

A *nisf-khirájdár* enjoys the further privilege of paying for the waste land of his estate only one-eighth of the rate assessed on ordinary *rupit* land in the neighbourhood. *Nisf-khiráj* estates generally are settled for a term of ten years throughout the Brahmaputra Valley.

Three-fourths of the total number of *nisf-khiráj* estates are situated in the district of Kámrúp and date from the last period of Ahom rule, when the seat of Government had been transferred from Garhgáon to Gauháti, and the Ahom kings gave away lands wholesale with all the zeal of recent converts to Hinduism. The *lákhiráj* or *debottar* grants, on the other hand, are usually of older date, the most ancient being ascribed to kings Dharmapál and Vanamála, who are said to have reigned between 1100 and 1200 A.D.

These estates are, like the *chamuas* and *khiráj-kháts* already mentioned, ordinarily cultivated by sub-tenants, who, when their superior landlord is (as is generally the case) a religious institution,

are known as *paiks* or *bhakats* of the temple or *chattra*; they usually
pay only the Government rates as rent, but are in addition bound
to do service for their superior landlord.

175. The history of the permanently-settled portion of Goálpára

Goálpára.

has been given above (paragraphs 80 and
81). It consists of nineteen permanently-
settled estates and eight small temporarily-settled holdings. These
between them cover the whole district, excluding the Eastern Duárs.
Twelve of the nineteen permanently-settled estates are those
of the border *Chaudhuris* described in paragraph 89. The remaining
seven consist of lands held originally revenue free on invalid titles,
which were resumed in consequence, and settled at a *jama* fixed in
perpetuity. The eight temporarily-settled estates include five *chars*,
which are farmed yearly to the highest bidder. Of the remaining
three, two are resumed *lákhiráj*, and the third was acquired by
Government as a free gift from the zemindár.

176. The Eastern Duárs comprise five separate tracts, *viz.*,

Eastern Duárs.

Bijni, Sidli, Chirang, Riphu, and Guma. The
last three are the sole property of Government,
and are managed on the same system as the *raiyatwári* tracts of
Assam Proper, the only difference being that cultivation is entirely
on annual leases, and that the revenue rates are lower than those
prevailing in Assam. Bijni and Sidli, with the exception of the
submontane forests which have been excluded from them and
brought under conservancy, are the estates of the Rájas of the
same names. But they are at present managed by Government on
the same terms as the remaining three Duárs, a fixed percentage of
the revenue realised being paid over to the zemindárs.

177. The land tenures in the district of Sylhet (excluding

Sylhet.

Jaintia, which was not annexed to the district
until 1835) present a remarkable contrast to
those of all the districts of permanently-settled Bengal except
Chittagong. In no other district was the permanent-settlement
preceded, as in these, by a survey; in no other district were the
zemindárs passed over at that settlement in favour of the superior

Section 1.
_Land
Tenures._

raiyats or middlemen called mirás-dárs or taluqdárs* (*cf.* the Chitta-gong tarafdárs). The consequence of the survey is that all lands within the surveyed portion of the district which were not settled in 1791-92, the date of the decennial settlement, and have not since been specially settled in perpetuity, are the property of Government and held under temporary settlement. The result of the settlement having been made with a large number of middle-men is that while in the districts of permanently-settled Bengal estates are counted by tens or hundreds, in Sylhet they are counted by thousands, and the individual revenue of each estate is generally very small. Of 49,946 permanently-settled estates at the close of the years 1892-93, only 469 paid a revenue of over Rs. 100, and 20,621 paid under one rupee. Thus, Sylhet is distinguished (1) by the large proportion of its area which is not permanently settled, and (2) by the extremely small payments of revenue due from individual estates, which make the collection (in the absence of *mufassal* revenue establishments, entertained nowhere in permanently-settled districts) a peculiarly difficult and complicated task.

178. The permanently-settled tenures of Sylhet are all held on the same conditions, but have received the names given below with reference to their revenue history :

Permanently-settled tenures.

(1) *Dassana*, estates included in the decennial settlement of 1791-92, which in 1793 became permanent ; in 1892-93 these numbered 25,967, and paid a revenue of Rs. 3,16,838.

(2) *Bázyáfti Dáimi*, lands resumed by the Special Commis-sioner appointed under Regulation III of 1828, and then permanently settled. Number 23,028 ; revenue Rs. 39,605. Of these, 33 estates paying a revenue of Rs. 402 are in the Jaintia parganas.

(3) *Iláhi* lands settled permanently (see below under tempora-rily-settled estates). Number 9 ; revenue Rs. 26.

---

* The above statement does not apply to (1) parganas Taraf, Bamai, and Putijuri, forming zila Laskarpur in the Habiganj subdivision, which were transferred to Sylhet from the Dacca and Mymensingh districts after the assessment for the decennial settle-ment had been effected and (2) certain parganas in the Sunámganj subdivision which could not be surveyed on account of difficulties with the Khásis. In other parts of Sylhet also, the settlement was occasionally made with the zemindárs, and not with the raiyats.

(4) *Khás Dáimi*, permanently-settled estates purchased by Government at sales for arrears of revenue and sold again as permanently-settled. Number 435; revenue Rs. 5,782.

(5) *Hálábádi*. The term *hálábádi* literally means "recently cultivated," but in Sylhet it is applied to all lands not included in the decennial settlement of 1791-92. The so-called *hálábádi* (also known as *ábádi* or *janpal ábádi*) *pattas* or *sanads* were granted between the years 1791 and 1807. They contained no express limitation of the term of settlement, and in 1869 were held by Government to have been settlements in perpetuity. Number of estates 474; revenue Rs. 2,767.

(6) *Khás hálábádi*, estates belonging to class (5) which, having been bought in by Government at sales for arrears of revenue, have been resettled permanently. Number 31; revenue Rs. 1,337.

(7) *Permanently-settled waste land grants*. The proprietors of three *hálábádi* estates paying a revenue of Rs. 9-5-3 claimed a large tract in the Raghunandan hills. Their claims were compromised by the grant in perpetuity of two estates covering an area of 1,659 acres and paying a revenue of Rs. 9-6-0.

(8) *Dhali Mujrai*, *maháls* exempted from assessment on condition of the holders furnishing *dhali* servants for the Sylhet Collectorate. At present two such servants are furnished. There are 41 such estates in Sylhet, covering an area of 377 acres.

179. The temporarily-settled estates of Sylhet Proper are also

Temporarily-settled tenures.

known under different names, but by far the most extensive class is that called *ilám*. In consequence of the success met with in Behar in bringing under assessment land not included in the decennial settlement which afterwards became permanent, the *pargana pátwáris* were, in 1802, directed to prepare and submit schedules of lands in their respective *parganas*, which had not been included in that settlement. On receipt of these schedules, the Collector issued proclamations (*iláms*) inviting claimants to any of the lands to come forward; but no one appeared to claim them. These lands have thus acquired the name of *ilám* or proclaimed lands. During the years 1829 to 1834, these *ilám* lands were surveyed, and in

Y

1835, those that were found cultivated were settled with the occupants if willing to engage ; otherwise they were farmed. The term of the first settlement was ten years for cultivated and fifteen years for jungle lands, and it was subsequently renewed on its expiry for successive further periods. In 1869, a systematic survey was commenced, and revised rules of settlement and a form of *patta* were drawn out. These rules were again revised in 1875 and modified in 1876. The resettlement commenced in 1871, and was practically concluded in 1881. On resettlement, all waste lands in excess of one-fifth of the cultivated area of an estate were, as a rule, excluded from the settlement. In order to protect the rights of Government in these excluded lands, and to prevent encroachment by the neighbouring permanent settlement-holders, a special form of farming lease was sanctioned in 1889. Holders of these leases have no right to resettlement. Holders of *ilám pattas*, on the other hand, have a permanent and heritable right of occupancy subject to payment of the revenue assessed and to acceptance of the terms of settlement. But, as the proprietary right vests in Government, they have no title to *málikána* if they refuse to engage. The last settlement of *ilám* lands in zilas Parkul and Latu, which expired on 31st March 1893, has been extended for one year. The settlement in the rest of the district will expire on different dates between 1st April 1894 and 31st March 1896. There are 3,262 *ilám* estates, with a total area of 97,571 acres.*

So much of the *ilám* area as was not included in the settlement of 1835 and subsequent years has been entered in the waste land register as waste at the disposal of Government; much of it has been taken up by tea planters on the tenures to be described in the next section.

The rest of the temporarily-settled area in Sylhet falls apart into two divisions : first, the small tenures settled on the same principle as *ilám* lands, but different in their origin ; and, secondly, the areas held *khás* by Government, in which, instead of making over definitely the use and occupancy of the land to a settlement-holder

---

* Exclusive of *ilám* lands in parganas Pratabgarh and Egárasati, which have been cadastrally surveyed.

who may eventually become a middleman, the Government has retained the management in its own hands, and deals directly with the cultivators.   The first class consists of 2,428 *maháls* covering an area of 24,214 acres, and technically known by the following names :

(1) *Nánkár patwárigari.*—Lands formerly held by the *pargana pátwáris* as *nánkár, i.e.,* in lieu of salary.   The *pátwáris* were abolished in 1833, and the lands were ordered to be assessed in 1835.

(2) *Char-bharát.*—Alluvial accretions, which in Sylhet all belong to the State.

(3) *Bil-bharát.*—The silted-up beds of *bils*, which were excluded from the permanent settlement because they were then useless.

(4) *Izád.*—Surplus lands discovered after the permanent settlement (but not formally proclaimed as the *ilám* lands were), and thus not included in it.

(5) *Resumed revenue-free land.*—Resumed because found to be held on invalid titles.

(6) *Khás.*—The *khás* lands in Sylhet are, for the most part, originally *ilám* estates, the settlement of which has for various reasons broken down ; in some the holders as a body refused to accept resettlement with joint responsibility ; in some, Government has bought in the estate at sales for arrears of revenue ; in some the settlement has been cancelled for default in payment of revenue. These estates are, for the most part, situated in the Karimganj subdivision of the Sylhet district, which contains a large area of waste land stretching south to the Tippera Hills. They are managed by the tahsildárs of the Pratabgarh and Hakaluki tahsils upon principles in general similar to the *raiyatwári* settlement of Assam Proper. Certain fixed rates are laid down, and raiyats are free to take up land when they please at those rates, after application to the tahsildár. The *khás* lands in the Pratábgarh tahsil have been cadastrally surveyed.

In addition to the above, the term "*khás*" includes also petty permanently-settled estates of little value, bought in by Government at sales for arrears of revenue and not resettled in perpetuity.

A full account of the last settlement of the estates in classes (1) to (5) and of the petty estates in class (6) will be found in

SECTION I.
Land Tenures.

paragraph 51 of the Administration Report for 1880-81. This settlement will expire in 1906-7.

180. The Jaintia parganas have, since they first came under

Jaintia parganas.

British rule, been temporarily settled.[*] The first regular settlement was made in 1838-40, when the tract was professionally surveyed and measured. It was made for a term of five years, at the end of which it was further extended for ten years, and then again extended, so that the settlement of the whole area expired in 1856. In that year the whole of Jaintia was resettled, without remeasurement, for twenty years. This settlement expired in 1876, when a new settlement was begun, which, owing to errors in the classification and assessment of land, was not finally completed until 1882. The term of settlement will expire in 1894, and resettlement operations are now in progress, the tract having been cadastrally surveyed for this purpose.

181. Besides these permanently and temporarily settled

Lákhiráj estates.

estates in Sylhet, there are, as in other districts, valid *lákhiráj* or revenue-free estates. There are in all 11,489 revenue-free estates, with an area of 41,914 acres, including—

(1) 178 grants, which were declared valid after resumption proceedings under Regulations II of 1819 and III of 1828.

(2) 6,345 petty grants, mostly under 10 *bighas* in area, which were exempted from assessment under order of the Bengal Government in 1841.

(3) *Kasba Sylhet.*—These estates are nominally all less than 10 *bighas* in extent, but many, as a matter of fact, greatly exceed this area. This anomaly probably originated through fraud, but it is hard, if not impossible, to rectify it now. Resumption proceedings were initiated many years ago, but the cases were struck off for no apparent reason. The number of these estates has been returned as 2,554, with an area of 4,560 acres.[†]

---

[*] With the exception of 33 permanently-settled and 29 revenue-free estates. The former consist of lands claimed as revenue-free, but resumed by the Special Commissioner appointed under Regulation III of 1828 and subsequently permanently settled.

[†] These figures, which are taken from a *chitha* drawn up by a former Collector for the purpose of assessing chaukidári tax, are only approximate.

(4) 2,412 redeemed estates, consisting of *ilám* estates paying

a revenue of Re. 1 and under, which were sold at auction revenue
free and other estates redeemed on payment of twenty or twenty-
five times the annual revenue.

182.   In the plains portion of Cachar there is, excluding the
waste land grants, but one form of revenue-
paying tenure, that known as *mirásdári*.
Cachar.
The peculiarity of the system as found in this district is that joint
responsibility for the revenue prevails among all the holders of
a *mahál*, who are usually numerous.   In this district, on the
margin of cultivation and settlement, it has been the custom from
the days of the native rulers to the present time for bodies of
cultivators, often consisting of persons of quite different castes,
and even of combinations of Hindus, Musalmans, and hillmen, to
join together in a coparcenary body in obtaining the settlement
of new land.   The Government deals with them as a single holder,
and they arrange among themselves the distribution of the revenue
payable, the joint responsibility, however, remaining.   This system
is a curious survival of primitive conditions which is now tending
to break up, though division of responsibility is not yet formally
recognised in Cachar.   Whether in long-settled *maháls*, or in new
allotments of waste (the latter being known as *jangalburi* grants
and given on a progressive assessment), the *mirásdári* tenure is,
in face of Government, the same.   The cultivators have a permanent, heritable, and transferable right of use and occupancy of the
land, subject to payment of the revenue assessed and to acceptance
of the terms of settlement.   The settlement of Cachar, like that of
the temporarily-settled lands in Sylhet, is for a term of years.   The
existing settlement, which is for a term of fifteen years, will expire
on the 31st March 1898.*

There are a few *lákhiráj* or revenue free estates in Cachar,
being the grants held by dependents of the old royal family, or
dating from the time of native rule.   These are known as *bakhsha*

* The *Jangalburi* Rules have since been be repealed, so far as future applications for
land are concerned, by settlement rules framed for the Surma Valley under sections 12
and 29 of the Land and Revenue Regulation.   The draft of these rules does not provide
for the settlement of waste land at progressive rates.

lands, and are revenue-free only so long as they remain in possession of the grantee and his heirs; when alienated, they are liable to assessment like other *mirásdári* lands.

183. In the hill districts there is no land revenue settlement

Hill districts.

properly so called, except in a few isolated tracts. The strip of plains land which encloses the Gáro Hills on three sides is managed on the system of settlement which obtains in Assam Proper, save in one portion, where the zemindárs of Mechpára hold certain land as part of their permanently-settled estates, and manage it themselves. The terms of tenure are similar to those of the annual *patta*-holders of Assam. In the Khási and Jaintia Hills, a class of land known as *rajháli*, in the Jaintia Hills subdivision, has since the year 1886 been assessed to land revenue under special rules, the rate charged being 10 annas per *bigha*. In the Nága Hills district there is also some land in the Nambar forest, which is held on annual *patta*. In the rest of these districts Government does not assess the land, but the houses. Each village, however, in the Gáro, Khási and Jaintia, and Nága Hills has its own known lands, in which rights of private ownership are recognised to a degree which seems surprising in so primitive a state of society. The system of cultivation by *jhúm*, which prevails throughout the greater part of this area, demands long periods of rest during which the land becomes reclothed with forest; and it is often difficult to believe that what seems an uncared-for wilderness is really the jealously-guarded private property of a clan, family, or village. But the case is so ; and no quarrels have been more enduring or more bitter among these people than those relating to land. The customs of land tenure among these primitive races are often strangely complicated and full of interest ; but they have as yet been insufficiently explored, and it is impossible to describe them at length here. The practice of taxing houses, instead of assessing the land, prevails also in certain remote parts of the plains districts, such as the North Cachar subdivision and the Mikir Hills in Nowgong, while from the Miris in Lakhimpur and the Tipperas in Sylhet a poll-tax is collected in lieu of land revenue.

SECTION 2.—WASTE LAND TENURES.

184. In a province like Assam, thinly peopled and sparsely cultivated, with a boundless extent of waste, inviting new settlers, the terms upon which land is allotted for extension of cultivation have always naturally been a subject of much consideration. The discovery of indigenous tea in Assam and of the possibility of growing this important staple on a large scale in the plains portion of the province, has given a special impetus to the taking up of waste, and the various rules which have from time to time been issued have generally had the extension of tea cultivation in view.

Importance of grants of waste land in Assam.

185. It is not intended in this section to deal with the ordinary tenures, common to all revenue-paying lands in the district, on which land under tea, like that under any other crop, may be held. There is a considerable extent of land in Assam Proper, amounting at present to 86,382 acres, held by planters under the ordinary *raiyatwári* leases described above, the greater part of which is under tea, and in Cachar the *mirásdári* tenure is the favourite form in which land is now taken up for tea cultivation. The *jangalburi* or reclamation lease in this district, which is allotted to any applicant whose appropriation of the land will not prejudicially affect existing rights, gives a lease at favourable rates for twenty years, for the first two years of which the land is revenue free, for the next four it is assessed at 3 annas an acre, for the next four at 6 annas, and for the remaining ten at 12 annas, after which the land is assessable at the ordinary district rates for lands of similar description.

Waste taken up on ordinary tenures.

186. The following is an account of the special terms under which waste land grants are held from Government in the various districts of the province. Only one of these systems, *viz.*, the Thirty-years' Lease Rules, is now actually in force for new applications; but grants made under

Special tenures.

all of the prior rules actually exist, and are governed by the conditions in force at the time when they were given.

I. The first special grant rules were those of the 6th March 1838, and related to Assam Proper only. No grant was to be made of a less extent than 100 acres, or of a greater extent than 10,000 acres. One-fourth of the entire area was to be under cultivation by the expiration of the fifth year from the date of grant, on failure of which the whole grant was liable to resumption. One-fourth of the grant was to be held in perpetuity revenue free. On the remaining three-fourths no revenue was to be assessed for the first five years if the land was under grass, ten years if under reeds and high grass, and twenty years if under forest; at the expiry of this term, revenue was to be assessed at 9 annas per acre for the next three years, after which the rate was to be for twenty-two years Re. 1-2 an acre. At the close of this period (the thirtieth year in the case of grants of grass lands, thirty-fifth in the case of reed lands, and forty-fifth in the case of forest lands), the three-fourths liable to assessment were to be assessed, at the option of the grantee, either at the market value of one-fourth of the produce of the land, or at the average rate of revenue paid by rice lands in the district where the grant was situated; the revenue was thereafter to be adjusted in the same manner at the end of every term of twenty-one years.

Very few grants under these rules still exist. There are now only two in Kámrúp and sixteen in Sibságar, with a total area of 5,533 acres.

II. The next rules were those for leasehold grants of the 23rd October 1854, commonly called the Old Assam Rules. Under these rules, no grant was to be less than 500 acres in extent (afterwards reduced to 200 acres, or even 100 acres in special cases). One-fourth of the grant was exempted from assessment in perpetuity, and the remaining three-fourths were granted revenue-free for fifteen years, to be assessed thereafter at 3 annas an acre for ten years, and at 6 annas an acre for seventy-four years more, making a whole term of ninety-nine years; after which the grant was to be subject to resurvey and settlement " at such moderate assessment as might seem proper to the Government of the day the proprietary right remaining with the grantee's representatives under the conditions generally applicable to the owners of the estates not permanently-settled." One-eighth of the grant was to be cleared and rendered fit for cultivation in five years, one-fourth in ten years, one-half in twenty years, and three-fourths by the expiration of the thirtieth year ; and the entire grant was declared to be liable to resumption in case of the non-fulfilment of these conditions. The grants were transferable, subject to registration of transfer in the Deputy Commissioner's office. These rules were extended to Sylhet and Cachar in 1856, and were in force until 1861, when they were superseded by rules for grants in fee-simple, which at the same time allowed holders of leasehold grants under the prior rules to redeem their revenue payments, on condition that the stipulated area had been duly cleared, at twenty years' purchase of the revenue at the time payable. This permission is still in force, and has been largely taken advantage of. Two hundred and seventy-one grants, with an area of 238,206 acres, have thus been redeemed, and 36 grants, with an area of 35,451 acres (most of which are in Cachar), remain upon the original terms.

III. To these succeeded a new policy, that of disposing of land in fee-simple. The first fee-simple rules were those issued by Lord Canning in October 1861. The Secretary of State took objection to some of their provisions, and a fresh set of rules was issued on the 30th August 1862. The rules issued by Lord Canning provided for the disposal of the land to the applicant at fixed rates, ranging from Rs. 2-8 to Rs. 5 per acre. The rules of August 1862 provided that the lot should be put up to auction. Grants were to be limited, except under special circumstances, to an area of 3,000 acres. In each case the grant was ordinarily to be compact, including no more than one tract of land in a ring fence. The upset price was to be not less than Rs. 2-8 an acre, and in exceptional localities it might be as high as Rs. 10. Provision was made for the survey of lands previous to sale, and for the demarcation of proper boundaries where applicants for unsurveyed lands were, for special reasons, put in possession prior to survey, and also for

z

the protection of proprietary or occupancy rights in the lands applied for. The purchase-money was to be paid either at once or by instalments. In the latter case, a portion of the purchase-money, not less than 10 per cent., was to be paid at the time of sale, and the balance within ten years of that date, with interest at 10 per cent. per annum on the portion remaining unpaid. Default of payment of interest or purchase-money rendered the grant liable to re-sale.

These rules were in force till August 1872, when the Lieutenant Governor of Bengal stopped further grants under them, pending revision of the rules.

IV. Revised fee-simple rules were issued in February 1874 just before the constitution of the province as a separate Administration, which raised the upset price of land sold to Rs. 8 per acre, and made more careful provision for accurate identification of the land, and for consideration of existing rights and claims, before its disposal. These rules continued in force till April 1876.

There now exist in the province 319 fee-simple grants (excluding redeemed leasehold grants already mentioned), covering an area of 192,734 acres.

V. The existing special rules under which applications for waste land for the cultivation of tea, coffee, or timber trees are dealt with, were originally issued in April 1876, and were revised and re-issued under sections 12 and 29 of the Land and Revenue Regulation in 1887. The land is leased (for thirty years) at progressive rates, and the lease is put up for auction sale, but only among applicants prior to its advertisement in the Gazette, at an upset price of Re. 1 per acre, under the provisions of Act XXIII of 1863. The progressive rates are as follows :

For the first two years	revenue free.
„ next four „	3 annas an acre.
„ „ four „	6 „ „
„ „ ten „	8 „ „
„ „ ten „	1 rupee „

After the expiration of the last mentioned term, the land is to be assessed under the laws in force, " provided that no portion of the said land shall at any time be assessed at a rate higher than that then payable on the most highly-assessed lands in the said district, cultivated with rice, pulses, or other ordinary agricultural produce." The grantee is required to pay the revenue punctually on the due date; to devote the land only to the special crops for cultivating which it is granted; to personally reside in the district, or have an agent residing there; to erect, and maintain in repair, proper boundary marks; not voluntarily to alienate any portion of the land, unless the estate is transferred as a whole; and to give notice to the Deputy Commissioner of all such transfers. On breach of any of these conditions, the concession of the favourable rates of assessment on which the land is held is liable to be withdrawn, and the estate is liable to be assessed at the ordinary district rates. There were altogether, at the end of 1892-93, 645 estates, covering 244,011 acres, held on this tenure in Assam.

Mention should here be made of a special tenure, compounded of the lease under the rules of April 1876 and the terms on which *ilám* land is held in the district, on which certain tea planters have been allowed to hold land for tea in South Sylhet. When the *ilám* resettlement was in progress in this district, it was found that several planters had recently acquired considerable areas of waste land held under *ilám pattas*. One of the rules of the *ilám* settlement was that waste land within the boundaries of the *patta* which exceeded the proportion of one-fifth of the cultivated area should be cut off and resumed by Government. But it was precisely in order to obtain this waste land that tea planters had acquired the *ilám pattas*. A compromise was, therefore, made in 1879. The land already under tea was assessed at Re. 1-8 per acre; of the waste, an area equal to one-fifth of the cultivated area was allowed at 8 annas an acre; and the rest was permitted to be held on the terms and at the rates specified in the waste land rules of 1876. There are 61 such estates in Sylhet, with an area of 26,317 acres.

From the above summary it will be seen that from 1838 to 1861 the principle on which waste lands were granted for tea cultivation was that they should be held on a leasehold tenure for

SECTION 3. long terms at low rates of assessment, the cultivation of the land
System of being secured by stringent conditions as to clearance: from 1861
Survey and
Settlement. to 1876 the policy was to alienate land free of revenue demand,
and without any clearance conditions: while from 1876 to date
the principle of leases has again been reverted to, but this time
without any special stipulations as to the area to be brought under
cultivation within the term of lease. The total area held on these
special terms for tea cultivation in the province is no less than
992,598 acres, or 1,550·93 square miles.

SECTION 3.—SYSTEM OF SURVEY AND SETTLEMENT.

187. The nature of the *raiyatwári* tenure in the Assam Valley
has already been described. Estates held
Settlements in Assam   on annual lease are resettled every year,
Proper.
while the ten-year settlements undergo no
alteration during the length of their term, save such as may be
caused by the raiyat's relinquishing some fields of his holding, and
such relinquishments are naturally less common in decennially-
settled lands, where the nature of the cultivation affords some
guarantee of permanence, than in those tracts where the system of
annual settlements continues to prevail. In either case settlement
is preceded by measurement, which, like the assessment, is effected
by the tahsildár or mauzadár with the help of his subordinate
officials, called mandals. The position and duties of these officers
have already been prescribed (*ante*, paragraph 109). A mauza is,
as already explained, a defined revenue circle averaging 11·589
square miles (though the area varies exceedingly in different parts
of the same district), while a mandal's charge averages nearly 20
square miles of gross area. These figures include unoccupied waste,
of which most parts of the valley contain an enormous extent,
and waste land grants, with which a mauzadár has nothing to do.
Excluding these, the average assessed area under a mauzadár is
about 7,023 acres, and that in charge of a mandal about 1,936 acres.

188. The old system of making these measurements was by
measuring up the four sides of the field with
Measurement.
a 30-foot chain and multiplying together the

mean length and breadth thus ascertained. The result of this
method was usually to give areas in excess of the reality, but this
tendency was more than compensated by the omission to measure
up the gradual extensions of cultivation which take place on the
edges of waste. This system is still followed in tracts which have
not yet come under survey; but whenever the land has been
cadastrally surveyed, its place has been taken by a regular survey.
All new fields are connected with permanent points (prisms, theo-
dolite stations, and the like), and are carefully plotted on the
village map, old and permanent cultivation being distinguished
from lands newly taken up by the use of different coloured lines.
In all cases alike the area is recorded in terms of *bighas*, *káthas*,
and *lessas*, a *bigha* (14,400 square feet) being equivalent to 5 *káthas*
and 20 *lessas*. The registers in which the results of the measurements are recorded are two in number,—a field register or *jamábandi*, and a *dág chitha* or revenue roll. The former shows the
number borne by each field in the mandal's circle, the raiyat's name,
the area and the class of soil; in non-cadastral tracts the boundaries and dimensions are also entered. The *jamábandi* is a record
of the fields constituting each raiyat's holdings, their area, soil class,
and assessment. Separate *dág chithas* and *jamábandis* are maintained for lands held on annual and lands held on decennial leases.
These measurements are made, and registers kept, by the mandals,
who answer to the *patwáris* of other parts of India, and of whom
there are usually three or four in a mauza.

189. In the five upper districts of the Brahmaputra Valley, the
soil is divided into three main classes,— *basti*,
Assessment. *rupat*, and *faringáti*. The first mentioned is the
land on which the raiyat's house stands, with the garden enclosure
around it; *rupit* land is that on which the winter crop of transplanted rice (*sáh*) is grown, as well as the low swampy lands
devoted to the cultivation of *bao*; the term *faringáti* denotes the
higher and lighter soils which produce *áhu* or summer rice, sugarcane, mustard, oil-seeds, and other crops.

Until the present year, no attempt had ever been made to proceed
further in the direction of classification. Advantage has now been

taken of the expiry of the decennial leases to revise the assessment; and, while securing to Government its fair share of the increased value of the produce, to introduce a more equitable system of classification. The main classes of soil already mentioned have each been divided into three sub-classes, the revenue payable on each being as follows:

			First class.	Second class.	Third class.	
			Rs. a.	Rs. a.	Rs. a.	
Basti	...	...	2 0	1 8	1 4	per *bigha*.
Rupit	...	...	1 4	1 0	0 12	,,
Faringáti	...	...	1 0	0 12	0 10	,,

The considerations taken into account in classifying land into these sub-classes are the demand for land as shown by the density of population and the proportion of settled to total area, etc., the productiveness of the soil, and the facilities for disposing of the crops. Special rates have been sanctioned for lands held by tea planters, and also for lands newly taken up.

In the Eastern Duárs no attempt has yet been made to go beyond the old three-fold classification of *basti*, *rupit*, and *faringáti*. The rates current in that tract are *basti* and *rupit* 8 annas and *faringáti* 4 annas per *bigha*.

190. The settlement year begins on the 1st April, and the tahsildár or mauzadár is responsible for seeing that all his books are sent to the Deputy Commissioner (or in subdivisions to the subdivisional officer) on the date fixed by them (usually about July). The accuracy of the assessments is checked in the Deputy Commissioner's office, and a settlement statement is then prepared and submitted to the Commissioner for confirmation. Each raiyat or occupier of the land receives a *patta* for his holding, and executes a *kabuliyat* in exchange, binding himself to pay the Government revenue. The *pattas* are issued under the signature of the Deputy Commissioner, or subdivisional officer, or, in the case of tahsils, the tahsildár.

Settlement statement.

The settlement above described is called the main or regular settlement of the year, and includes all lands taken up for cultivation in the first half of the year to which it relates. A supplementary settlement, however, is needed, in order to assess the lands which are broken up for oil-seeds and pulses in September and October, when the floods subside. The measurements for this purpose are conducted during the winter months; the papers of the *dariabadi* or supplementary settlement are filed before the close of the financial year; and the settlements are reported to the Commissioner for confirmation in the same manner as the main settlements concluded in the July preceding. In the following year these *dariabadi* lands come into the main settlement.

The revenue is paid in two instalments of three-fifths in November and two-fifths in February; but *dariabadi* lands, being settled too late for the November instalment, pay the whole year's revenue in a lump sum in February.*

191. In paragraph 188 reference has been made to the cadastral survey. Prior to 1883, maps showing the cultivation in each village did not exist, and the only record of the fields occupied by the raiyats was that contained in the mandal's *dag chitha* and *jamabandi*. It was then decided, wherever practicable, to replace this inaccurate system by the exact record of a regular survey, and with this object operations were commenced by a professional survey party in November 1883. During the cold weather of 1883-84, 228 square miles were cadastrally surveyed in Kámrúp, and between that year and 1890-91 the whole of the more permanent and densely cultivated tracts in the five upper districts of the valley (consisting in all of 4,460 square miles) were brought under survey. As the survey progressed, steps were taken to ensure the proper maintenance of the maps and other records by increasing the number of Sub-Deputy Collectors (there is now one of these officers in each subdivision), who are held directly responsible for all survey and settlement operations by appointing a new class of officers known as supervisor kánungos, whose duty it is to be constantly on the move, checking the work done by the mandals and training those whose knowledge is deficient; and, lastly, by improving the status of the

Cadastral survey.

---

* In certain mauzas, where the cultivation of mustard is considerable, the whole revenue is paid in one instalment, on the 15th February.

Section 3.
*System of
Survey and
Settlement.*
mandals themselves. Formerly, the latter were all paid at a uniform rate of Rs. 6 per month : now they are divided into three grades drawing Rs. 12, Rs. 9 and Rs. 6 respectively, and promotion to the higher grades is made directly dependent on their qualifications as surveyors.

The principal statistics connected with the cadastral survey are set forth in the following statement :

Year of cadastral survey.	Locality surveyed.	Area surveyed.	Cost.		Increase of revenue.	Percentage of increase.	
			Total cost of finally compiled papers.	Cost per square mile.		To previous revenue.	To cost of acres.
		Sq. miles	Rs.	Rs. a. p.	Rs.		
1883-84 ..	Nine mauzas in Kámrúp ..	72·19	1,13,635	40 15 9	6,0·5*	4·24	5·24
1884-85 ..	Twenty-one ditto ..	47·55	1,61,229	3·6 14 4	8,317*	3·29	5·18
1885-86 ..	Twenty-two ditto ..	168·51	1,58,16	2·8 7 6	13,307*	5·63	10·20
1886-87 ..	Thirty-six mauzas in Mangaldai ..	547·02	1,53,150	279 15 9	979†	0·31	0·64
1887-88 ..	Twenty-five ditto in Nowgong ..	586·50	1,35,981	243 12 0	22,222†	9·41	20·65
1888-89 ..	Thirty-two mauzas in Sibsagar ..	656·90	1,48,291	225 11 5	68,510†	17·04	46·20
1889-90 ..	Thirty-two ditto ..	715·49	1,29,870	182 0 5	29,482†	12·69	22·70
1890-91 ..	Twenty-four mauzas in Kámrúp and Nowgong, and two mauzas (in part) in Darrang (two transferred to Nowgong) ..	781·69	1,24,989	160 0 9	18,152†	10·84	14·52

The main features brought out by this statement are the annually decreasing cost of survey operations and the large variations from year to year in the increase of revenue resulting therefrom. Taken as a whole, the survey has produced a total increase of revenue amounting to Rs. 1,74,301, which represents 7·94 per cent. on the original revenue and 15·67 per cent. on the cost of the operations. It must, however, be remembered that

* Calculated both on the *khiráj* and the *nisf-khiráj* areas.

† Calculated on *khiráj* area only, as the mauzadárs' figures for *nisf-khiráj* area are not available, and therefore the increase thereon cannot be ascertained.

‡ In calculating the increase, the area of five mauzas of Kámrúp (Barpeta) and one mauza of Nowgong have been excluded, as the mauzadars' figures for these areas are not available.

these figures do not take into account the normal increase in revenue that would in any case have taken place, nor the fact that revised definitions of *basti* and *rupit* land, which were issued while the survey was in progress, would in any case have produced a considerable gain under the head of reclassification; neither do they allow for the increased cost of survey and settlement operations due to the necessity of maintaining the more elaborate system which the survey has inaugurated. But, even after making allowance for all this, it must be conceded that the operations have proved a fair financial success; and it must, moreover, be borne in mind that the more powerful supervising staff now placed at the disposal of district officers, together with the increased facilities for checking afforded by the survey maps, will be of permanent benefit to the revenue by making it almost impossible for concealed cultivation to exist in the area over which the survey has extended.

The work of the professional party has now come to an end, as no tracts remain of sufficient extent and cultivation to render it profitable to carry out their survey through this expensive agency. But it has been the steady policy of Government throughout the course of the survey to employ as many mandals as possible as amins, and thereby to secure a trained staff in every district; and it is now intended to utilise the services of these men for the gradual extension of the surveyed area wherever there is sufficient cultivation to render this course desirable. Small areas will be selected annually in each district for survey by trained mandals from adjacent mauzas, under the supervision of the Sub-Deputy Collector and the supervisor kánúngo of the circle; and by these means, in course of time, the whole of the cultivated area in the Brahmaputra Valley will be brought under cadastral survey.*

192. In Sylhet the temporarily-settled portions, as already explained, consist of the Jaintia parganas and the *ilám* and other miscellaneous *maháls* not included in the permanent settlement.

Sylhet.

---

* The practicability of this scheme has been proved by an experimental survey at Barpeta, where 111 square miles were surveyed by the ordinary revenue staff at a total cost of Rs. 50·45 per square mile.

Settlement in Jaintia.

183. The history of the Jaintia settlement has already been partly given. In 1838-40 a cadastral or professional *khasra* survey was made of these parganas, and the maps of this survey formed the basis, with additional surveys by amins where fresh land had been taken up, of the resettlement made in 1856. At this settlement, the rates of assessment were determined on local enquiry by the Settlement Officer and his subordinates, according to the nature of the soil and its capabilities. The rates varied from 2 annas 6 pie to Re. 1-0-3 per acre; but these rates were pitched extremely low in consequence of the successful opposition of the cultivators to the imposition of any higher assessment.

This settlement expired in 1876; but, owing to errors committed in the classification and assessment of the land, the new settlement was not finally completed until 1882. A survey and reassessment are now being carried out with a view to the introduction of a new settlement for ten years from the 1st April 1892. For this purpose, land is divided into four main classes,—(1) homestead, (2) cultivation, (3) fallow, and (4) waste. The seventeen parganas, covering an area of 159 square miles, are further divided into homogeneous net profit tracts, after taking into consideration the productiveness of the soil, cost of cultivation, proximity to markets, liability to ravages by wild beasts, &c. In each of these tracts the four main classes of land are subdivided into four sub-classes, called first, second, third, and fourth class homestead, cultivation, &c. Differential rates are fixed for these sub-classes in each homogeneous circle, the ultimate result for all the parganas taken together being that homestead land bears six different rates of assessment, varying from 10 annas to 3 annas 9 pie per *bigha*; cultivation (seven rates), varying from 7 annas to 2 annas $7\frac{1}{2}$ pie; fallow (seven rates), varying from 2 annas to 9 pie; and jungle (eight rates), varying from 1 anna to $4\frac{1}{2}$ pie per *bigha*.

Ilam and miscellaneous temporarily-settled estates.

194. The resettlement of *ilam* and other miscellaneous temporarily-settled estates in Sylhet has been conducted under rules sanctioned in 1876 by the Government of India. Before settlement,

the lands were measured with chain and compass by native amins, a plan of the estate on the scale of 16 inches to the mile was prepared, and the area was calculated in both *bighas* and acres. These measurements were tested by the Settlement Deputy Collector. The rates of assessment have not been scientifically determined with reference to the advantages of situation or productivity of the soil, but were fixed in each case by the Settlement Officer (himself a zemindár of the district) with regard to the rates paid by cultivators for similar lands in the neighbourhood. From these rates, a deduction of 15 per cent. was made to cover cost of collection and risks, and the remainder was fixed as the assessment of the *mahals*. The resultant assessment is considerably in excess of the former revenue derived from these *mahals*, but is not, so far as can be judged, in itself burdensome, being considerably lower in its incidence than the revenue rates, which are found to be paid with ease in the more backward and less civilised districts of the Assam Valley. These settlements will all expire in 1907 A.D.

195. The last settlement of the Pratabgarh tahsil was effected

Pratabgarh tahsil.

in 1881-83, the previous one having broken down, owing to the rates having been fixed at too high a figure. At this settlement, the land was divided into four classes (homestead, *dofasal*, *ekfasal*, and *chena*), the rates varying from Re. 1 to 7 annas per acre. This settlement expired in 1887, since which time it has been extended from year to year, pending a fresh survey which is now at last approaching completion. For the purposes of this settlement, the land has been divided into ten classes, some of which are again divided into first and second sub-classes, according to the productiveness of the soil. The rates per *bigha** which have been proposed vary from 3 annas to Re. 1-2-0.

196. The first regular settlement of Cachar was made in 1838-

Cachar.

39 for a term of five years, and was based on a somewhat imperfect survey. In 1841-42 the district was surveyed on the same plan as the adjacent Jaintia parganas. The cultivated land in the several mauzas was surveyed field by field, and so much of the uncultivated area as seemed likely to come under cultivation was also surveyed and divided

* 3·025 *bighas* = 1 acre.

into numbered *dágs* or plots, the intention being that, as cultivation extended, these plots should afford the means of determining its site and a basis for a detailed map of its area. In 1843-44 a re-settlement, based upon this survey, was made for fifteen years. Then followed the settlement of 1859, made for twenty years, which expired in 1879. This also was based on the survey of 1841-42, the fresh cultivation since that was made being measured up by native amins. The land was divided into two classes, called *arwal* and *duam* respectively; and within these classes it was ranged, according to situation, distance from navigable rivers, and exposure to the ravages of wild beasts, in four grades. The local measure of land in Cachar is the *hál*, or plough (also called by the Arabic name *halbah*), which is equal to 4·82 acres; and the rates imposed varied from Rs. 3-8 to Rs. 3-0 for first-grade land to Rs. 2 to Re. 1-8 for fourth grade. Waste land producing thatching-grass and reeds, which are valuable products in the densely-peopled Surma Valley, was settled at the full rates of revenue charged for cultivated land in the neighbourhood. Forest jungle, which required much clearing, was settled for three years revenue-free, and then at a progressive *jama*, rising to the full rates charged for adjacent lands at the end of the term, twenty years.

197. On the expiry of this settlement, a fresh survey was made,

and a settlement was effected for fifteen years, which extends up to 31st March 1898. For the purpose of this settlement the three fiscal divisions, known as the Katigora tahsil, the Hailákándi tahsil, and the sadr tahsil, were dealt with separately. In each tahsil the soil was divided into four classes, *viz.*, homestead, cultivation, tea, and waste, and each class was again subdivided into four circles, the constitution of the circles being based on a consideration of the productiveness of the soil, the facility or otherwise of communication, the liability to inundation, the exposure to the ravages of wild animals, and the proximity to dense forests.

The rates fixed at this assessment vary from Rs. 8-4 to Rs. 4-12 per *hál* for homestead land, from Rs. 7-2 to Rs. 3-12 for cultivation, and from Rs. 7-2 to Rs. 6-0 for tea. Waste was assessed at a uniform rate of Re. 1 per *hál*.

CHAPTER V.

Civil Divisions of British Territory.

198. The province of Assam is divided, for administrative purposes, into twelve districts, *viz.*, the six districts of the Brahmaputra Valley, the two
districts of the Surma Valley, and the four hill
districts. These districts, their administrative headquarters, the
subdivisions into which they are divided, their area, and their population according to the census of February 1891, are shown below:

General administrative
divisions.

CIVIL
DIVISIONS.

Name of district.	Headquarters.	Subdivisions.	Area, in square miles.	Population.
Surma Valley—				
Cuchar	Silchar	Silchar	1,952	267,673
		Hailakandi	520	99,869
		Total	2,472	367,542
Sylhet	Sylhet	North Sylhet	1,018	482,711
		Karimganj	1,122	351,635
		South Sylhet	828	345,379
		Habiganj	957	508,854
		Sunamganj	1,500	413,344
		Total	5,414	2,154,593
Total Surma Valley	....		7,886	2,522,135
Brahmaputra Valley—				
Goálpára	Dhubri	Dhubri	2,381	317,781
		Goálpára	1,570	134,323
		Total	3,951	451,334
Kámrúp	Gauháti	Gauháti	2,353	498,544
		Barpeta	1,307	135,705
		Total	3,660	634,249

CIVIL
DIVISIONS.

Name of district.	Headquarters.	Subdivisions.	Area in square miles.	Population.
Darrang	Tezpur	Tezpur	2,173	125,637
		Mangaldai	1,245	182,124
		Total	3,418	307,761
Nowgong	Nowgong		3,754	344,141
Sibságar	Sibságar	Sibságar	890	160,304
		Jorhat	918	181,152
		Golaghat	917	115,818
		Total	2,855	457,274
Lakhimpur	Dibrugarh	Dibrugarh*	2,563	190,619
		North Lakhimpur	1,161	63,434
		Total	3,724	254,053
Total Brahmaputra Valley	....		2,800	2,149,782
Hill Districts—				
Gáro Hills	Tura		3,970	121,570
Khási and Jaintia Hills	Shillong	Shillong	2,955	132,383
		Jowai	2,086	64,521
		Total	6,041	197,504
Nága Hills	Kohima	Kohima	5,110	96,151
		Mokokchang	600	26,316
		Total	5,710	122,867
North Cachar†	Gunjong		1,768	18,941
North Lushai Hills‡	Aijal		5,520	43,634
Total Hill districts	....		20,419	504,916
Grand total	....		42,094	5,476,833

* Including Saikya.

† North Cachar is really a subdivision of Cachar, but is here shown as a separate district for the reasons stated in the foot-note to paragraph 1.

‡ The area and population shown against " North Lushai Hills " are only estimates.

At each headquarters station there is a Deputy Commissioner, and at each subdivisional station other than that of the headquarters sub-division an Assistant or Extra Assistant Commissioner, or, in one or two cases, a police officer.

The six districts of the Brahmaputra Valley constitute the charge of the Commissioner of the Assam Valley Districts, whose headquarters are at Gauháti.

199. In the eight plains districts and the Khási and Jaintia Hills the area is further subdivided into thánas, or jurisdictions of police stations.

Police divisions.

There are 46 thána areas in these districts. Some of the larger thánas are again divided into outposts, of which there are 58 in the province. These areas, though they originally define police jurisdiction, are convenient for other purposes : thus, the jurisdiction of the munsifs in Sylhet is arranged by thánas ; the registration sub-districts are similarly arranged ; Muhammadan Marriage Registrars and Kázis in the Surma Valley are also appointed for thána and outpost areas.

200. In Assam Proper and the Eastern Duárs the district is portioned out for revenue purposes into mauzas. The average area of these mauzas is 115·89 square miles. They thus correspond in size rather to the pargana or *tappa* than to the mauza of Upper India. In Assam there is little cohesion in the village society, and almost nothing which represents the complex social organization of the North-Western Provinces or the Punjab. Hamlets of a few houses are scattered about the whole mauza area ; and though the boundaries of the lands recognised as belonging to a particular village are in some districts (*e.g.*, parts of Kámrúp) known to the people, they do not imply any definite appropriation of the soil to that village ; anyone applying for it can settle upon Government waste wherever it is situated.

Revenue divisions.

Formerly, each of these mauzas was under a mauzadár or revenue contractor (see paragraph 109 *ante*) ; but since 1882 the tahsildári system has been partially introduced into Kámrúp, Darrang, Nowgong, and Sibságar, each tahsil being under a tahsil-

dár paid by salary and not by commission, and consisting of a
collection of from three to eleven of the old mauzas. This system
is still being extended as opportunity occurs, and the entire dis-
appearance of the old mauzadári system is now only a matter of
time. The following statement shows the extent to which mauzas
have already been amalgamated into tahsils :

District.	Area.	Revenue.	Number of mauzas.	Already included in tahsils.			Not included in tahsils.		
				Area.	Revenue.	Number of mauzas.	Area.	Revenue.	Number of mauzas.
	Acres.	Rs.		Acres.	Rs.		Acres.	Rs.	
Kámrúp	2,312,400	9,79,317	72	1,693,495·6	8,46,276	65	618,902·4	1,33,071	7
Darrang	2,187,680	4,96,682	51	526,363·6	2,78,586	35	1,661,325·4	2,18,096	16
Nowgong	2,084,956	5,41,144	36	265,383·6	2,16,009	13	1,819,562·4	3,25,045	23
Sibságar	1,806,188	8,72,184	50	316,096	2,66,975	14	1,194,692	6,05,319	56

In Sylhet and the plains of Cachar, as well as in permanently-
settled Goálpára, the ordinary revenue division into parganas,
which dates from times prior to British rule, is in force. In the
two former districts, however, these parganas are very small, and
much interlaced one with another. In Sylhet, there are 186 parganas, so that their average area is less than 29 square miles ; 15
are less than one square mile, and 42 are more than one and less
than two square miles. In the plains of Cachar there are 24 and
in Goálpára 19 parganas, the last representing separately-settled
estates of the permanent settlement.

These parganas are grouped, in Sylhet and Cachar, into larger
areas for the purposes of revenue payment. In Sylhet these areas
are called zilas, of which there are ten, besides the Jaintia parganas,
which latter are divided into two tahsils or collection areas. The
zilas are made up of parganas, and the revenue is paid at each
subdivisional headquarters for the zilas included in its jurisdiction.
In the Jaintia parganas there are two collecting centres, one at
Kanairghat, and the other at Sylhet. In Cachar, the plains portion

of the district is divided into three tahsils, the offices of which are located at Silchar, Hailákándi, and Katigora.

In the hill districts different divisions for revenue purposes prevail. In the Gáro Hills, the strip of plains land which surrounds the hill area on three sides is managed by two mauzadárs, who, however, are not contractors, as in Assam, but officers on a fixed salary. The hill area is also portioned out into five mauzas; but the mauzadár here is merely the superior officer who receives the house tax from the *lushkars*, or Gáro headmen of groups of villages. These again collect from the *lakma* or *nokma*, the head and representative of each village.

In the Khási Hills, as already mentioned, there is not much British territory, the area being generally included in the States of the Khási Seims, Sardars, Longdohs, or other petty chiefs. Only 25 villages, or groups of villages, are British, and these pay house tax through a village headman. In the Jaintia Hills there are 19 circles of villages, each of which is managed by a dolloi or headman, who collects the house tax and pays it in, receiving commission. There are, besides, four Sardarships, the management of which is hereditary, the headmen being Kuki or Mikir chiefs.

In North Cachar, the assessment and collection of house tax were formerly carried out by a special tahsil establishment, but this has been replaced since 1884 by mauzadárs, who are remunerated by a commission of ten per cent., and occupy much the same position as the mauzadár in the Brahmaputra Valley.

In the Nága Hills, part of the district is in charge of mauzadárs (the Mikir and Rengma Hills and the land revenue paying villages in the Nambar forest), and in part (the Angámi, Rengma, Sema, Lhota, Ao, and Kacha Nága villages on the main range) the house tax is collected by village headmen, called *lambárdars*, who receive a commission varying from $12\frac{1}{2}$ to 20 per cent.

CHAPTER VI.

Details of the last Census (1891).

Census.   **201.** The last census of Assam was taken on the 26th February
1891 in all those portions of the province in
Manner of taking the   which it was synchronous, that is to say,
census.
throughout the plains and in some parts of
the hill districts. In the greater portion of the latter a more
gradual enumeration was carried out, but the total number of
persons included in the non-synchronous returns amounted only
to about 100,000, or less than 8 per cent. of the total population.
A census was taken of Manipur, but all papers connected therewith
were destroyed in the disturbances which took place in the
following March, and no statistics are, therefore, available for that
State. In the North Lushai Hills the Civil and Military population was censused on the 26th February, while, for the Lushais,
an estimate of the population was prepared by the Political Officer,
based on enquiries made by him during his tours. The figures
furnished for the last mentioned tract are, of course, only approximate, but it is believed that they are very fairly accurate. The
report and tables were issued in June 1892, or about fifteen
months after the census was taken. A brief summary of some of
the more important results is given below.

202. As stated in the last chapter, the area of the province
is about 49,004 square miles, and the popu-
Area and density.   lation 5,476,833, or on the average 111
persons per square mile, which is less than in any other part
of India, except only in Burma and Coorg. The details of the

population in each district are shown in the following state- CENSUS.
ment :

District.			Area, in square miles.	Population.	Number of persons per square mile.	Number of persons per house.	Number of females to 100 males.
Cachar (plains)	...	...	2,472	367,542	148·6	4·4	89·09
Sylhet	...	...	5,414	2,154,593	397·9	4·9	95·70
Goálpára ...	...	...	3,954	452,304	114·3	5·5	91·14
Kámrúp ...		...	3,660	634,249	173·2	5·0	97·56
Darrang ...	...	...	3,418	307,761	90·0	4·8	90·70
Nowgong	...	...	3,258	344,141	105·6	5·1	93·56
Sibságar ...		...	2,855	457,274	160·1	4·6	89·74
Lakhimpur		...	3,724	254,053	68·2	4·5	86·25
North Cachar	...	...	1,728	18,941	10·9	5·0	103·53
Nága Hills		...	5,710	122,867	21·5	3·5	97·53
Khási and Jaintia Hills		...	6,041	197,904	32·7	5·0	109·18
Gáro Hills	...	...	3,270	121,570	37·1	5·0	98·60
North Lushai	...	...	3,500	{ 2,044° } { 41,590† }	12·4	5·0	91·05
Total	...	...	49,004	5,476,833	111·0	4·8	94·23

° Civil and Military.　|　† Estimated.

The Khási and Jaintia and the Nága Hills districts stand first in respect of area; but they consist, to a large extent, of rocky and unculturable uplands, and their population is consequently sparse. Their combined area is double that of Yorkshire, but they contain only about one-ninth of the population of that county. The next largest district is Sylhet, which contains very nearly two-fifths of the total population of the province. With the exception of a large belt of jungle at the foot of the hills along the southern boundary and of a smaller similar tract towards the north, the whole of the district is very densely peopled. It is equal in area to Durham, Cumberland, Northumberland, and Westmoreland; its population is larger by 33 per cent. than that of these four counties taken together. The next district, Goálpára, is about the size of North Wales, and is equally densely peopled. Lakhimpur comes next in size, and then Kámrúp, with an area equal to that of Lincolnshire and Nottinghamshire, but only about 70 per cent. of the combined population of these counties. The smallest district in the province is North Cachar, which is somewhat larger than Somersetshire, but has less than 4 per cent. of its population.* As a general rule, it may be said that the density of the population is greatest in the west, and decreases gradually towards the east, the main reason for this result apparently being that in the days of native rule the eastern districts suffered more from wars and a disturbed frontier than those further west.

203. For census purposes a house was defined to be "the homestead where the members of one family reside under a common head with their servants." That the definition was well understood is shown by the great uniformity in the average number of persons per house returned in the different districts. With the exception of the Nága Hills and Goálpára, the average in all districts lies between

Houses and house room.

---

* North Cachar is administratively a subdivision of the Cachar district, but, owing to the wide physical and ethnological differences between it and the plains portion of Cachar, it was treated as a separate district for the purposes of the census.

5·0 in Kámrúp, Sylhet, and three out of the four hill districts, and 5·3 in Nowgong, where the figures are higher than they otherwise would be, owing to the great number of Mikirs living in the district, amongst whom it is customary for large groups of relatives to reside together under a common roof. The materials of which houses are constructed in Assam are extremely plentiful, and can be got everywhere at a very trifling cost; in fact, in most parts they cost nothing more than the labour involved in cutting them and bringing them to the homestead. So far, therefore, as their houses are concerned, the condition of the people is one of great comfort, and overcrowding is practically unknown.

204. The number of males exceeds that of females in every

Proportions of the sexes. district except the Khási and Jaintia Hills and North Cachar, which are peopled mainly by aboriginal tribes. In the Nága Hills and the Gáro Hills districts the preponderance of males is very slight, and is due entirely to the Hindu and Musalman population. In the province generally, not only does the number of males exceed that of females, but this excess is more marked now than it was in 1881, males having increased by 316,000, or 12·62 per cent., and females by 279,407, or 11·75 per cent. The explanation of these figures will be found in the fact that amongst the immigrant population males largely outnumber females. In 1881 there was a foreign-born population of 280,609, viz., males 163,664, and females 116,945. The total foreign-born population now numbers 510,672, including 297,301 males and 213,371 females, that is to say, the excess of immigrant males over females is greater by 37,211 than it was in 1881. Excluding immigrants, 50·79 out of every 100 persons are males and 49·21 are females.

Census.

Towns and villages.

205. The statement below displays some of the most prominent facts regarding the distribution of the population over towns and villages :

District.	Towns.			Villages.					
	Number.	Population.	Percentage to total population of district.	Number.	Population.	Percentage to total population of district.	Average number of persons per village.	Average number of acres per village.	Proximity or average distance between each village, in miles.
Cachar (plains)	1	7,523	2·9	635	500,010	98·0	575	2,475	2·11
Sylhet	5	27,205	1·2	6,717	2,127,268	98·8	320	531	0·98
Goálpára	2	16,265	2·2	1,098	442,622	97·8	411	2,230	2·03
Kamrup	2	20,159	3·1	1,503	614,090	96·9	404	1,194	1·64
Darrang	1	4,041	1·3	1,116	303,693	98·7	273	1,358	1·87
Nowgong ..	1	4,815	1·3	909	339,326	98·7	378	2,501	2·03
Sibságar	3	9,019	2·1	1,306	447,953	97·9	349	1,595	1·58
Lakhimpur ..	1	9,576	2·8	782	234,177	96·2	324	3,042	2·34
North Cachar ..	..	....	....	216	18,947	100·0	90	5,205	3·08
Nágá Hills ..	1	1,781	1·4	649	121,086	98·6	191	5,704	3·20
Khási and Jaintia Hills	1	6,720	2·2	1,729	191,184	96·7	113	2,603	2·29
Gáro Hills ..	..	....	....	1,905	121,570	100·0	129	2,082	1·93
North Lushai Hills	..	....	....	29	42,633	100·0	1594·5	....	....
Total	18	102,074	1·8	17,149	5,324,789	98·2	313·54	....	....

The urban population is extremely small, being only 1·8 per cent. of the total population of the province. The corresponding percentage in Bengal amounts to 5·3, in Bombay to 17·8, and in England and Wales to 66·6. The reasons for the absence of large towns in Assam are that the country is still very sparsely populated; there are no large industries to encourage the growth of towns, and the main occupation of the great bulk of the people is agriculture. The figures regarding the number of villages are of very little statistical value, as the definition adopted for census purposes in the different districts was far from uniform. In the cadastrally-surveyed portions of the Brahmaputra Valley and Cachar, the area which formed the revenue survey village was taken as a "village"; elsewhere it was taken to be a group of houses bearing a separate name, outlying hamlets being included in, or excluded from, the parent village according to the requirements of the work of enumeration. The total number of "villages" returned is 17,160, and the average population per village is 319. Nearly half of the population reside in villages containing from 200 to 499 persons, and nearly half of the remainder in villages containing more than 500 and less than 1,000; 13 per cent. of the people live in hamlets, where there are less than 200 persons, and only 19 per cent. in places of which the population exceeds 1,000.

Variations in the population.

CENSUS.

206. The next statement shows the variations in the population which have taken place since the previous census:

District.	Population, 1891.				Population, 1881.				Percentage of increase or decrease.			
	Total.	District-born.	Immigrants. From other districts.	From other provinces.	Total.	District-born.	Immigrants. From other districts.	From other provinces.	Total.	District-born.	Immigrants. From other districts.	From other provinces.
Cachar	365,542	249,565	25,380	92,597	293,728	190,831	21,667	78,949	+25·1	+30·6	+2·8	+18·6
Sylhet	2,154,723	2,033,631	5,882	115,070	1,962,009	1,922,604	5,756	41,249	+9·4	+5·8	+2·3	+178·9
Goálpára... ...	452,304	401,827	5,538	45,139	416,292	405,276	997	22,959	+1·36	—4·8	+435·4	+95·5
Kámrup	634,049	616,949	6,688	11,412	644,960	635,627	2,448	5,885	+1·6	—3·2	+173·2	+93·9
Darrang	307,761	251,290	47,765	11,596	273,833	251,134	18,972	3,727	+12·6	......	+143·6	+213·14
Nowgong ...	341,141	319,487	7,755	16,889	310,279	297,463	3,568	9,248	+10·81	+7·22	+131·41	+82·30
Sibságar... ...	457,974	354,924	13,067	89,983	370,274	314,129	3,629	52,516	+23·49	+12·76	+259·62	+71·31
Lakhimpur ...	254,053	164,012	8,404	80,737	175,893	135,457	3,619	40,587	+44·42	+21·71	+132·21	+97·05
Naga Hills ...	...	...	...	...	...	...	...	...	...	...	...	...
Khási and Jaintia Hills.	197,004	191,119	3,857	2,898	169,300	165,873	1,707	2,280	+16·65	+15·55	+125·3	+27·1
Garo Hills ...	121,570	107,645	5,853	8,072	109,518	98,077	3,088	8,323	+10·95	+9·76	+80·7	+1·96
Total of the Province (excluding the Naga Hills*).	5,291,391	4,689,588	127,020	474,714	4,686,426	4,402,361	67,801	265,364	+11·90	+5·7	+87·4	+78·93

* Details for 1881 are not available in the case of the Naga Hills.

The general result of the statistics for the different districts appears to be that the population of the eastern portion of the province is advancing far more rapidly than that of the western districts. The natural increase in Cachar is more than three times as great as in Sylhet. In the Brahmaputra Valley, Goálpára shows a considerable decrease in its natural population, and so also does Kámrúp, though to a less extent. The population of Darrang is stationary, that of Nowgong is growing at the rate of 10 per thousand per annum, and that of Sibságar at the annual rate of 11·5 per thousand, while in Lakhimpur the rate reaches 17·3 per thousand, which is approximately the same as in Cachar, the eastern district of the Surma Valley. The growth of the population in the hill districts cannot be stated with any degree of accuracy. The total increase in the people of the province is contributed to by all districts except Kámrúp and the North Cachar subdivision, where there is a decrease of 10,711 and 1,179, respectively, due, in the former case, to the prevalence of *kála-azár*, which also accounts for the comparatively small increase in Goálpára, and, in the latter, to the migrations of Kacháris and other tribes. The largest additions to the population are in Sylhet (185,584), Sibságar (87,000), Lakhimpur (74,160), and Cachar plains (73,804). The largest percentage of increase is in Lakhimpur (41·22), Sibságar (23·49), and Cachar (25·12), in all of which districts immigration, due to the extension of the tea industry, accounts for the greater part of the excess of the present figures over those of 1881. Excluding the Nága Hills, where the increase is mainly due to the inclusion of the newly-formed Mokokchang subdivision, the Khási and Jaintia Hills district furnishes the largest proportional increase (16·85 per cent.) amongst the districts in which tea is not largely cultivated. The population of the lower portion of the Brahmaputra Valley, where the land is not very favourable to tea cultivation, and which has, moreover, suffered considerably from *kála-azár*, has been stationary, the nominal increase in Goálpára and Mangaldai being more than counterbalanced by the decrease in Kámrúp.

207. The increase in the number of immigrants from other
provinces is remarkable. The number of
*Immigration and emi-
gration.*
persons born elsewhere is 510,672, against
280,710 in 1881, being an increase of nearly
82 per cent. in the course of the decade. It has been estimated
that out of the total number of immigrants, about 424,000, or 83
per cent., are probably persons who originally came to the province
as garden coolies, and that of the remainder, some 61,000, or
nearly 12 per cent., are cultivators from adjacent districts of
Bengal. The Census Superintendent calculates that, on the average, an annual immigration of close upon 39,000 persons must
have taken place, in order to keep up the number of immigrants
censused in Assam in 1881 and to produce the increase over that
number which has been recorded at the present census.

The loss to the province by emigration during the inter-censal
interval has been very slight. The total number of persons born
in Assam who were censused in other provinces in 1881 was
41,038, and the number has now risen to 43,611, so that the
net increase of persons born in the province, who have emigrated
during the decade, over the number of such persons who were
absent in 1881, but have since returned, is only 2,573. The total
net emigration of persons born in Assam is, therefore, represented
by this figure, *plus* the number required to keep up the
emigrant population of 1881, which, at the assumed death-rate
of 35 per thousand, would involve an annual exodus of 1,687
persons.

208. The distribution of the population according to the religion returned by them is given below :

Religions. District.	Hindu.		Musalman.		Christian.		Animistic.		Buddhist.		Others.	
	Number.	Percentage.	Number.	Percentage.	Number.	Percentage.	Number.	Percentage.	Number.	Percentage.	Number.	Percentage.
Cachar (plains) ...	239,934	65·28	112,846	30·70	809	·22	13,899	3·78	2	·0007	52	·01
Sylhet ...	1,016,068	47·15	1,123,984	52·16	643	·02	13,818	·64	8	·0003	72	·003
Goálpára ...	209,482	46·31	124,455	27·51	1,632	·36	116,112	25·67	112	·02	511	·11
Kámrúp ...	445,197	70·19	55,350	8·72	948	·14	131,759	20·77	613	·12	182	·02
Darrang ...	195,937	63·66	18,454	5·99	849	·27	91,870	29·85	519	·16	132	·04
Nowgong ...	214,260	62·26	14,137	4·10	417	·12	115,044	33·42	49	·011	234	·06
Síbságar ...	418,725	91·56	19,805	4·33	1,365	·29	16,243	3·55	987	·21	149	·03
Lakhimpur ...	227,234	69·44	8,086	3·18	1,606	·63	12,546	4·93	4,462	1·75	119	·04
North Cachar ...	8,221	43·40	15	·07	1	·005	10,704	56·51	...	...	...	...
Nága Hills ...	4,438	3·61	209	·17	231	·18	117,007	95·71	350	·29	22	·01
Khási and Jaintia Hills ...	4,567	2·30	820	·41	7,144	3·60	185,364	93·66	21	·001	7	·003
Gáro Hills ...	11,393	9·37	5,597	4·60	1,184	·97	103,004	84·72	393	·32	...	...
North Lushai Hills (Civil and Military)	1,607	78·62	216	10·56	15	·73	205	10·03	...	...	1	·002
North Lushai Hills (estimated)	...	...	...	...	...	...	41,590	100·00	...	...	...	...
Total for the Province ...	2,997,072	54·72	1,483,974	27·09	16,844	·30	969,765	17·70	7,697	·14	1,481	·20

Speaking generally, it may be said that nearly 55 per cent. of the total population profess the Hindu religion, that 27·09 are Muhammadans, 0·30 Christians, and 0·14 Buddhists, while 17·70 per cent. consist of persons whose tenets have been described as Animistic. Under the head "Others" are included the Jains, who are all immigrants, and also a few Theists and Agnostics. The Hindu religion predominates most largely in Sibságar and Lakhimpur, where the influence of the Vaishnava Gosains is greatest. It includes amongst its adherents more than half the population of Cachar, Kámrúp, Darrang, and Nowgong, and slightly less than half of the people living in Sylhet and Goálpára. In the hill districts, the number of Hindus is nominal. The prevalence of the Muhammadan religion is precisely that which one would expect from the previous history of the province. Musalmans constitute slightly more than half of the population of Sylhet and very nearly one-third of the population of the Cachar and Goálpára districts. Higher up the Brahmaputra Valley, the proportion of Musalmans steadily decreases, while in the hill districts the number is almost nominal. There has been very little change during the decade in the proportion which Musalmans bear to the total population. In 1881 the percentage was 26·98, and it is now 27·09. The primitive beliefs of the different Mongolian tribes have been classed together under one head, "Animistic," partly because too little is known about them to enable any more minute classification to be adopted, and partly because their general characteristics are everywhere much the same. The following description of them is taken from the last Census Report :

There is a vague but very general belief in some one omnipotent being, who is well disposed towards men, and whom, therefore, there is no necessity for propitiating. Then come a number of evil spirits, who are ill-disposed towards human beings, and to whose malevolent interference are ascribed all the woes which afflict mankind. To them, therefore, sacrifices must be offered. These malevolent spirits are sylvan deities, spirits of the trees the rocks and the streams, and sometimes also of the tribal ancestors. There is no regular priesthood, but some persons are supposed to be better endowed with the power of divination than others. When a calamity occurs, one or more of these diviners, *shamans*, or soothsayers, is called on to ascertain the particular demon who is offended, and who requires to be pacified by a sacrifice. This is done either by devil-dancing, when the diviner works himself into a paroxysm of drunkenness and excitement, and then holds converse with the unseen spirits around him, or by the examination of omens,—eggs, grains of rice, or the entrails of a fowl. There is a profound belief in omens of all sorts ; no journey is undertaken unless it is ascertained that the fates are propitious, while persons who have started on a journey will turn back, should adverse omens be met with on the way. One peculiarity in connection with their sacrifices may be mentioned. On all necessary occasions goats, fowls, and other animals are offered to the gods ; but it is always assumed that the latter will be contented with the blood and entrails ; the flesh is divided amongst the sacrificer and his friends, the presiding soothsayer usually getting the lion's share.

The great majority of the people in the hill districts are still animistic, and so also are from 20 to 30 per cent. of the population of Kámrúp, Darrang, and Nowgong. Elsewhere the number are comparatively small, owing to the proselytising influence of Hinduism, which has almost effaced the identity of the non-Aryan constituents of the Surma Valley population, and is rapidly doing the same in Upper Assam, where the Vaisnava Gosains are especially active, and the observances which they enforce in the case of new converts are few and light. Owing to defects in the form in which information on the subject was collected in 1881, it is impossible to furnish figures to show at what rate the process of conversion is proceeding to-day, but there is no doubt that it is steadily going on.

CENSUS.   The figures for Christians are given in greater detail below:

District.	Number of Christians.						Percentage on total population.	
	1881.		1891.				1881.	1891.
	Europeans and Eurasians.	Natives.	Europeans and Eurasians.			Natives.		
			Total.	Europeans.	Eurasians.			
Cachar (plains) ..	291	476	321	273	48	488	·26	·22
Sylhet ..	115	264	387	278	109	256	·04	·02
Goalpara ..	121	392	85	52	33	1,547	·11	·06
Kamrup ..	101	265	72	52	20	876	·05	·14
Darrang ..	176	235	207	183	24	642	·13	·27
Nowgong ..	50	2·4	63	63		554	·08	·12
Sibsagar ..	342	462	317	274	43	1,048	·21	·29
Lakhimpur ..	227	610	363	305	58	1,243	·46	·63
North Cachar ..			1	1		..	..	·005
Naga Hills ..	22	3	20	20		211	·02	·18
Khasi and Jaintia Hills ..	212	1,430	203	164	33	6,941	1·24	3·60
Garo Hills ..	14	656	30	21	9	1,154	·61	·97
North Lushai Hills (Civil and Military) ..		..	13	13		2	..	·73
Total for the Province ..	1,631	5,462	2,092	1,609	383	14,762	·14	·30

In Assam there are several missions. Judging by their results, the most important of these is that of the Welsh Calvinistic Methodists already referred to, who for many years past have been working amongst the Khásis. This race appears to be more than usually receptive of Christianity, and the number of Christians amongst them has risen from 1,895 in 1881 to 6,941 at the census taken two years ago. The next missions to be mentioned are those of the American Baptists, who have stations at Tura, Gauháti, Nowgong, Sibságar, and Mokokchang. A fair amount of success has attended their efforts, and the number of native Baptists now reported amounts to 3,718, against 1,475 at the previous census. Census. The greater part of the increase is found in Goálpára and the Gáro Hills. In Nowgong the number is almost stationary, the increase during the last ten years being only 29, or less than three new converts a year. Next, in point of numbers, come the missions of the Society for the Propagation of the Gospel, whose converts have risen from 640 to 1,324. There is a small colony of Sonthals of the Lutheran Church in Goálpára ; but this is rather a settlement of persons converted to Christianity elsewhere than a centre of mission work in the generally accepted use of the term. The total number of native Christians has risen during the last ten years from 5,462 to 14,762. A small proportion of the increase is due to the immigration of Christian Uriyas and Sonthals, but by far the greater part is the result of the labours of the missionaries of different denominations within the province.

The other religions may be dismissed in a few words. The persons shown as Bhuddhists in Sibságar, Lakhimpur, and the Nága Hills are chiefly the descendants of persons who immigrated from the Hukong valley about a hundred years ago ; those in Kámrúp and Darrang are Bhutias, of whom numbers visit these districts every cold weather ; and those in Goálpára and the Gáro Hills are the relics of the Burmese occupation at the beginning of the century.

209. The age statistics have been discussed in the Census Report, and it would be superfluous to reproduce them here. It will suffice to say that an examination of the figures recorded seems to indicate a birth-rate of 49 and a death-rate of 42 per thousand, and an average duration of life of rather less than 24 years ; but the age returns are so unreliable that it would be unsafe to accept these figures as anything more than a rough approximation to the truth. Assuming that men are fit for work between the age of 15 and 59, and women from 15 to 44, it has been calculated that 63 per cent. of the male and 46 per cent. of the female population of the province are capable of adding to the material prosperity of the community.

210. The proportion of the married, single, and widowed of each sex per ten thousand of the population in the different districts is as follows :

Marriage.

District.	Unmarried.		Married.		Widowed.	
	Males.	Females.	Males.	Females.	Males.	Females.
Cachar (plains)	5,337·0	4,040·5	4,326·7	1,480·7	336·3	1,420·8
Sylhet	5,932·1	3,786·9	3,849·5	4,147·2	318·6	2,065·9
Goálpára	5,234·1	3,928·2	4,368·3	4,261·7	367·6	1,897·1
Kamrúp	5,620·2	4,273·4	3,911·4	3,996·6	468·4	1,730·0
Darrang	5,553·4	4,379·1	4,050·8	4,228·8	386·8	1,392·1
Nowgong	5,527·4	4,864·3	3,679·9	3,815·6	49·7	1,272·1
Sibságar	5,607·1	4,701·4	3,768·5	4,081·7	621·4	1,217·9
Lakhimpur	5,405·9	4,620·9	4,019·1	4,246·0	575·0	1,133·1
North Cachar	5,867·2	5,073·2	3,759·9	3,517·4	372·9	1,409·4
Naga Hills	5,031·7	4,186·1	4,521·5	4,493·5	446·8	1,310·4
Khasi and Jaintia Hills ..	5,697·7	4,669·0	3,978·4	3,932·7	323·9	1,398·3
Garo Hills	5,362·9	4,242·1	4,505·9	4,882·6	232·2	865·3
North Lushai Hills (Civil and Military)	5,281·9	....	4,505·8	....	212·4	....
Total of the Province ..	5,915·5	4,024·4	5,065·9	4,970·1	2,019·1	7,909·8

The proportions of the married, single, and widowed at the different age periods and amongst the various religions have been fully discussed in the Census Report, and it is unnecessary to discuss the subject further here.

211. The census returns deal with four infirmities,—insanity, deaf-mutism, blindness, and leprosy.

Infirmities.

Infirmity.	Total number afflicted.						Average number of persons of whom one is afflicted.		Average number of females to 100 males afflicted.
	1891.			1881.			1891.	1881.	
	Total.	Males.	Females.	Total.	Males.	Females.			
Insanity ..	3,022	1,737	1,285	1,318	919	399	1,396·5	3,215·6	74
Deaf-mutism ..	4,691	2,693	1,998	2,578	1,629	949	1,161·3	1,855·4	74
Blindness ..	5,832	3,031	2,801	3,210	1,846	1,364	951·9	1,520·6	92
Leprosy ..	6,727	5,128	1,599	3,313	2,408	905	807·9	1,472·9	31

The large increase in the total number of persons afflicted is attributed to better enumeration and a more perfect system of tabulation, rather than to any spread of these infirmities during the decade. The figures for insanity and leprosy show that these infirmities are more prevalent in Assam than in most parts of India, but the number of the insane is nevertheless far lower than that recorded in European countries. The proportion of deaf-mutes is much the same in Assam as in other Indian provinces, while that of the blind is considerably smaller, the reasons for the latter result being apparently the dampness of the climate and a less general prevalence of small-pox.

The high proportion of lepers is somewhat unexpected; the liability of the people to this loathsome complaint was first noticed in a report by the Civil Surgeon of Sibságar to Mr. Mills, on his visit to the province in 1853.

212. The census returns display a great variety of language.

Languages.

The province is peopled by numerous different tribes, and each tribe has its own peculiar dialect. The list of languages is further swollen by the various tongues spoken by the large immigrant population. The indigenous languages may all be classed under four main families, between the individual members of which verbal and grammatical resemblances are sufficiently numerous, and the differences are, generally speaking, not more marked than one would have anticipated from the former isolation of the different tribes and the fact that their languages are, as a rule, unwritten. First come two languages of the Aryan family, Bengali and Assamese, the former being spoken by some two and three quarter millions of people, residing chiefly in the Surma Valley and Goálpára, while the latter is the parent tongue of nearly one and a half millions in the five upper districts of the Brahmaputra Valley. Next to be mentioned is the Assam branch of the great family of Tibeto-Burman languages, which, with the exception of the small Khási family, includes all the tongues spoken by the Non-Aryan tribes whose residence in the province dates from pre-historic times. More than 800,000 persons still speak languages of this stock, chief amongst which may be reckoned Kachari, spoken by 200,000 persons, Gáro, spoken by 120,000, and Manipuri, by 72,000. These languages have been

CENSUS.   classified into groups, of which, so far as our knowledge at present
extends, that known as the Bodo group is the most homogeneous,
and at the same time the largest, containing, as it does, more than
half the total number of persons returned as speaking one or other
of the Tibeto-Assam languages.   One of the most interesting
pieces of information derived from the returns of the last census
is the proof afforded us that these languages, especially those of the
Bodo group, are rapidly dying out.   Two Bodo dialects (Moran
and Chutiya) have entirely disappeared from the realms of spoken
speech ; and Koch, Rabha, Kachari, and Lalung are also showing
signs of a rapidly approaching extinction.   It is only in the hills,
where contact with other languages is very slight, that these dialects
still retain their hold over the tribes to which they belong.   The
Khási family, referred to above, consists of Khási and three allied
dialects (Synteng, Dyko, and Langam), which are spoken in all by
over 178,000 people.   This family is noteworthy as being altogether
distinct from the Tibeto-Burman dialects spoken from the tribes
around it, and in fact from all other non-Aryan languages in India.
No allied language is known anywhere, except perhaps that spoken
in Anam.   The only family remaining to be referred to is the Shan,
of which several dialects are spoken in this province by people whose
ancestors immigrated within comparatively recent years.   The older
Shán settlers (the Ahoms and many of the Noras) have abandoned
their ancestral forms of speech, and now talk Assamese, while the
Turungs, another Shan tribe, speak the language of the Singphos.

213. The number of castes and tribes returned at the census
is very great, and only a very brief reference
can be made to the subject here.   The
following table shows the strength of the professional classes under
which the castes were tabulated :

Caste.

Class.	Strength.	Percentage on total population.
Class A.—Agricultural	2,465,767	45·02
,, B.—Professional	245,669	4·43
,, C.—Commercial	11,086	·20
,, D.—Artizan	1,089,632	20·04
,, E.—Vagrant and minor artizans	24,671	·47
,, F.—Races and nationalities ...	1,598,418	29·40

Each class was subdivided into groups, but space forbids a detailed examination of the scheme. It may, however, be said that the most numerous Hindu castes included in class A are the Kalita (222,606), Halwa Das (143,536), Koch and Rajbansi (377,807), Kewat (91,129), and Kaibartta (67,324), and that the aboriginal hill tribes, which number in all 1,188,974, are also classified under the same head. Chief amongst these tribes are the Kacharis (243,378), the Gáros (119,754), the Khásis (117,891), the Mikirs (94,829), the Meches (70,201), the Chutiyas (87,691), the Rabhas (69,774), the Lálungs (52,423), the Syntengs (51,739), and the different Nága tribes, numbering in all 102,085. Class B includes 102,569 Brahmans, 92,395 Káyasthas, and 23,739 Ganaks. Class C is almost entirely composed of immigrants belonging to the different Baniya castes. In class D, group 40—"Fishermen, Boatmen, and Palki bearers"—is numerically the most important; it includes 205,053 Doms, 180,539 Chandáls, and 58,100 Máhimals, the last mentioned being a Musalman fishing caste of Sylhet. Other important castes in class D are the following:

Jugi	...	...		177,746
Shaha		...	...	51,971
Bhuimáli	...	...	...	50,940
Teli	...	...	...	...	35,624
Nápit	...	...	...	...	32,989
Kámár	...	...	...	...	29,654
Kumar	...	...		25,441
Dhoba	...	...	...	24,299

In class F have been included—non-Asiatic foreigners (1,698) [amongst whom English (1,381) and Europeans unspecified (237) are the most numerous], Eurasians (383), Christian converts (14,756), and "non-Indian Asiatic races" (1,573,237). The last mentioned group is artificially swollen by the inclusion in it of all Musalmans who described themselves as Sheikh (1,377,015), Saiad (12,127), Moghal (2,126), or Páthán (13,088). It is well known

CENSUS. that the vast majority of the persons thus returned have no foreign blood in their veins, and are simply natives of the country, who have assumed these titles on conversion to Muhammadanism ; and it would, therefore, have been more correct ethnologically, had these persons been classified under some other head. Their entry under this head was made under instructions laid down for the whole of India by the Census Commissioner. It should be mentioned that the Ahoms (153,528), Khamtis (3,040), and other tribes of Shán extraction have been included in this class, as the country from which their ancestors emigrated lies outside the British boundary.

214. The occupations returned at the census were classified under seven classes, twenty-four orders, and seventy-seven sub-orders. The following statement exhibits the distribution of the people per 1,000 over the seven main classes in the province generally, in town and country and in the three principal divisions,—the Surma Valley the Brahmaputra Valley, and the hill districts :

Occupation.

Class.		Total population.			Surma Valley.	Brahmaputra Valley.	Hill districts.
		Total.	Town.	Country.	Total.	Total.	Total.
A—Government	..	8·49	131·69	0·13	10·43	8·33	14·15
B—Pasture and agriculture	..	777·85	131·02	790·23	699·79	849·51	823·83
C—Personal and domestic services	..	16·37	94·31	14·48	22·30	12·14	6·49
D—Preparation and supply of material substances	..	127·38	368·89	121·75	184·27	81·95	67·82
E—Commerce	..	16·26	112·54	11·42	20·95	13·23	6·81
F—Professions	..	19·10	73·45	15·07	29·09	12·67	4·18
G—Indefinite occupation	..	34·55	88·41	22·52	31·07	25·18	86·72
Total ..	..	1,000	1,000	1,000	1,000	1,000	1,000

Taking the province as a whole, 777 persons in every 1,000, or nearly four-fifths of the total population, derive their support directly from agriculture, and 127, or rather more than one-eighth, from the preparation and supply of material substances. Only 19 per thousand are returned as belonging to the professional class, and only 16 to the commercial. The proportion of persons supported by personal and domestic services is also 16 per 1,000. Government employment supports 8 per 1,000.

In the proportional statement given in the margin, persons who combine agriculture with some other non-agricultural occupation have been shown under the latter. The number of persons in each class who combine the occupation under which they have been classified with some means of livelihood connected with the soil, and the proportion which they bear to the total strength of the class, are

Class.	Total number of persons in each class.	Total number of persons in each class combined with agriculture.	Number in 1,000 persons.
A—Government	46,144	16,653	360·59
B—Pasture and agriculture	15,623	2,578	165·05
C—Personal services	85,955	28,915	334·34
D—Preparation and supply of material substances	692,312	335,973	485·29
E—Commerce, transport, and storage	89,393	30,506	345·12
F—Profession	101,858	42,405	406·37
G—Indefinite and Independent	187,785	23,700	126·25
Total	1,222,956	480,740	393·08

shown in the margin. More than a third of the persons employed under Government, in commercial pursuits, and in the profession, are also partly dependent for their subsistence upon agriculture, and the same remark is true of nearly half the total number of persons in class D. Out of the total population shown as following non-agricultural occupations, no less than 480,740, or 39 per cent., derive a portion of their sustenance from cultivation. If these be added to those already shown under "Agriculture" in the table, the number of persons connected with the soil rises to 4,692,997, or 86·34 per cent. of the total population. Assuming that, on the whole, these persons are supported by agriculture and their other occupations in equal proportions, the former is found to be the means of subsistence of 82·2 per cent. of the people.

Turning to the distribution by classes in the three main divisions of the province, the proportion of persons supported by Government service is highest in the hill districts, where the regiments and police battalions form a comparatively large proportion of the population, and is next highest in the Surma Valley, where out of a total of 26,568 persons in this class, 18,155 are members of the rural police force and their families.

The proportion of persons whose occupations are purely agricultural is highest in the Brahmaputra Valley, where it amounts to

CENSUS. 819 per thousand. In the hill districts, it is somewhat lower, owing to the figures for the Khási and Jaintia Hills, where a large number of persons were returned as general labourers. It is lowest in the Surma Valley, which is the most advanced portion of the province, and in which the smaller number of agriculturists is partly due to a larger number of persons engaged in the preparation and supply of material substances, and partly to the fact that many cultivators follow also other occupations, and have thus been entered under the latter.

Next to the large proportion of cultivators, the primitive condition of the people of this province is best illustrated by the exceptionally small number of persons engaged on personal and domestic services. In the hill districts only 6 persons per thousand, and in the Brahmaputra Valley only 12 per thousand, derive their support from this source, while in Sylhet and Cachar the ratio only rises to 22 per thousand.

The number of persons engaged in the preparation and supply of material substances is 184 per thousand in the Surma Valley; in the Brahmaputra Valley it falls to 81, and in the hill districts to 57 per thousand.

The commercial and professional classes are small everywhere, but are better represented in Sylhet and Cachar than in the Brahmaputra Valley, and in the latter than in the hill districts.

CHAPTER VII.

Frontier Relations and Feudatory States.

215. The only Feudatory States with which the Assam FRONTIER RELATIONS. Administration has political relations are Manipur and the petty States in the Khási Hills. Of the latter, sufficient has already been said in Chapter II, Section 5, of this report. A list of these States, their population, revenue, and the names of their rulers will be found among the statistical tables appended (Part I, Tables B1 and 2).

Feudatory States.

216. Manipur is a protected State lying between Burma on the east, the Nága Hills on the north, Cachar on the west, and the Lushai Hills and the country of the Sukte Kukis on the south. It is almost entirely a hill country, the exception being the valley of Manipur in its centre. Its area is between 7,000 and 8,000 square miles, and its population, according to the census of 1881,* 221,070 souls. Of these, 85,288 are returned as hill tribes, the remainder being by religion Hindu or Muhammadan, and consisting of the population of the valley of Manipur, in which is situated the capital of the State. The claim of the Manipuris to be Hindus, however, rests on no better foundation than the same claim on the part of Ahoms, Kacharis, or Tipperas (with all of whom the Manipur ruling family has intermarried); and while their features clearly show that they belong to the Indo-Chinese stock, their language is closely allied to those of the Kuki tribes which border them on the south.†

Manipur.

---

* It was explained in the last chapter that the records of the Census taken in Manipur in 1891 were destroyed during the disturbances of the following March.

† Although the above is true of the present people of Manipur, there is some reason for believing that this territory was the road by which Hindu influence from the west was first brought to bear upon the Burmese races of the Irrawaddy Valley (see Phayre, "History of Burma," pages 3, 4, and 15).

The kingdom of Manipur first emerges from obscurity as a neighbour and ally of the Shán kingdom of Pong, which had its capital at Mogaung. The regalia of the royal family are said to have been bestowed by king Komba of Pong, who at the same time added the valley of Khambat to Manipur. In 1714 a Nága, named Pamheiba, became Rája of Manipur, and adopted Hinduism, taking the name of Gharib Nawaz. His people followed his example, and since that date have been conspicuous for the rigidity with which they observe the rules of caste and ceremonial purity. Gharib Nawaz, during his reign of forty years, was engaged in constant warfare with Burma, and this state of things continued during those of his successors. Manipur was frequently invaded by the Burmese, whose last occupation of the country began in 1819. The three Manipuri princes, Márjit, Chaurjit, and Gambhir Singh, were compelled to escape to Cachar, which country, as has already been related, they occupied. With them large numbers of Manipuris emigrated, and many of their descendants, together with emigrants of later date, are still to be found in Cachar and Sylhet.

When war was declared against Burma by the British Government in 1824, and the Burmese had been expelled from Cachar, assistance in arms and money was given by the Company to Gambhir Singh in an attempt to recover possession of Manipur. In this he was successful, occupying not only the valley in which the capital is situated, but also the Kubo Valley down to the Ningthi or Chindwin river, lying to the east of the former boundaries of the State, and peopled by Sháns (called Kabau in Manipuri). The treaty of Yandabu with Burma, executed in February 1826, declared (article II) that should Gambhir Singh desire to return to Manipur, he should be recognised by the king of Ava as Rája thereof.

Gambhir Singh being thus established on the throne, the levy with which he had effected the reconquest of his country was placed under the management of two British officers, and supplied with ammunition, and also with pay, by the British Government. In 1833 the British Government agreed to annex to Manipur the

ranges of hills on the west, between the eastern and western bends
of the Barák, giving that State the line of the Jiri and the western
bend of the Barák as its boundary, on condition that the Rája
removed all obstructions to trade between his State and Cachar,
kept in repair the road between Manipur and British territory,
and promised to assist the Government, in the event of war with
Burma, both with carriage and with troops. In 1834 Gambhir
Singh died, and his death was followed by the regency of Nar
Singh, his minister, and a great grandson of Gharib Nawaz, on
behalf of the dead king's son, Chandra Kirti Singh, then one year
old. In the same year, the British Government decided to restore
the Kubo Valley to Burma, the Government of which had never
ceased to remonstrate against its separation from that country.
The valley was given back, and a new boundary laid down in the
presence of British Commissioners by an agreement dated the 9th
January 1834, and at the same time the British Government
bound itself to pay a monthly stipend of Rs. 500 to the Rája of
Manipur in compensation for its loss. In 1835 the assistance
formerly given to the Manipur levy was withdrawn, and a Political
Agent was appointed to reside at Manipur.

In 1844 the Queen Dowager, widow of Gambhir Singh and
mother of Chandra Kirti, attempted to poison Nar Singh, the
Regent; her attempt failed, and she fled from the country with
her son. Nar Singh then assumed the *ráj* in his own name, and
ruled till his death in 1850. He was succeeded by his brother
Debendra Singh; but this prince ruled for only three months,
Chandra Kirti Singh, with the help of Nar Singh's three sons
succeeding in ejecting him and recovering possession of the
throne. This was followed by some disorder in the State; but in
February 1851 the Government of India decided upon recognising
the succession of Chandra Kirti Singh, guaranteeing the *ráj* to him
and his descendants, and preventing, by force of arms if necessary,
any attempts by rival chiefs to dislodge him.

In 1851 Debendra Singh's and Nar Singh's sons attempted a
rising. In 1852 another attempt occurred, led by Kanhai Singh,
son of Márjit, Gambhir Singh's brother. In 1857 some of the

rebellious sepoys from Chittagong, who had found their way to Cachar, were used by one Narendrajit, a younger son of Chaurjit, to raise a disturbance. Narendrajit was transported. In 1859 Maipák, a descendant of Gharib Nawaz, invaded the valley, but was defeated and fled. In 1862 he again, in conjunction with another Rajputra, named Khaifa Singh, headed an attack, and penetrated to the Rája's palace, where he was captured. Kanhai Singh made another attempt in 1865, when his followers were attacked and dispersed by British troops and police. Another raid was perpetrated by Gokul Singh, a younger son of Debendra Singh, in 1866. His enterprise failed, like the rest, but he escaped for the time. He was captured in 1868, tried in Cachar, and sentenced to seven years' imprisonment.

In the Nága war of 1879 the Mahárája of Manipur distinguished himself by rendering loyal assistance to the British Government. He furnished a force, which under the leadership of the Political Agent, Colonel (now Sir James) Johnstone, raised the siege of Kohima by the Nágas, and prevented a great catastrophe. In recognition of this service the Government of India bestowed upon the Mahárája Chandra Kirti Singh the dignity of K.C.S.I. Another series of events, which gave occasion for much correspondence, was the raids of certain Kukis known as Chasads on the eastern frontier of Manipur territory. It was believed that these raids were abetted by the Shán *Tsawbwa*, or chief of Samjok in the Kubo Valley; and, as there was much indefiniteness in the frontier north of the Kubo Valley proper as set forth in the agreement of 1834, it was determined by the Government of India to send a Commission to define and demarcate the boundary of Manipur in this direction. This task was accomplished in the cold weather of 1881-82, and the Burmese Government (who were invited to co-operate in the demarcation, but did not do so) were informed that the boundary so laid down would be maintained by the Government of India. The raiding Kukis, who were favoured in their enterprise by the uncertainty of the frontier, were found to be settled within Manipur territory, and some of them were induced to move further in, and were thus brought under stricter control.

On the death of Chandra Kirti Singh in 1886, Bara Chauba the eldest son of Nar Singh, who had been Maháraja from 1844 to 1850, made an attempt to get possession of the *gadi*, but was eventually defeated by a detachment of the Cachar Military Police, after which he gave himself up, and was deported with his relatives to Hazaribagh.

The last event to be recorded in the history of this State is the terrible disaster which took place in March 1891. In September 1890 the Maháraja Sura Chandra Singh was driven from his palace by his two youngest brothers, at the instigation of the Senapati, Tekendrajit Singh, and took refuge with the Political Agent. Notwithstanding the advice given by the latter, he declared his intention of abdicating, and left Manipur for Brindaban. On reaching British territory, he repudiated any intention of abdicating, and requested the assistance of the Government of India to regain the *gadi*. The Government of India, after duly considering the matter, decided that the Jubraj should be confirmed as Rája, but that the turbulent Senapati should be removed from Manipur. To carry out this decision, Mr. Quinton, who was then Chief Commissioner, proceeded to Manipur early in 1891 with an escort, and ordered the Senapati to surrender himself. This he refused to do. Troops were sent to arrest him in his house in the palace enclosure. They were fiercely attacked by the Manipuris, and the engagement continued until the evening, when an armistice was agreed to, and firing temporarily ceased. The Chief Commissioner and four other officers were then induced, under a promise of safe conduct, to enter the "Pat" and hold a Darbar in the Darbar hall at the entrance to the Rája's citadel. No agreement being found possible, the officers started to return to the Residency ; but on the way the crowd closed in on them, and the Political Agent, Mr. Grimwood, was fatally speared and Lieutenant Simpson severely wounded. The Chief Commissioner and his companions were then kept prisoners for two hours, after which they were marched to the green space in front of the dragons, and there beheaded by the public executioner. The attack on the Residency was then resumed, and the

FRONTIER RELATIONS. defenders, thinking it untenable, retreated to Cachar. These events took place on the 24th March. On the 27th April the place was entered by three columns of British troops, marching from Silchar, Kohima, and Tammu. The Regent and his brothers had fled the night before, together with the Tangkhul Major, the Senapati, and other persons implicated in the outrage, but all were subsequently captured. The Senapati, Tangkhul Major, and some others were sentenced to death and executed, and the Regent and his brothers were transported for life. The future of the State had then to be considered, and it was eventually decided by the Government of India to regrant the State and to place upon the throne a youth named Chura Chand, a scion of a collateral line. During his minority the administration of the State is to be conducted by the Political Agent, and numerous reforms, including the introduction of better judicial tribunals, the abolition of the system of *lalup*, or forced labour, etc., have already been effected.

The Political Agent in Manipur was till 1879 only partly under the control of the Chief Commissioner, with whom he corresponded only in regard to matters connected with Assam and its frontier, but in that year he was made directly subordinate to the Chief Commissioner. On the regrant of the State in 1891, his designation was changed to " Political Agent and Superintendent of the State. "

217. The frontier States and tribes which adjoin the province of Assam, commencing at the north-west corner, are the following :

Frontier States and tribes.

(1) Bhutan,
(2) Bhutias subject to Thibet,
(3) Independent Bhutias,
(4) Akas,
(5) Daflas,
(6) Miris,
(7) Abors,
(8) Mishmis,
(9) Khamtis,
(10) Singphos,
(11) Nágas,
    (here Manipur intervenes, and then follow)—
(12) Lushais, and
(13) Hill Tippera.

218. With the Deb Rája of Bhutan the Chief Commissioner, has now no direct relations. Whenever it may be necessary to communicate with him,

Bhutan.

this is done through the Commissioner of Koch Bihar, a copy of
the communication being sent at the same time to the Government
of Bengal. Although this State adjoins Assam to the north of the
districts of Goálpára, Kámrúp, and Darrang, as far east as the
Doishám river, no official intercourse other than complimentary
interviews with local officials is kept up.

On the conquest of Assam, the northern portion of Kámrúp,
consisting of the Bijni, Chappakámar, Chappaguri, Banska, and
Garkalia Duárs was found in possession of Bhutia chiefs, who
paid a tribute of Rs. 3,019 yearly to the Assam Rájas. To the
east of the Bornadi the two Duárs of Khaling and Buriguma were
held by the Bhutias for eight months of the year, and by the
Assam Rája for the remaining four (the rainy season). The payment of tribute by the Bhutia *Jungpens* during the first fifteen
years of our rule was very irregular, and the frontier was continually harassed by dacoities and outrages perpetrated on our subjects, which necessitated frequent armed reprisals. At last, in
1841, it was determined (since the possession of these tracts by
the Bhutias was of recent date) to resume the Duárs, and bring
them under British management, paying to the Bhutan Government an annual sum of Rs. 10,000 as compensation for their loss.
This sum was regularly paid until the outbreak of the Bhutan war
in 1864, when it was stopped, and the seven Assam Duárs (as
well as the five Eastern Duárs north of Goálpára, by name
Guma, Ripu, Chirang, Sidli, and Bijni, and the seven Western
Duárs north of Koch Bihar, were finally annexed to British territory.
At the same time the Fort of Diwángiri and its neighbourhood,
which commands the passage down to the bázárs of Kámrúp, was
occupied and retained as British territory.

The Bhutias come down during the cold weather for pasture
and trade into the north of Kámrúp and western Darrang, but few
of them appear to visit the thinly-peopled submontane tract of
Goálpára. Most of their trade is done at Subankhata, Kumori
Kata, and Genbári in the Kámrúp district south of Dewangiri,
and at Ghagrapara in Darrang. There are a few Bhutia settlements in British territory at the foot of the hills, but their condi-

tion is not very prosperous, and they seem to be a survival of the old days of Bhutia supremacy, rather than the beginning of a more extended immigration.

During their visits to the plains it is not uncommon to hear of exactions made by the Bhutias visiting the Kámrúp district, who take advantage of the timorous nature of the villagers to force upon them chillies and salt and extort in exchange large quantities of rice and other articles. These exactions have of late become so bad that it has been found necessary to place an additional guard at Kakolábári, the cost of which is deducted from the *posa* of the Rája.

216. The Bhutias of the Kariápára Duár, which lies east
of Bhutan Proper and extends from the Doisham to the Rota river, are dependent upon Towang, which is a dependency of the Government of Lhassa. The chiefs of this Duár, called the Sát Rájas, used, like their neighbours of Bhutan Proper, to levy dues from the inhabitants of the adjoining plains. In 1844 their claims were bought out by the British Government on payment of an annual sum of Rs. 5,000. Our relations with these people since the composition of 1844 have only once been disturbed. In 1852 one of the Gelongs, or Thibetan officials appointed from Lhassa to supervise the local chiefs, having some misunderstanding with his superiors, fled to British territory. His surrender was peremptorily demanded by the authorities of Lhassa, and a Thibetan army moved towards the frontier. A British force was assembled at Udalguri, with two guns. But no hostilities actually occurred; the Thibetans retired, the fugitive Gelong was removed to Gauháti, and the Duár was reopened for trade. This pass is specially interesting, as it is the only place in many hundred miles of Himálayán barrier where the British power is in actual contact with Thibet. The hillmen, including Thibetans from the higher ranges, resort in considerable numbers during the cold weather through this Duár to the annual fair at Udalguri, which lies due south of the gap through which the Dhansiri river issues from the hills.

Exactions, similar to those referred to in the last paragraph have occasionally been reported; but these acts of oppression are now comparatively rare. Owing to the fall in the price of salt imported from England, the Bhutias find their trade less profitable than it used to be, and the number who visit the plains is decreasing every year.

220. Next to these Bhutias subject to Towang come the Sát Rájas of Charduár, chiefs who live at villages called by the people of the plains Rúpráigáon and Shergáon. They claim to be independent of Towang, and rule the face of the hills from the Rota to the Diputa river. The Thebengia Bhutias are a distinct race and live several days' journey into the hills, but they used, in conjunction with the Sát Rájas, to levy contributions from the people of the adjacent plains. From 1839 to 1844 these people were excluded from the plains by the British Government, in punishment for outrages committed by them. On their submitting and executing a formal agreement to refrain from aggressions, they received annual pensions,—the Shergáon and Rúpráigáon Bhutias of Rs. 2,526-7 a year, and the Thebengia Bhutias of Rs. 145-13-6. They come down annually to receive their pensions at Tezpur. They also hold an annual fair at a place beyond British territory, in the gorge of the Belsiri river, called Daimára, where some trade is done with the people of the plains, which is registered by a police post at the boundary pillar on the frontier.

Independent Bhutias.

221. Next to the Bhutias come the Akas, who occupy the sub-Himálayán region as far east as the issue of the Khari-Dikarai river. This tribe is divided into two sections, called by the Assamese the Hazárikhoas and the Kapáhchors.* The former received a

Akas.

---

* The first of these names probably indicates that a thousand *gots* of *paiks*, or individual groups of revenue-payers, was set aside to provide a stipend for the tribe: *khoa* (eater) is the usual Assamese termination, indicating that a person is supported from the revenues of any place or people. *Kapáhchor* means cotton-thief, this class of Akas being famous for their night attacks, in which they lurked in the cotton-fields with a primitive sort of dark lantern, waiting their opportunity.

FRONTIER
RELATIONS.

posa * or stipend, from the Assam Rájas, and the latter levied
contributions without having any such title. Both tribes are
believed to be very limited in number ; but to the north of them is
an allied race called the Mijis, of whose strength nothing certain is
known. Though small, however, this tribe has a great reputation
for violence and audacity. For many years Tági Rája, the chief
of the Kapáhchor Akas, gave us much trouble by his robberies
and murders in the plains. In 1829 he was captured, and lodged
for four years in the Gauháti jail. In 1832 he was released, in
the hope that he had learnt a lesson, and would be quiet in future ;
but he immediately resumed his attacks, and in 1835 massacred
all the inhabitants of the British village and police outpost of
Bálipára. For seven years after this he evaded capture, his tribe
remaining outlawed in the hills. At length, in 1842, he surrendered, and it was decided to use his influence with the other chiefs
to secure the peace of the border. An agreement was made, under
which the Kapáhchor Aka chiefs receive Rs. 520 a year as pension. The Hazárikhoas receive a pension of Rs. 180. Both tribes
have certain small areas of land in the plains allotted to them for
cultivation. The Kapáhchors threatened in 1875 to give trouble,
claiming an extensive tract of forest and other land on the Bharali
river, which was cut off by the demarcation of the boundary in
1874-75. Nothing further occurred at the time, and the new
boundary was quietly accepted.

This dispute, however, coupled with one or two other grievances
of a very minor nature, is believed to have been the cause of the
acts of aggression which resulted in the expedition of 1883-84.
In October 1883, Lakhidhar mauzadár, who had visited the village
of Medhi, the Kapáhchor Aka chief, to ask him to supply articles
for the Calcutta Exhibition and to send down a man and a woman

---

* The word *posa* or *pacha* (पछ) literally means a collection or subscription for a
common purpose ; it is probably connected with the word *panch* (five), and recalls the
Mahratta *chouth*, or fourth. The word is still well understood in this sense in Upper
Assam. In its special sense of payment to a hill tribe, it strictly denotes the subscription
which the village raised in order to meet the customary demands of their visitors from
the hills, in other words, blackmail. It is not properly applicable to a fixed stipend,
paid, as in these cases, by Government in accordance with treaty ; but it has now come
to include such stipends.

to be modelled there, was forcibly detained, and shortly afterwards Medhi's brother, Chandi, carried off a clerk and forest ranger from Bálipára. A punitive expedition was despatched, and Medhi's village was occupied, the Akas taking refuge in the jungle. They gave up their captives (except Lakhidhar, who had died) and sent in some rifles and other articles which they had carried off; but the chiefs themselves did not come in before the departure of the troops, which took place only fourteen days after their arrival, and appears to have been somewhat premature. The expedition was followed by a blockade of the frontier, which was maintained until 1888, when the Aka chiefs appeared before the Deputy Commissioner and tendered their submission. Since that time they are reported to have been perfectly well behaved and contented.

222. Next to the Akas come the Daflas, who, with the Hill Miris

Daflas.

and the Abors, occupy the whole of the rest of the sub-Himálayán hills until the Mishmi country is reached. These three races speak languages which are said to be mutually intelligible, and they are evidently, though differing in arms and style of dress, nearly akin. The Daflas and Miris were, like the Akas, in receipt of *posa*, or pensionary allowance, under the Assam Government, as a condition of their refraining from aggression on the northern tracts of Darrang and Lakhimpur, and these allowances have been continued by the British Government. There are two divisions of the Daflas, one called the Paschim, or Western, Daflas, and the other the Tagin Daflas, who live to the east of these. For many years the Daflas have been quiet neighbours. Previous to 1837 their raids on the frontier were numerous, but in that year the system of annual pensions was settled. The only occasion since then when they have given trouble was in 1872 and 1873, when the Tagin Daflas broke the peace on two occasions by seizing some plains Daflas who were believed by them to have caused sickness in the hills. These outrages were punished first by a blockade ; on this proving ineffectual in obtaining the surrender of the captives, an expedition was sent into the hills north of the Dikhrang river in the cold weather of 1874-75, which was followed by the release of the prisoners and the

2 F

submission of the tribe. Since then our relations with the Daflas have been peaceful. Considerable numbers of this people, whose superstitions in regard to sickness and witchcraft lead them to frequent attacks by one village upon another, have settled in the plains of Darrang and Lakhimpur as Government ryots. The last census showed 1,137 Daflas as settled in these districts, against 549 in 1881 and 418 in 1872.

223. The Miris are a quiet and inoffensive race. They receive an annual allowance in money, salt, and rum from the North Lakhimpur treasury. It is

Miris.

believed that they stand in some sort of servile relation to the Abors, to avoid which large numbers of this people have settled in Upper Assam as British subjects. In the plains they still preserve their customs of building houses on piles, and of cultivating by *jhum* ; they are expert and fearless boatmen, and always settle on the banks of a river. Retaining their own language among themselves, they also speak Assamese, to which is due the name by which they are known in Assam (Miri, or Mili, meaning go-between or interpreter), as they act as a channel of communication with the Abors of the hills. The total number of Miris settled in Assam is 37,430, of whom all except about 3,000 are found in Sibságar and Lakhimpur.

224. The Abors, who call themselves Pádám (*Ábor* being an Assamese word designating an independent, remote, and unknown savage), occupy the

Abors.

hills east of the Miris as far as the Dibong river. They bear a very different character from the latter, and the want of population on the north bank of the Brahmaputra from opposite Dibrugarh to Sadiya is chiefly due to dread of their raids. Their principal villages are in the hills about the course of the Dihong, but several recent settlements have been founded in the plains. Murders and outrages committed by them on Government ryots, in some cases close to the headquarters station of Dibrugarh, have led to several punitive expeditions. In 1858 one was sent to punish the massacre of a Bihia village by the Bor Meyong Abors, but was not successful in its object. In 1859 a second expedition was sent, and met with better fortune. In 1861 another massacre of Bihias, a few miles from Dibrugarh, on the south side of the Brahmaputra, occurred. This was followed by preparations for establishing a line of outposts along the north bank of the Brahmaputra, connected by a road, to guard against such attacks in future. The Abors appear to have been impressed by these operations. They made overtures, which were responded to, and a meeting took place in November 1862 between them and the Deputy Commissioner. A treaty was arranged with eight communities of the tribe, promising them, on condition of good behaviour, an annual allowance of iron hoes, salt, rum, opium, and tobacco. Later, in November 1862 and in January 1863, some other powerful villages made similar agreements. The last concluded was made with the remaining communities in April 1866. All these agreements recite that the British territory extends to the foot of the hills. The allowance to the tribe is paid at the Darbár held annually at Sadiya; but on several occasions the Abors have held sulkily aloof, and have not presented themselves at the Darbár.

In 1881 it was apprehended that certain villages of Abors, who had expressed an intention to cross the Dibong river and settle upon the hills beneath those occupied by the Chulikáta Mishmis, would carry their hostilities with the latter tribe into British territory, and cut them off from access to Sadiya. The execution of this plan was prevented by the despatch of a mixed force of troops and police to occupy the post of Nizámghát, where the Dibong river issues from the hills north of Sadiya, and another lower down, opposite the Abor village of Bomjur.

In 1889 two Meyong villages combined to decoy four British subjects, Miris, beyond the Inner Line, where they murdered them, the object apparently being to establish a claim for *posa*. A fine of 20 *mithans* was imposed upon them, and the whole of the Passi and Meyong Abor frontier was blockaded pending payment. The fine was paid in less than a year, and no trouble has since been given by this tribe.

225. The Mishmis, who occupy the hills from the Dibong to the Brahmakund in the north-eastern corner of the valley, are divided into three tribes,

Mishmis.

called respectively the Chulikáta or crop-haired Mishmis, the Tain or Digáru Mishmis, and the Mizhu or Midhi Mishmis. The first named have on several occasions attacked Khámti settlements in the neighbourhood of Sadiya, and have threatened to give trouble. Of late years, however, they have become embroiled with the Abors, and have looked to the British Government for protection and assistance. They resort in considerable numbers to the Sadiya fair, and are active traders. The Digáru Mishmis are a quiet, inoffensive people, and act as guides to the pilgrims to the Brahma-kund. Of the Mizhu or Midhi Mishmis, who are the most remote of the three, we know little. In 1854 two French priests, M. M. Krick and Bourry, who endeavoured to pass through their country from Assam to Thibet, were murdered by a party of these Mishmis under a chief named Kai-i-sha. This outrage was avenged in February 1855 by an expedition under Lieutenant Eden, who with 20 Assam Light Infantry and 40 Khámti volunteers reached Kai-i-sha's village, stormed it, and took the murderer prisoner. In December 1885, Mr. F. J. Needham, Assistant Political Officer at Sadiya, accompanied by Captain E. H. Molesworth, Commandant of Military Police, and three police orderlies, succeeded in penetrating through the Mizhu Mishmi country and in entering the Thibetan province of Zayul, and thereby establishing the identity of the Sanpo with the Dibong.

The Chulikáta Mishmis were blockaded from 1884 to 1887 in consequence of the murder of an Assamese at Dikrang in revenge, it is said, for the death of a Chulikáta chief, Lako, on his return from the Calcutta Exhibition, for which the superstitious tribesmen believed the British Government to be responsible. The blockade was raised in 1887 on the payment of a fine of Rs. 2,000.

None of the Mishmi tribes receive any *posa*, nor do formal treaties or agreements with them exist.

226. The Khámtis settled about Sadiya have already been mentioned in paragraph 75 of this report.

Khámtis.

They are immigrants from a Shán State beyond the Pátkoi range, formerly tributary to Burma, and known to the Assamese as Bor Khámti. They are of the same race as the Ahoms, but differ from the latter in being Buddhists. They are a literary and cultivated people, and much more civilised than any of their neighbours, not excluding the Assamese. They first settled in Sadiya during the latter part of the eighteenth century. When the Burmese were expelled from Assam, the Khámti Gohain, or chief of Sadiya, executed an agreement of allegiance to the British Government, and Sadiya was selected as the residence of the Political Agent in Upper Assam. In 1839, after the death of the Khámti chief, with whom we made the agreement, the Khámtis of Sadiya suddenly rose, and massacred the Political Agent, Colonel White, and many of his guards and attendants. A war followed, ending in the transportation of the Khámti chief's son and his followers to a distant part of British territory. In 1843 some chiefs of this race were again allowed to settle about Sadiya ; and in 1850 a new immigration from Bor Khámti took place. The Khámtis living about Sadiya and Saikwa are British ryots, and pay revenue. Those living on the Tengápáni beyond the Inner Line acknowledge allegiance to the British Government, but pay no revenue. A small force of 24 men, known as the Khámti Volunteers, are employed for the protection of the villages about Sadiya. They receive a trifling yearly pay from Government, and have been supplied with muskets and ammunition. They patrol the paths to the north and east of Sadiya by which the Mishmis come down to that place. This force is gradually being abolished, and no new appointments are being made to replace losses by death, &c. The last census showed 3,040 Khámtis to be resident in Assam.

227. The Phákials, or Phake, are said to have left Mogaung for Assam about 1760 A.D., immediately after the subjugation of that province by Alompra.

Phákials and Turungs.

Colonel Hannay tells us that, prior to their immigration into this province, they were resident on the banks of the Turungpáni, and were thus apparently near neighbours of the Turungs. On reaching Assam, they at first settled on the banks of the Buri Dihing, whence they were brought by the Ahoms, and settled near Jorhát. When the Burmese invaded Assam, they and other Shán tribes were ordered by the Burmese authorities to return to Mogaung, and they had got as far as their old settlement on the Buri Dihing when the province was taken by the British.

Their language closely resembles that of the other northern Shans. Like the Khámtis and Turungs, they are Buddhists. They seldom marry outside their own community ; and, as this is very small, their physique is said to be deteriorating. They are adepts in the art of dyeing. The total strength of the Phákiáls is only 565 ; all of whom are found in the Sadr subdivision of the Lakhimpur district.

The Turungs immigrated into the province less than seventy years ago. Their own tradition is that they originally came from Mungmang Khaosang on the north-east of Upper Burma, and settled on the Turungpáni, whence the name by which they are now known. While there, they received an invitation from the Norás, who had preceded them and settled near Jorhát, and in consequence they started across the Pátkoi *en route* for the Brahmaputra Valley. They were, however, taken prisoners by the Singphos and made to work as slaves, in which condition they remained for five years. They were released by Captain Neufville, along with nearly 6,000 Assamese slaves, in 1825, and continued their journey to the Jorhát subdivision, where they are still settled.

228. The Singphos, who live intermixed with the Khámtis on
Singphos. the New and Old Dihings, the Tengápáni, and the mountains beyond, are, like the latter, but an outlier of the main population of the same race who occupy in force the hilly country between the Pátkoi and Chindwin river, where they are nominally subject to Burma. To the Burmese they are known as *Kakhyens*, and *Singpho* is but the word in their language meaning " man." They are, apparently, from what is known of their language, related to the Nága tribes in their neighbourhood, to whom, however, they stand distinctly in the position of masters and superiors ; where brought in contact with the Khámtis they have borrowed something of the civilisation and outward appearance of the latter, and have also in some cases been converted to Buddhism. They are, however, probably quite distinct by race.

The Singphos are recent arrivals in Assam, having made their appearance at the head of the valley during the troubles of Rája Gaurináth Singh with the Moámáriás about 1793. It was through their country that the Burmese invaders passed into Assam in 1818 and 1822 ; and the ravages of the Singphos, added to those of the Burmese, contributed greatly to the depopulation of the Matak country and Sibságar. When Assam was conquered from the Burmese, the chiefs of the Singphos, after several engagements with our troops, tendered their allegiance, and entered into agreements not to disturb the peace of the frontier. Great numbers of Assamese slaves, who had been carried off by them in the early years of the century, were released, and the wealth and power of the tribe were in this manner much reduced. In 1839 they joined the Khámtis in their attack on Sadiya ; but by 1842 they had again been brought to acknowledge their subjection. Many of the Singpho immigrants, with whom agreements were made in 1826, have since retired across the frontier into Hukong.

The Duániás, or Singpho-Assamese half-breeds (so called from the Assamese *duán* = language, because they act as interpreters), are the offspring of the intercourse between these slaves and their captors. They are chiefly settled along the Buri or Old Dihing, and are quiet subjects.

The now universal habit of opium-eating is believed to have contributed largely to the present quiet attitude of the Singphos and Khámtis. The chiefs of these people meet annually at the full moon of Mágh (in the end of January or beginning of February) at Sadiya to present themselves, with the chiefs of the Mishmi and Abor tribes, before the Political Officer, who receives their offerings, and gives them in return small presents. They pay no revenue except where settled within the Inner Line.

229. The tribes known to the Assamese as Nágas stretch un-
Nágas. interruptedly from the Pátkoi along the southern frontier of the Lakhimpur and Sibságar districts, to the valley of the Dhansiri and North Cachar. Of the Nágas in the British district of the Nága Hills (the Angámis, Kácha Nágas, Rengmás, Semás, Lhotás, and Aos) mention has already been made. Our relations with the remaining tribes are conducted through the Deputy Commissioners of Dibrugarh and Sibságar. From the Tiráp river eastward to the Pátkoi, the Nágas are com-

pletely in subjection to the Singphos, and are apparently a very
quiet race. West of this point begins a succession of groups of
villages known to the Assamese by the names of the passes or Duárs
through which their inhabitants resort to the plains,— as the Námsángias, Borduárias, Pániduárias, Mithonias, Banpheras, Jobokas,
Bhitarnámsángias, Játungias, Táblungias, Assiringias, etc. The
outer tribes of this region are in constant communication with the
plains, and in the times of the Assam Rájas used to make annual
offerings of elephants' tusks and other such articles. They do a
considerable trade in cotton and other hill produce, and carry back
large quantities of salt and rice. The inner tribes, known to the
Assamese as *Abors*, or wild men, are kept from access to the plains
by these outer or *Bori* (subject, civilised) Nágas, who thus keep the
carrying trade in their own hands. Besides, for purposes of trade,
these outer Nágas come down in considerable numbers to labour in
tea plantations and on roads during the cold weather. Unlike the
Angámis, Semás, and Lhotás, who are intensely democratic in their
social economy, many of the Eastern Nágas appear to acknowledge
the authority of Rájas and minor chiefs among themselves.

With the internal affairs of these people we hardly meddle at
all ; but they are prohibited from carrying their quarrels into the
settled British territory, and, if they do so, are tried and punished
by our courts. On this frontier, a system prevails by which
the Nágas of each group have allotted to them certain Assamese
agents, called *kotokis*, who manage small plots of revenue-free land
called *Nága kháts*, on behalf of the tribes. When the attendance
of the chiefs in the hills is required for any purpose, they are summoned through these *kotokis*. If satisfaction for robberies and
other outrages is not in this way obtained, the Duár or pass through
which the tribe visits the plains is blocked, and no one is allowed to
come down or go up. This system has rarely failed to secure
reparation : and, on the whole, the conduct of the Nágas on this
frontier, when left to themselves, has been peaceable and quiet,
so far as the settled lands of the plains are concerned. Among
themselves, however, their feuds are incessant, and are only composed to break out anew. The easternmost tribes of Borduárias

and Námsángias have thus been prosecuting a quarrel for over fifty years, each group taking, when it can, the lives and heads of some of the others. With these feuds it has not been our policy to meddle, though attempts have occasionally been made to mediate between contending tribes.

The Nága country up to the Pátkoi range is nominally British territory by inheritance from the rulers of Assam and by our treaties with Burma. It has from time to time been explored by survey parties, and on one of these occasions, in February 1875, a party sent into the hills south of Jaipur was treacherously attacked at Ninu, a village four marches from the plains up the valley of the Disang, and Lieutenant Holcombe, the Assistant Commissioner accompanying the party, with eighty coolies and followers, was killed, Captain Badgley, the survey officer, and fifty others being wounded. This was followed by a punitive expedition, by which the villages which took part in the massacre were attacked and destroyed. During the same season the survey party in the western Nága Hills was attacked by Nágas; and in December 1875 Captain Butler, the Political Agent, who was accompanying the survey party, was again attacked near the Lhota Nága village of Pángti, and received a wound of which he died a few days later. The village was at once destroyed by the force which accompanied the survey party.

230. Passing by the British district of the Nága Hills and Manipur already described, we come to the country of the Lushai Kukis lying south of Cachar.

Lushais.

From the earliest period of which we have any knowledge, the hills lying to the south of Manipur, Cachar, and eastern Sylhet have been inhabited by various tribes known to the Bengalis by the common name of Kukis. These tribes have always, so far as we know, been divided into numerous families, each family acknowledging a chief or ruling house, and these houses being generally engaged in warfare with one another. Each village had its chief, whose object it was to extend the fame and power of his village by fighting with his neighbours. As among the Gáros and

2 G

FRONTIER other wild tribes in this part of India, the gathering of heads was
RELATIONS. the object of many of these attacks and of raids upon the adjacent
plains. During the weak rule of the last Rájas of Cachar, the
valleys in the south of that district were almost depopulated by
attacks from these hillmen, and at the same time the district began
to be invaded by refugee bodies of Kukis who had been driven out
of their own country by more powerful chiefs, and sought protection
from the rulers of Cachar. Many of these communities settled
across the Baráil in North Cachar, where they were comparatively
safe from pursuit. Those who settled in the southern hills were
often followed up by their conquerors and massacred. The older
immigrants of this period (none of whom probably date from before
the beginning of the present century) are known to the Kacharis
as "old Kukis," those who have immigrated since British rule
began being called the "new Kukis." Govind Chandra is said to
have employed Kukis in his contest with Tularám Senápati, and
this no doubt increased their numbers in North Cachar.

The Kuki families whose feuds first attracted most attention,
and from whose raids we suffered during the first years of British
rule, were the Thángams, Changsels, Thadois, and Poitus. The
Lushais* were not heard of until about 1840, when they made their
appearance on the Chattachura range, from which they were
driving the Poitus. Their chiefs are all descendants of Chunglunga,
whose successor, Lallula, had four sons,—Lalpuilena, Lalienvunga,
Mangpor, and Vuta. The descendants of the first mentioned are
the Eastern chiefs, of whom Lengkám, Lálbura, and Poiboi are
names of note in our recent relations with the Lushais. Of the
descendants of Lálienvunga, Lálhai may be mentioned ; of Vuta-
Laleya and of Mangpor-Lenkhunga, Khálkám, Lengpunga,
Thánruma, Lálrima, and Thángula, all of whom, with the excep-

---

* Lushai is said to be derived from *Lu*=head and *sha*=cut. This name is not
known to the people so designated, who are said to call themselves *Zho*. This name is
said to "include all the hill tribes of this region who wear their hair in a knot resting on
the nape of the neck. The tribes further south and east are distinguished under the
generic title of Poi : these wear the hair knotted upon the temple." Between the Lushais
and the Pois are the Howlongs and the Kamhows, and east of the Pois are the Suktes.

tion of the last mentioned, are sons or grandsons of Sukpilál, who died in 1880, and who at the time of his death was ruler over the whole of the Western Lushais.

The first atttacks upon British territory made by the Lushais after their advance northwards were in November 1849, when almost at the same time a party of woodcutters was massacred, a village of Tipperas was burnt, and another village was plundered, in the Singla valley in Sylhet, west of the Chättachura range, and an attack was made by Mora, son of Lálienvunga, on three villages of refugee Thadoi Kukis within ten miles of the station of Silchar. To punish these outrages, the first expedition was led against the Lushais by Colonel Lister, who in January 1850 surprised and destroyed Mora's village, situated a little way south of the great peak of Nisapwi, between the Dhaleswari and the Sonai rivers. This expedition secured peace for many years. The Lushais gradually withdrew their advanced posts southwards, and we ceased to have much communication with, or information about, them. A raid was committed in 1862 on Hill Tippera and South Sylhet near Adampur, which two years later was discovered to have been perpetrated by Sukpilál; but this was followed only by negotiations. A meeting was held between the Deputy Commissioner of Cachar and Sukpilál's agents, and it was arranged that the captives taken should be surrendered, and that Sukpilál should receive an allowance for keeping the peace of the frontier. A similar arrangement was made with Vonpilál, son of Mora. But, although four of the captives were surrendered, these arrangements were never actually carried much further. In November 1868 the Eastern Lushais began a series of attacks on Manipur. In December of the same year Sukpilál carried his feuds with the Poitus into Sylhet. In January 1869 the tea garden of Noárbánd in Cachar was plundered and burned, several coolies being killed, by Lálruma, son of Lálpunga and brother of Poiboi. On the 14th January, Dántáu, son of Vonolel and brother of Lengkám and Lálbura, attacked the garden of Monierkhál, which he burned and plundered. In February a combined attack was made upon the Kála Nága stockade in Manipur. It was determined to punish these outrages by an expedition, one portion of which was to go up the Dhaleswari river to attack Sukpilál, and another up the Sonai, while a Manipuri force was to march south and join the second. The season, however, was too late for effective measures, and the expedition was practically a failure. Emboldened by this result, a new series of attacks was planned by the Lushais in the cold weather of 1870-71. A new family now appeared on the scene. While the Eastern Lushais of the family of Vonolel (Lálbura and Lengkám, his sons, and his nephew Thondong) led an attack on the Monierkhál stockade, the Bengali village of Nagdirgrám, and the Nágas in Manipur, the Howlongs of Lálpitang's house, who dwell south of Sukpilál's Lushais, and the western Poitu Kukis raided down the Hailákándi valley, and attacked the tea garden of Alexandrapur, where they killed a number of coolies and the manager, Mr Winchester, and carried off his daughter and several other captives, besides much plunder. A subsequent attack on a neighbouring garden, Katlacherra, was repulsed. Upon this it was determined to send a thoroughly effective expedition to march through the hills and exact reparation. Two columns were despatched in the cold weather of 1871-72, one from the Chittagong side, which marched northwards through the country of the Sylus and Howlongs and recovered the captives taken from Alexandrapur; and the other, which advanced, *viâ* Tipaimukh, southwards into the country of Vonolel and his sons. This expedition was completely successful in procuring the submission of the chiefs and satisfaction for the outrages; and from its termination down to 1892, no raid was made on territory under the Assam Administration.

In 1889, however, a raid was made in the Chengri valley on the Chittagong frontier, and a number of captives were taken, whom the chiefs concerned (Lengpunga and his brother Zarok) declined to release, and an expedition was accordingly undertaken in the cold weather of 1889-90. The main column marched through the Lushai Hills from Chittagong, and were met by a detachment of 400 Military Police from Silchar. The captives were surrendered, but Lengpunga escaped for the time. His village was burnt, and the troops then left the country. Previous to this raid, the policy of Government since 1872 had been to maintain a line of outposts connected by patrol paths, and, while cultivating, as much as possible, a friendly intercourse with the chiefs, to abstain from interfering in their internal affairs. It was now decided to endeavour to put down raids once for all by proving our power to occupy their country and establishing military outposts in their midst. Two such outposts (at Aijal and Changsil) with a garrison of Military Police were established in the portion of the Lushai Hills bordering on the Cachar district, and Captain Browne was deputed thither as Political Officer. For a time, the Lushais appeared to have accepted the situation, and, amongst other proofs of friendship, the leading chiefs attended a darbár held by Captain Browne, and killed a metna and swore an oath of friendship to the British Government. But the hopes thus raised were soon dissipated. Suddenly, without a word of warning, they rose in a body, attacked simultaneously the stockades at Aijal and Changsil, and killed Captain Browne, who was marching from Saireng to Changsil with a small escort of four sepoys. This was on the 10th September 1890. Three days later a relieving force of 200 Military Police left Silchar under Lieutenants Swinton and Tytler. Lieutenant Swinton was killed on the passage up the river Dhaleswari, whereupon Lieutenant Tytler assumed command, and reached Changsil and relieved the garrison under Lieutenant Cole, on the 28th September. The force at Changsil was further augmented by a detachment of 200 men of the 40th Bengal Infantry under Lieutenant Watson, who arrived at Changsil on the 30th. Mr. McCabe, who had been deputed to Cachar on special duty, reached Changsil on the 5th October 1890, and on his arrival offensive operations were at once commenced, with such success that within two months all but one of the Western Lushai chiefs had been arrested. The three ringleaders, Khálkám, Lengpunga, and Thángula, were deported, and the others were released on payment of the fines imposed on them. A few months later Khálkám and Lengpunga put an end to their existence by hanging themselves with ropes, which they had surreptitiously manufactured from their clothes.

These operations resulted in the complete pacification of the Northern Lushai villages west of the Sonai river and the unconditional surrender of all the chiefs implicated in the rising, with the exception of Thánruma, who fled for refuge towards the east, and who is still at large. At the commencement of 1891, the Lushais were peacefully employed in *jháming* and in rebuilding their villages, many of which had been destroyed by our troops as a punishment. The feeling of insecurity which our operations had occasioned was beginning to wear off, and Lushais came readily to trade at the newly reopened bázár at Changsil and to barter vegetables and live stock with the garrison of Fort Aijal. Requisitions for the supply of coolies to work on roads and carry stores and baggage, &c., were promptly complied with by all the chiefs so requisitioned except Lálbura, in consequence of whose non-compliance, Mr. McCabe, with an escort of 100 Military Police under Lieutenant Tytler, marched to his village, where he halted for the night. Next day, as Lálbura refused to come in, Mr. McCabe commenced collecting supplies and making other arrangements for halting in the village. Shortly afterwards 300 armed Lushais were observed to advance towards the north crest of the hill commanding his camp. The Political Officer promptly ordered them to be fired on, and at once commenced to make dispositions for the defence of the camp. Before they could be completed, however, the Lushais attacked the camp from all directions, and set fire to the village. They were driven off, and the fortification of the camp was then proceeded with. Stores of paddy were collected from the jungle where they had been hidden by the Lushais; a bridle path from Aijal to the Sonai was pushed on with great rapidity; and a reinforcement of 100 Military Police was at once sent to Mr. McCabe's assistance from Aijal. The fact was recognised that it would be impossible to undertake punitive measures in a satisfactory way with the small force then available, and it was therefore decided to bring up 300 men of the 18th Bengal Infantry from Silchar to hold Aijal and Changsil, and thus enable the whole of the Military Police stationed at those places to join the force with Mr. McCabe. In the meantime, skirmishing

parties were sent out daily to disperse the Lushais in the neighbourhood of the camp, and search for further stores of paddy. The
Lushais soon found that it was hopeless to try to take the camp,
and confined themselves to ambuscading small parties.

Enquiries showed that Lálbura was assisted in his rising by all
the Lushais east of the Sonai, and also probably by the Howlongs ;
but that the Western Lushais had profited by the lesson taught
them in the previous year, and had stood aloof. The attack at
Lálbura took place on 1st March 1892. On the 10th April, the
punitive force, consisting of 225 men of the Military Police and
75 of the 18th Bengal Infantry under Captain Loch, left Aijal.
Lálruya, Poiboi, Lálhai, Bungteya, Maite, and other villages were
occupied in turn, and all the chiefs submitted, except Lálbura,
who fled, accompanied by only twenty followers, to the impenetrable
jungles on the Manipur frontier. These operations were followed
by the complete submission of the Eastern Lushais, who now, like
the Lushais west of the Sonai, appear at last to have recognised
that it is far better to submit willingly to our rule than to suffer
the inevitable consequences of fighting against it.

In the course of these operations, the inconvenience of dividing
the Lushai country amongst three Administrations—Assam, Bengal,
and Burma—was found to be considerable. It has now been
settled that the portion administered from Bengal will shortly be
made over to Assam. The Burma portion will, however, for the
present at least, continue to be under the control of the Chief
Commissioner of Burma.

231. With the State of Hill Tippera this Administration has
no direct relations ; all communications for
the Mahárája are forwarded through the
Government of Bengal. The State is conterminous with Sylhet,
along the whole of the southern border of that district, and considerable intercourse takes place up and down the valleys of the rivers
which flow northwards from the Tippera Hills. The Mahárája's
boundary was laid down on this side by a joint Commission in
1865-66. The Mahárája is the zemindár of considerable estates in
Sylhet, and is to that extent subject to our revenue jurisdiction.

Hill Tippera.

232. In the preceding paragraphs reference has been made to the "Inner Line." This expression denotes a boundary which, in accordance with the policy to which effect was given by Regulation V of 1873, has been laid down in certain districts as that up to which the protection of British authority is guaranteed, and beyond which, except by special permission, it is not lawful for British subjects to go. The Inner Line Regulation was the result of much correspondence between the Government of Bengal and that of India on the subject of frontier policy. It was believed that many complications were caused by permitting persons from the plains to penetrate into the hills or submontane forests inhabited or frequented by wild tribes, where no effective protection could be given by Government, and where disputes relating to buying and selling frequently occurred. At the time the Regulation was passed, the great demand and competition for India-rubber brought down by the hillmen gave special prominence to these considerations : and it was decided that the best way to prevent these complications was to stop, as far as possible, the access of strangers to tracts where adequate control could not be exercised. An Inner Line has been laid down in the following districts :—In Darrang, towards the Bhutias, Akas, and Daflas ; in Lakhimpur, towards the Daflas, Miris, Abors, Mishmis, Khámtis, Singphos, and Nágas ; in Sibságar, towards the southern Nágas ; and in Cachar, towards the Lushais. The line is marked at intervals by frontier posts, held by Military Police or troops, and commanding the roads of access to the tract beyond ; and any person from the plains who has received permission to cross the line has to present his pass at these posts. At the close of 1892-93 there were 5 such outposts in the Darrang district, 4 of which were manned by detachments of the Military Police and the other by troops ; 13 garrisoned by Military Police in the Lakhimpur district ; one at Abhaypur in Sibságar garrisoned by Military Police ; and 7 in Cachar, all held by troops.

The Inner Line.

.

www.ingramcontent.com/pod-product-compliance
Lightning Source LLC
Chambersburg PA
CBHW030311270326
41926CB00010B/1327